EDGAR ALLAN POE

Thank Heaven! the crisis —
The danger is past,
And the lingering illness
Is over at last —
And the fever called 'Living'
Is conquered at last.

For Annie

Edgar Allan Poe

David Sinclair

J.M. Dent & Sons Ltd
London, Melbourne and Toronto

Printed in Great Britain by
Heffers Printers Limited, Cambridge

and bound at the Aldine Press, Letchworth, Herts
for
J. M. DENT & SONS LTD
Aldine House, Albemarle Street, London

First published 1977

This book is set in 11 on 12pt IBM Journal

British Library Cataloguing in Publication Data

Sinclair, David
    Edgar Allan Poe.
    1. Poe, Edgar Allan 2. Authors, American —
    19th century — Biography
    818′ .3′09   PS2631

ISBN 0-460-12003-4

Contents

List of Illustrations   6
Acknowledgments   7
Introduction The Unquiet American   9

1   All the World's a Stage   15
2   The New World and the Old   31
3   Birth of a Poet   47
4   Learning the Hard Way   59
5   The Good Soldier Perry   75
6   Officer's Mess   91
7   All in the Family   115
8   Back to Old Virginia   133
9   The Demon Drink?   149
10 The Child Bride   163
11 Tricks of Fate   179
12 Down and Out   197
13 War of Words   207
14 Affairs of the Heart   227
15 The Final Tragedy   245

Epilogue   259
A Note on Sources   263
Select Bibliography   265
Index   269

Illustrations

Between pages 128 and 129

1   Edgar Allan Poe
2   Elizabeth Arnold Poe
3   Frances Valentine Allan
4   John Allan
5   Elmira Royster Shelton
6   Virginia Clemm Poe
7   Maria Clemm
8   Marriage bond of Edgar Allan Poe and Virginia Clemm
9   Illustration for 'The Raven'
10 Map of central Richmond in Poe's day
11 Manuscript of 'Annabel Lee'
12 Russell Square, London
13 Poe's house in Amity Street, Baltimore
14 Church Home and Infirmary, Baltimore
15 Poe's grave, Baltimore

Acknowledgments

I am indebted to the following people and organizations, and profoundly grateful for their help and kindness:

Miss Denise Bethel and Mr Sergei Troubetskoy, of the Poe Foundation Inc., Richmond, Virginia; the Valentine Museum in Richmond, and especially Mrs Stuart Gibson and Mrs Robert Anderson; the Enoch Pratt Free Library, Baltimore, Maryland, and in particular Mrs Averill Kadis; Washington State University, Pullman, Washington, and particularly Mrs Kathleen McLean, of Poe Studies; Mr Alexander Rose, President of the Edgar Allan Poe Society, Baltimore; the Virginia State Library, Richmond; the Church Home and Infirmary, Baltimore. I am also indebted to the doctor to whom I took the medical questions raised in this book, and who for professional reasons cannot be named.

On an entirely personal level, my thanks are due to Bob and Irene Fischl, of North Stamford, Conn., Caroline Arcier, of New Canaan, Conn., and Auziville and Estelle Jackson, of Richmond, Va., for their hospitality and for helping to smooth the path of an Englishman on his first visit to the United States.

Finally, I must express my gratitude to Peter Shellard, for his advice and encouragement; to my wife, Ruth, who helped with the research, took some of the photographs, and who has graciously entertained the ghost of Edgar Allan Poe; and to my family, who endured my anti-social behaviour throughout the preparation of this book.

America has been found out; and Poe has not; that is the situation. How did he live there, this finest of fine artists, this born aristocrat of letters? Alas! he did not live there: he died there, and was duly explained away as a drunkard and a failure, though it remains an open question whether he really drank as much in his whole lifetime as a modern successful American drinks, without comment, in six months.

George Bernard Shaw,
The Nation, 1909

The Unquiet American

There is something of Edgar Allan Poe in all of us, lurking in the shadows of our souls and manifesting itself in our unreasoning dread of the unknown. Fear of darkness, horror of madness, abhorrence of decay, the crippling sense of powerlessness in the face of death — all these sensations, which we tend to keep locked in our subconscious minds, Poe touches like a needle hitting a nerve. In his tales we can see our nightmares brought out into the open for analysis and rationalization, yet the identification of our fears in no way diminishes them, because all the time Poe is pushing us towards the brink of a greater and still more terrifying awareness. Those nightmares are merely vehicles for a journey into the farthest recesses of our own psyches. The secret of Poe's appeal, of his power over readers who will readily accept fantastic plots and characters and believe what, on more objective examination, may turn out to be hoaxes, is that he is leading us towards the edge of that most profound human fear, the fear of self-revelation. His characters are our blackest visions of ourselves and their situations are the stuff of our worst imaginings.

Poe knew, with his poet's intuition (and he always thought of himself as a poet, though we know him better as the writer of some of the most powerful and haunting short stories in the English language), that man can face almost anything except himself. For his strengths and successes, man will happily take the credit, but for his failures and weaknesses he puts the blame on God, luck, the stars, Fate, Nature, destiny, the Devil, or anything that is likely to prevent him from meeting his own imperfections head-on. Poe himself, with his morbid self-pity, persecution mania, blinkered pride, and pathetic dependence upon others, was guilty of passing the buck: he saw himself as the victim of a terrible destiny, just like his hero in 'The Fall of the House of Usher'. At the same time, however, he felt that there must be escape routes: perhaps through the power of analytical thought (like Dupin, his detective in 'The Murders in the Rue Morgue' and other stories, or like Legrand, who solved the riddle of 'The Gold Bug'); or through some kind of liberation of the soul, as expressed in some of his poems; or maybe in some cases through the acquisition of great wealth and its use in the pursuit of Beauty ('The Domain of Arnheim'). But Poe never travelled very far along these routes except in his imagination, so his truly unforgettable characters are those who, like their creator, are trapped in their own private hells, mirroring the human condition, albeit in a realm somewhere beyond conscious experience.

What I am considering in this book is Poe's particular hell – how he came to it, how he tried to escape from it, how it swallowed him up, and how he managed to triumph over it through his work. The story of Edgar Allan Poe is one of the great tragedies of literature. His life was as grim as anything in his tales. On the one hand he was a self-proclaimed aesthete, a handsome, passionate, romantic poet in love with beauty and idealism, while on the other he was obliged to spend his adult life in poverty, misery and sickness, and to die a failure in the eyes of his contemporaries. Yet who today, almost a hundred and thirty years after his death, has not heard of Edgar Allan Poe? His tales are popular all over the world, and many of them have been the basis for highly successful films. His poetry is recited in schools, and some of it has been set to music. Millions of words have been written about him, and he is frequently referred to as a genius. It looks like the classic story of the man out of his time, the artist scorned or, worse still, ignored while he lived and recognized only after his death. But that is only half the history of Edgar Allan Poe.

It was Poe's misfortune to be born into an America obsessed with democracy and economic development, and careless of what it considered to be the less profitable aspects of civilization, such as education and the arts. George Bernard Shaw may have been over-stating the case when he said in 1909 that Poe and Walt Whitman were the 'only two men born since the Declaration of Independence' whose advocacy could save America from damnation on the Judgment Day, but it is hard to dismiss the assertion of Ralph Waldo Emerson that between 1790 and 1820 New England, the 'cultural centre' of the newborn United States, produced no book, speech, conversation or thought worthy of note. Shaw was being only too accurate when he wrote that Poe was 'explained away as a drunkard and a failure' by his fellow countrymen, who had judged him by their laws of success and found him wanting. The fault, however, was not only America's. It was also Poe's. He had weaknesses which probably would have destroyed him even if he had achieved success by nineteenth-century America's standards.

One of Poe's handicaps, I suggest, was physical: after a youth spent in robust health, he was attacked by a chronic illness and this produced a disastrous effect when combined with another of his weaknesses – a tendency to seek escape from miserable reality through alcohol. His other failings were psychological. Pride caused him to cling to an image of himself which never had a chance of being realized; in his own eyes he was a genteel, scholarly man of letters to whom the world owed its appreciation, its help, and its rewards, and when these were not forthcoming he became bitter and resentful. It was pride, too, that drove him to lie about his age (in order to make himself appear a prodigy) and to glamorize his early life to cover up the fact that he had served in the army as an enlisted man, which he thought would not be socially acceptable. Yet his pride was no match for his sense of grievance and self-pity, which sometimes led him to cringe before those who could help him or give him money. And behind all this was his often pathetic dependence upon women, arising in part from the early loss of his mother and also from his lifelong pursuit of the ideal of love and beauty.

Such a man as I have described might seem an unlikely candidate for the title of genius, but Poe had great strengths as well as dangerous weaknesses. For a start there was his inborn talent as a writer, and this was supported by his ability to go on writing in spite of hardship, illness, disappointment and rejection. But his greatest strength lay in his unique faculty for probing into his own neuroses and translating them into stories of breathtaking power. Whether he did this consciously or not is a question for a pyschologist rather than a biographer, but that he did so is obvious from the handful of his tales and poems which can be identified as direct reflections of his life.

To take a general example, it is clear from Poe's 'horror' stories, and many of his poems, that he was obsessed with the idea of death, and a study of his life indicates that he had good reason for such an obsession. But in its passage from actual experience into literature, this awful fascination takes on a different and vastly more significant character. Poe attempts to reach some sort of understanding of or even arrangement with death. He recognizes the connexions between sleep and death, between trance states and death, and between the disorganized ('mad') mind and death — connexions which are very much the concern of scientists, doctors, psychologists and medico-legal experts today as they struggle to define 'death' in the light of the awesome possibilities and problems stemming from heart trans-plants, the ability to maintain what is called life by artificial means, and the moral aspects of euthanasia. We ask the question today, is death merely a state of disorganization? Poe asked it more than a century ago. His gloomy explorations of his own fears and night-mares are really expressions of problems which have troubled scientists and philosophers throughout history and which still trouble them now. Therein lies the seed of Poe's genius.

In his own time and in his own country, though, the genius of
Edgar Allan Poe was not recognized. His importance was realized,
towards the end of his life, in France, where his prose was translated
by Baudelaire, and his verse by Mallarmé (and his work later
influenced the early writings of Guy de Maupassant). He was noticed
in England, too, principally by Elizabeth Barrett (later Mrs
Browning) and Charles Dickens. But it took America the best part of
a century to see that it had overlooked its first home-grown truly
original writer. Since the light dawned, however, the literary
establishment has spared no effort to atone for the short-sightedness
of its forebears. 'Poe scholars' must by now have weighed, dissected,
X-rayed, crystallized, distilled, measured and found the specific
gravity of almost every word the unfortunate Edgar ever wrote. And
yet the effect of the personal notoriety, the ill-natured gossip and the
ignorant criticism that kept Poe in the wilderness for so long persists
even today. A substantial majority of people who enjoy Poe's tales
and poems, and who never read academic books, treatises and essays,
still regard him as a drug-crazed pervert or a drunken waster. To
correct that distorted picture is my purpose.

This is not a 'literary' biography, or a 'critical' one. Neither is it an
exercise in rehabilitation nor an apology for Poe, who needs
justification no more than he deserves damnation. What he requires is
understanding. He must not be viewed, as he sometimes is in
America, as an artist to be protected because of his literary
importance. Equally, he should not be seen as a hopelessly
inadequate character who, in spite of himself, managed to produce
work of value. He must be regarded as a human being, with all the
plus and minus factors that implies, and furthermore he should be
treated as a human being tormented by both inner turmoil and
external difficulty and deprivation. He was not only a writer but also
a man, and it was through the kind of man he was that he became
the sort of writer he was. That may seem obvious, but it has often
been ignored.

The chapters which follow, then, attempt to build up a picture of
Poe the man perhaps rather more than Poe the artist, and the
attempt is supported as far as possible by his own thoughts as he
expressed them in a variety of letters which reveal his personality so
well that I have quoted them extensively throughout the book, and
also by extracts from his writings which seem to have a direct bearing
on his life and his feelings. I have tried to keep in mind that a writer's
work may be his life but that his life is not necessarily his work: that
the writer, like any artist, shapes his thoughts, emotions and
experiences, and perhaps distorts them, in order to achieve the effect
desired in his work. As Poe himself said, 'I prefer commencing with

the consideration of ·an *effect*. Having chosen a novel, first, and secondly a vivid effect, I consider whether it can best be wrought by incident or tone . . .' So the life does not fully explain the work, and the work does not fully explain the life. The most that can be said is that the one can serve to throw some light upon the other, providing the distinctions between the two are maintained.

In Poe's case, further distortion arises from the fact that his physical survival depended entirely upon his writing — he wrote to live, therefore he had to write material that would sell. Thus the biographer has to decide how much of Poe's work really refers to himself and how much is mere reader-fodder. The difference is not always easy to see, and many of Edgar's contemporaries found evidence in the horrors of his tales to support the popular rumours of drug-taking, perversion and madness. I have done my best to avoid such confusion, and I hope that I have produced a balanced view of Poe which may help towards greater understanding of him and increased enjoyment of his work. While Poe's writing fits, rather uncomfortably, into an American context, it is steeped in the European tradition and indeed has truly international validity.

More than a century and a quarter after Poe's death, it is not easy to separate the facts of his life from the mass of fiction that surrounds it. As I have said, he himself was responsible for a number of false trails, and his first biographer added to the uncertainty with his lies (even to the extent of forging several letters). When Edgar was safely buried, rumour ran riot and many people added to it by claiming some association with Poe which he was not there to deny. Consequently, much of the evidence which has survived is unreliable but cannot be entirely disregarded because it provides the only clues to the many gaps in the Poe story. There are so many mysteries to consider. What was the illness that afflicted Poe so badly? What caused the breakdown in his relationship with his adoptive father? Why did he marry a thirteen-year-old girl? How did he come, at last, to be found in a Baltimore gutter, semi-conscious and wearing clothes that were not his own? I believe I can answer these questions. Occasionally, judgments have had to be made with very little information to go on, but I believe I have kept them to the minimum and that they are valid because they are made in the light not only of known facts but also of human nature, and Poe's character in particular.

Poe has suffered almost as much from biographers as he did at the hands of uncomprehending and intolerant editors and readers during his lifetime. Some have idealized him, others have patronized him, still others have sought to diminish him, and at least one has told downright lies about him. I have tried to tell the truth, as I see it and as far as my view can be reinforced by Edgar's own actions and thoughts. In the course of researching and writing this book, my attitude towards him has changed somewhat. I have always greatly admired his work, but as I have learnt more about him, his faults have become more obvious and I have been forced to admit that he himself was to blame for much of the misery in which he lived. On the other hand, it has become clear that he was a sick man, both physically and, to a lesser extent, mentally, and when this is borne in mind it is astonishing that he could have produced so much brilliant writing.

Should he be called a genius? I have my doubts. But of one thing I am certain: Edgar Allan Poe's ability to chart the disintegration of his soul, as D. H. Lawrence put it, is more than enough justification for his inclusion among the immortals.

Chapter 1

All the World's a Stage

On 29 November 1811, the *Enquirer* newspaper in Richmond, Virginia, published a touching appeal on behalf of one of the city's favourite actresses:

> To the humane heart. On this night, Mrs Poe, lingering on the bed of disease and surrounded by her children, asks your assistance, and asks it for perhaps the last time. The generosity of a Richmond audience can need no other appeal. For particulars see bills of the day.

The audience at the Richmond Theatre that evening did indeed respond generously, but the most that the money raised by Mrs Poe's benefit performance could do was to make her last days in a cheap boarding house a little more comfortable than they otherwise might have been. She died of consumption on 8 December, leaving three small children: the eldest, William Henry, would also be claimed by consumption, at the age of twenty-four; the youngest, Rosalie, would survive until 1874, when she would die in an old people's home; the middle child was destined to a life of misery, deprivation and tragedy, yet to become one of America's greatest writers and a potent literary force throughout the world — the man we know today as Edgar Allan Poe.

The loss of his mother a month before his third birthday was to affect Edgar Poe throughout his life. For thirty-seven years he would seek to re-create her in his relationships with other women, not only as a mother but also as an ideal woman, a goddess of love and beauty. The memory of her pale, fragile face and maternal tenderness remained ever before him, arousing an obsessive belief that his identity depended upon feminine care and affection, while the agony of parting from her — which he relived through the premature deaths of a succession of women he worshipped — produced the fear that love was a killer. The urge to love and be loved was central to Poe's life, and to his work, but his experience led him to associate love

with death. The resulting contradiction between his desire to give
and receive affection and his horror of the grave awoke in him
terrifying nightmares which upset the balance of his mind, driving
him inexorably towards his own destruction. Such was the legacy he
took away from the corpse of his mother.

But if love and death were to be powerful forces in Poe's life, they
would be matched equally by perversity, which showed itself in his
complete inability to act in his own best interests. That fault was
handed down from the father he hardly knew. It is difficult to escape
the conclusion that in view of the psychological inheritance he
received from his parents, Edgar Allan Poe was doomed from the
start.

Poe's forebears on his father's side were immigrants to colonial
America, having originated in County Cavan, in what is now the
Republic of Ireland, where one David Poe had been a tenant farmer.
Agriculture must have been an uncertain life in wild and watery
Cavan, where the land was generally poor and the climate damp and
cold. When David Poe died in 1742, his eldest son, John, scraped a
living for seven years (perhaps growing flax, one of the main crops of
the region) before setting off in search of new horizons in the New
World, arriving with his wife and family in Pennsylvania in 1750. Six
years later John Poe was dead, and the family — there were about ten
children by that time — was living in Baltimore, Maryland. How they
lived is not certain, but at least the eldest son, named David after his
grandfather, had a trade, for in 1776 he was to be found making 'all
sorts of Spinning Wheels, Clock Reels, Weavers' Spools &c', according to an advertisement he placed in the *Maryland Journal and
Baltimore Advertiser.* That notice appeared on 3 June: a month later
came the Declaration of Independence, and the revolutionary war
against the British, begun in Massachusetts in April 1775, was joined
in earnest.

David Poe, a staunch Whig, answered the call of George Washington and enlisted in Captain John McClellan's Baltimore Company,
rising to become the city's Deputy Quartermaster General, with the
rank of major, in September 1779. He carried out his duties
conscientiously and efficiently, using on at least two occasions his
own funds to purchase supplies, as witness a letter he wrote to an
army commander in 1782 pointing out that 'rather than the public
property should suffer, I shall struggle hard, as has ever been my
inclination, to endeavour by all means in my power to preserve it,
and will, therefore, once more try my credit, in order to procure
forage to preserve the horses from perishing'. Nor was that all.
Washington's renowned French ally, General LaFayette, visiting
Baltimore long after the war had been won, recalled 'my friendly and

patriotic commissary, Mr David Poe, who resided in Baltimore when I was here, and out of his own very limited means supplied me with five hundred dollars to aid in clothing my troops, and whose wife, with her own hands, cut five hundred pairs of pantaloons, and superintended the making of them for the use of my men'. Major Poe's patriotism and selfless devotion to duty were rewarded by shabby treatment from the new American government, which did not even make good his expenses in buying supplies, but the proud citizens of Baltimore accorded him the courtesy title of 'General'.

The heritage of Edgar Poe, then, was solid, honest and hardworking respectability — until it came to his father. David Poe Jr, fourth son of the 'General', born on 18 July 1784, grew up to be handsome and clever, with a gentlemanly charm and manner. However, his make-up also included a rebellious spirit and a large measure of wild Celtic temper, and one or other of these drove him, at the age of eighteen, to abandon a promising career in the law in favour of a roving, rootless and at best precarious life on the stage. What lay behind the young man's decision to embark upon a course for which, in the event, he proved to be quite unsuited, can only be guessed at. Perhaps the very worthiness and respectability of his father were a source of irritation to a nature that craved romance and excitement; perhaps there were rows because David Jr spent more time lost in vague dreams than in attending to his studies (a habit that would later cause trouble for his son); or perhaps he was simply stage-struck. Whatever the reason, David Poe Jr made his acting début in Charleston, South Carolina, on 1 December 1803.

By 1803, the woman David Poe would later marry had already become a seasoned and successful actress. Her name was Elizabeth Arnold Hopkins (she had been married, at the age of sixteen, to a fellow member of the theatre company in which she worked), and she had been 'born in a trunk', as the saying goes, in England. Of Elizabeth's father little is known, but he appears to have been an actor named Henry Arnold who married an actress named Elizabeth Smith on 18 May 1784 at St George's Church, Hanover Square, London. Henry's new wife did well on the stage, beginning with minor roles at the Theatre Royal, Covent Garden, and rising to be second lead in a popular comic opera, *The Maid of the Mill,* in January 1795. Exactly a year later she turned up in America, with her daughter Elizabeth but without her husband, who may have died. The merit of having an English background in the American theatre of the day is emphasized by the fact that when Mrs Arnold opened at the Federal Street theatre in Boston on 12 February 1796, in a musical comedy entitled *Love in a Village,* the *Massachusetts Mercury* recorded enthusiastically:

We have had the pleasure of a complete fruition of the
satisfaction a Boston audience would receive from the
dramatic abilities of Mrs Arnold. The theatre never shook
with such bursts of applause as on her first appearance, on
Friday evening last. Not a heart but was sensible of her
merits; not a tongue but vibrated in her praise; not a hand
but moved in approbation. Nor did these expressions of
satisfaction die with the evening, her merits have since
been the pleasing theme of every conversation.

Mrs Arnold, however, had not only won the hearts of Boston
theatregoers, but she had also conquered a gentleman by the name
of Mr Tubbs, a character almost as obscure as Henry Arnold. We
know that Tubbs arrived in America on the same boat as Mrs Arnold
and her daughter; we are told that he was a piano-player; and there
are records to show that he opened a theatre in Portland, Maine,
following 'a concert of vocal and instrumental musick' featuring 'Mrs
Tubbs, late Mrs Arnold of the Theatre Royal, Covent Garden', as the
Eastern Herald and Gazette of Maine put it. Whether Mrs Arnold had
married Tubbs in England and merely retained her former name until
she had become established on the American stage, whether they
married in America, or whether indeed they ever married at all, are
matters for conjecture, since no information has ever come to light.
What is recorded, however, is that Mrs Arnold's daughter, Elizabeth,
aged about nine (the date of her birth is uncertain), began her acting
career at the Tubbs theatre in Portland, though she had in fact made
her début before an audience in Boston as an interval attraction
during one of her mother's triumphs. She must have been a mature
nine-year-old, for in her first role in Portland she played a teenage
flirt with three lovers, and the *Eastern Herald* was moved to
comment that 'the Ladies, perhaps, ought not to attend till it is
known whether their ears are again to be offended with expressions
of obscenity and profanity'. The paper did admit, though, that Miss
Arnold's powers as an actress commanded admiration: 'Add these to
her youth, her beauty, her innocence, and a character is composed
which has not, and perhaps will not again be found in any theatre.'
  If the people of Portland were equally impressed by Miss Arnold,
it did not show in box-office returns. Mr Tubbs was obliged to close
his theatre on 17 January 1797, and he, his wife and the young
Elizabeth moved first to a company in Newport, Rhode Island, next
to Charleston, and then to the New Theatre in Philadelphia, where
Elizabeth Tubbs apparently died in 1798 — probably in a yellow
fever epidemic which swept the city that year and forced the closure
of the theatre for nine months. The young Elizabeth Arnold

remained in Philadelphia for the next four years (during which time Mr Tubbs disappeared from the scene; presumably he also died), moving to the Chestnut Street Theatre Company in 1800 and, through talent and sheer hard work, becoming one of its leading players. In 1802 she was married to Charles D. Hopkins, a successful comic actor, and the two of them moved to Alexandria, just south of Washington, to join Mr Green's Virginia Company.

The season at the Alexandria Theatre was almost over when the Hopkinses arrived in August, and they were employed for only about a month, Elizabeth doing little but singing and dancing. No record of their activities during the following winter is available, but they probably travelled around Virginia giving concerts, recitations and so on. March 1803 found them opening at the New Theatre in Norfolk, Virginia, where they appeared continuously until the middle of July. The company appears not to have been conspicuously successful, with a critic commenting that most of the players were '"weary, stale, flat and unprofitable" in the extreme'. There followed another break until December, when Mr Green took his company to the Richmond Theatre — where, in the summer of 1804, he engaged David Poe Jr.

David Poe had spent the winter of 1803 and spring of 1804 with Placide's Company in Charleston and in Savannah, Georgia, playing an amazing variety of leading parts for one who had not been trained as an actor. The fact that he was a native American in a profession dominated by the British was no doubt helpful, as were his good looks and gentlemanly bearing, but he certainly had difficulties to overcome, as the *Charleston Courier* pointed out:

> He is . . . extremely diffident; indeed so much so, that the slightest lapse in his speech throws him from the little confidence he has acquired, back into his first night's trepidation . . . He ought to practise before some judicious friends, and beg of them to set him right, when he is wrong.

Whether he took this advice or not, David clearly began to improve, for in a review of *Much Ado About Nothing* early in 1804, the *Courier* said: 'Young Poe being less than usual under the domination of that timid modesty which so depresses his powers, acted Don Pedro so respectably as to animate the hopes we have entertained of his future progress.' It must have been with high hopes, and quite a respectable reputation, that he made the journey to Richmond.

Less than a month after David Poe's début with Green's Company in June 1804, the management of the Richmond Theatre passed to

Charles Hopkins, as the result of some dispute, and he threw himself enthusiastically into an extensive programme of plays, making full use of his wife and David Poe. The actors spent a complete year in Richmond, with only two short breaks, then in 1805 went on tour, visiting Norfolk, Washington and Baltimore, Poe's home town (there is no record of whether the prodigal was acknowledged by his family). It was in Washington that destiny supervened, with the death of Charles Hopkins on 26 October. The stage was now set, so to speak, for a tragedy that would echo down the years. It opened on 14 March 1806, when David Poe visited Henrico County Court House in Richmond to file a bond for his marriage to Elizabeth Arnold Hopkins, which took place about three weeks later. The inheritance of Edgar Allan Poe was in the making.

Two questions arise: Had David Poe formed a romantic attachment to Elizabeth before her husband's death, and was the Hopkins marriage a love-match or merely the result of a young girl's desire to seek protection in what was then a rough profession? The young widow did indeed wait five months before accepting Poe's proposal, but from what we know of David's romantic nature it is reasonable to assume that he would have taken the time and trouble to court her properly. Then, she had been married to Hopkins for three years without producing a child, while she became pregnant almost immediately after her marriage to Poe, for their first child was born in January 1807. Hopkins may have been sterile or impotent – or Elizabeth's first marriage may have lacked the passion of her second. We shall never know the answer, but it is nice to think of the young gallant loving the beautiful actress from afar, until the death of her perhaps rather cold husband gave him the chance to reveal his true feelings. It is pleasant to imagine their happiness against the background of a beautiful, scented Virginia spring – for there was little enough joy to follow.

The Poes spent the early months of their marriage working in Philadelphia, then at a summer theatre in New York, and finally in Boston, where Elizabeth's mother had been so well received and where the new Mrs Poe had herself first appeared on a stage. Boston was to be their home for three years, and it was there on 19 January 1809 that Edgar was born. He would later lie about it, first adding to his age so that he could join the army and then reducing it to present himself as a precocious genius, but we can be sure of his date of birth because it was recorded in the Bible of the Allan family, into which, as we shall see, Edgar was later adopted: 'William Henry Poe was born on the 30th day of January, 1807. Edgar Allan Poe was born on the 19th day of January, 1809.' Further evidence of the birthdate comes from the *Boston Gazette* on 9 February 1809: 'We congratulate the frequenters of the Theatre on the recovery of Mrs Poe from her recent confinement. This charming little Actress will make her re-appearance To-morrow Evening. . .' What is less certain is where Edgar was born, a subject of some interest in the light of the Poe cult that has grown up over the years. For a long time local legend in Boston sited his birthplace at 33 Hollis Street, but this appears to have been based on a faulty reading of city records, and a Boston antiquarian named Walter K. Watkins produced in 1909 convincing evidence that David Poe rented a wooden house on Carver Street in 1808 and that he and his family remained there until after the birth of Edgar.

The Poes were not to remain in Boston much longer, however. They had been in financial difficulties ever since the birth of their first child, Henry — Elizabeth had been back on stage less than a month after the confinement — and two benefit nights within a month in 1808 had done little to improve things. (The benefit system gave the actor what was left of the evening's takings after all expenses had been paid.) On 21 March 1808 the *Boston Gazette* had announced:

> If industry can claim from the public either favor or support the talents of Mrs Poe will not pass unrewarded. — She has supported and maintained a course of characters more numerous and arduous than can be paralleled on our boards during any one season. Often she has been obliged to perform three characters on the same evening, and she has always been perfect in the text, and has well comprehended the intention of her author.
>
> In addition to her industry, however, Mrs Poe has claims for other favors from the respectability of her talents. Her Romps and Sentimental characters have an individuality which has marked them peculiarly her own. But she has succeeded often in the tender personations of tragedy; her conceptions are always marked with good sense and natural ability. We are confident to hope therefore that the Bostonians will not suffer her merits to be so slighted that poverty and distress are to result from her benefit night, as has been the case with other performers.

Such confidence in the Bostonians was misplaced, for in April Mr and Mrs Poe 'present their respects to the town of Boston and its vicinity, and beg leave to inform them that from the great failure and severe losses sustained by their former attempts, they have been induced, by the persuasion of friends, to make a joint effort for public favor, in hopes of that sanction, influence, and liberal support, which have ever yet distinguished a Boston audience'. The drawback to the benefit system was that if the performance made a loss, the actor meant to benefit was obliged to make it up financially to the theatre management.

So the Poes remained in 'poverty and distress', working hard to feed baby Henry, who was all too soon followed by Edgar. For the second time Elizabeth was back at work within a month of the birth, but now her husband was absent from the playbills. Between 10 February and 17 April 1809 he was off on a fund-raising trip in the course of which he made an appeal to his family, as his wealthy cousin George, who lived in Stockerton, Pennsylvania, noted in a letter to another relative on 6 March that year. In this document, which includes details of the only letter David Poe is known to have written, George wrote:

> One evening he came out to our house − having seen one of our servants (that is one of the two we keep) he had me called out to the door where he told me the most awful moment of his life was arrived, begged me to come and see him the next day at 11 o'clock at the Mansion House, said he came not to beg, & with a tragedy stride walked off after I had without reflection promised I would call − in obedience to my promise I went there the next day but found him not nor did I hear of him until a dirty little boy came to the door & said a man down at the tavern desired him to bring that paper and fetch back the answer − it is only necessary for me to copy the note here that you may see the impertinence it contains.

> Sir, *You* promised *me* on your honor to meet me at the Mansion house on the 23d − *I* promise *you* on *my* word of honor that if you will lend me 30, 20, 15 or even 10$ I will *remit* it to you *immediately* on my arrival in Baltimore. Be assured I will keep *my* promise at least as well as you did yours and that nothing but extreem [sic] distress would have *forc'd* me to make this application − Your answer by the bearer will prove whether I yet have 'favour in your eyes' or whether I am to be despised by (as I understand) a rich relation because when a *wild boy* I joined a profession which I then thought and now think an honorable one. But which I would most willingly quit tomorrow if it gave satisfaction to your family provided I could do *any thing* else that would give bread to mine − Yr politeness will no doubt enduce you to answer this note from Yrs &c

> D. POE Jr

To this impertinent note it is hardly necessary to tell you
my answer — it merely went to assure him that he need
not look to me for any countenance or support more
especially after having written me such a letter as that and
thus for the future I desired to hear not from or of him —
so adieu to Davy. . .

The family, then, had not forgiven David for 'disgracing' it, but
what is more significant is David's own attitude. Assuming that
George's version of the letter is correct, David expected to be re-
buffed and accordingly reacted to the snub before it had been
delivered. Also, if one is looking for a favour, one does not antag-
onize the prospective benefactor by failing to keep an appointment.
Probably David's pride had something to do with it. He knew he had
to beg for money but he could not find in himself the humility to do
it properly, so he went into a bar, had a few drinks to bolster his
confidence, and composed his aggressive note, knowing in his heart
of hearts that it was almost certain to annoy the one person who
could help him. This kind of reaction was to become only too
familiar to Edgar Poe, who attributed it to what he called 'The Imp
of the Perverse', a strange impulse to do the very opposite to what is
best for oneself. Edgar, too, would find himself frequently reduced
to seeking loans from people whom he had offended, but as he grew
older his ability to beg improved.

David Poe returned to Boston in April 1809, presumably little
better off than when he had left. He collected his family and in May
they all set out for New York in the hope of improving their circumstances. As it turned out, New York was to ruin David and break up
the family. The years in Boston had been successful in a professional
sense even if they had not brought adequate financial rewards. Both
the Poes had been 'stars' of the theatre company, taking a wide
variety of leading roles and even playing Laertes and Ophelia to the
Hamlet of the famous John Howard Payne. But then, as now, the
New York theatre was a demanding and fiercely competitive arena
presided over by critics who expected the best as of right and who
were unlikely to show kindness towards valiant efforts if they were
unsuccessful. Elizabeth Poe, though not perhaps as talented an
actress as her mother seems to have been, had beauty, charm and
ability. She could sing and dance, and also bring her skill to bear in
difficult dramatic roles. She might never be a great performer, but
she was workmanlike and would survive. After all, the theatre was in
her blood. David Poe, on the other hand, seems never to have been
more than a 'promising' or an 'improving' actor, if his critics are to
be believed. He had been successful in what were called juvenile or

gallant roles, but his lack of real training must have left him deficient in the more subtle techniques of the drama, and he had always encountered problems with his voice and diction. Then there was his character. He never took kindly to criticism of either himself or his wife. J. T. Buckingham, of the elegant literary magazine *Polyanthos*, recalled that during the Boston days David Poe 'called at my house to chastise my impertinence, but went away without effecting his purpose'. Such sensitivity was a weakness the New York critics could seize upon, and it was exploited most viciously by the gentleman representing *The Rambler's Magazine*, who first classified David Poe as 'never destined for the high walks of the drama; — a footman is the extent of what he ought to attempt'.

From that point a personal feud developed, with Poe apparently offering threats of violence to the man from *The Rambler's*, who replied:

> By the by, it has been said, that this *gentleman* has taken some of our former remarks very much in dudgeon; but whether this be true or not, we entertain very great doubts, for certainly we have said nothing but the truth, and that should give no man offence. If it is the case, however, we are sincerely sorry for it; for from his amiable *private character*, and high *professional standing*, he is among the last men we would justly offend. We owe this much to our friend . . . from having heard so much of his *spirit* . . .

That last remark might well have been a reference to David Poe's drinking habits. The magazine left its readers in no doubt when it further attacked Poe with a poem in French, entitled 'Sur un POE de Chambre' and ending with the lines,

> Son père était pot,
> Sa mère était broc,
> Sa grande mère était pinte

Or, 'his father was the tankard, his mother was the jug, his grandmother was the booze' (the word 'pinte' is old French for 'pint' but is also associated with the slang verb 'pinter', which means 'to booze'). The charges appear to have been not entirely without foundation. According to announcements in the New York press, David was often absent from the stage through 'indisposition', a contemporary theatrical euphemism for 'drunk'. Again we find a parallel with the life of Edgar Poe: he too would be viciously attacked in

New York journals, and he too would get into trouble through alcohol.

Drunk or sober, David Poe made his last appearance in the theatre on 18 October 1809, just nine months after the birth of his second son. Indeed, it was his last appearance anywhere, for all we know. Elizabeth remained in New York until July 1810, working constantly and by all accounts having some success, but of her husband there is no further mention. It has been generally assumed that he died, but I disagree with this conclusion, which it is impossible to confirm because the city kept no register of deaths at the time. It seems to me unlikely in any case, because no newspaper death notice referring to David has ever come to light, and I feel certain that one would have appeared in view of the publicity he had received in New York. I believe that David Poe, disillusioned with the life he had so perversely chosen and weary of the struggle against poverty and despair, went off to seek a happier life elsewhere.

It is important to try to establish what became of David Poe because John Allan, who was to become Edgar's guardian, would later use David's disappearance and the subsequent birth of a third child to Elizabeth to suggest that Edgar came from a tainted line. The whole matter hangs on the date on which that third child, Rosalie, was born.

Elizabeth Poe was appearing at the Richmond Theatre in August 1810, having recently left New York, but there is no evidence that her husband was with her. We know that his last theatre performance took place in October 1809, but he must have remained with his wife at least until the spring of 1810 if he was the father of Rosalie and if she was born on the date that is usually given, 20 December 1810. But that birthdate is based upon uncheckable evidence. It is said to have been recorded in the Bible of the Mackenzie family, who adopted Rosalie in Richmond in 1811, but that Bible has disappeared, and there is no copy of the record it contained. In the case of Edgar and Henry Poe, the note written in the Allan Bible was copied by the son of John Allan's business partner, and that copy can be seen in the Valentine Museum, Richmond. There is no such evidence for Rosalie's birth. The date could have been 20 December 1810, for Mrs Poe was absent from the Richmond boards for two months at the end of that year — but there is nothing to suggest she was having a baby, and since she was to die of consumption a year later it is reasonable to assume that she was already suffering periods of illness.

I believe that Rosalie may have actually been born earlier. Mrs Poe was not working in New York between 15 January and 23 February 1810, because the theatre was closed, and it would have been possible for her to have had a baby then without exciting the press comment which had accompanied her earlier confinements. If one accepts a date somewhere between January and February 1810, that would place the conception of Rosalie in April or May 1809, about the time David returned to Boston after a two-month absence. If David had not died by the spring of 1810 he had certainly been out of work for several months, and that would have placed the family in severe financial straits, making it unlikely for Elizabeth to take the risk of having another child. In the spring of the previous year, however, apart from the joy of reunion which would presumably have resulted in love-making, the couple were already thinking of heading for the bright lights of New York, with their promise of fame and fortune.

Of course, it is possible that John Allan's suggestion was correct, that Rosalie was not David Poe's child and that Elizabeth left New York before her birth to avoid scandal. But that theory depends on the acceptance of Rosalie's birthdate as 20 December 1810. I favour the earlier date, for the reason given, and I believe that having been hounded by the critics in New York, and facing the prospect of another mouth to feed, David Poe gave up the struggle. My idea is supported by a letter written on 2 November 1811, referring to Mrs Poe's last illness, in which a Richmond historian, Samuel Mordecai, stated that Elizabeth had 'quarrelled and parted with her husband'. There is no reason to assume, as some earlier biographers did, that the quarrel and parting were recent at the time of the letter, for the writer only mentions it in passing, as an extra piece of information about Mrs Poe. I think John Allan was merely repeating gossip when he claimed that Rosalie was illegitimate, and his reason for doing so was to cast doubt on Edgar's character, a purpose for which Allan felt he had good reason at the time.

But whatever had happened to her husband, Elizabeth Poe was warmly welcomed back to the Richmond stage in the summer of 1810. A letter in the *Enquirer* on 21 September noted:

> From an actress who possesses so eminently the faculty of pleasing, whose powers are so general and whose exertions are so ready, it would be unjust to withhold the tribute of applause. Were I to say simply that she is a valuable acquisition to the Theatre, I should dishonor her merit, and do injustice to the feeling of the public... On her first moment of entrance on the Richmond Boards she was saluted with the plaudits of admiration, and at no one moment since has her reputation sunk.

In spite of the fact that she must by then have been feeling the effects of the consumption that was soon to kill her, Elizabeth worked as hard as she had always done. She missed the last two months of the Richmond season, but January 1811 found her in Charleston with Placide's Company, and after that she played a season in Norfolk, where a theatregoer suggested that 'grief may have stolen the roses from her cheeks' — though disease was a more probable cause. It was back to Richmond in August, and the inevitable losing battle against death. She did not appear at her own benefit on 9 October, but two days later she gave her last performance in a benefit for another actress. By 29 November the theatre management was announcing a further benefit owing to 'the serious and long continued indisposition of Mrs Poe and in compliance with the advices and solicitations of many of the most respectable families'.

Richmond society had rallied round magnificently. Samuel Mordecai, in the letter from which I have already quoted, wrote: 'A singular fashion prevails here this season — it is — charity. Mrs Poe, who you know is a very handsome woman, happens to be very sick, and . . . is destitute. The most fashionable place of resort now is — her chamber — And the skill of cooks and nurses is exerted to procure her delicacies . . .' It was a measure not only of the kindheartedness of the Southerners and the popularity of the theatre in Richmond, but also of Elizabeth Poe's striking personality, her ability to impress almost everyone she met. Edgar was to grow up with the same gift, as well as his mother's capacity for hard work in difficult and demoralizing circumstances.

But all the sympathy and charity in the world could not save Elizabeth Poe. On 10 December 1811 the *Enquirer* announced:

> Died, on last Sunday morning, Mrs Poe, one of the Actresses of the Company at present playing on the Richmond Boards. By the death of this lady the Stage has been deprived of one of its chief ornaments. And to say the least of her, she was an interesting Actress, and never failed to catch the applause and command the admiration of the beholder.

We have no reliable details of her last days (indeed, we cannot even be certain of where she was living since it has been proved that the house revered in Richmond for many years as the place of her death did not exist in 1811), but there is an account (albeit highly coloured) in Mary Newton Stanard's sentimental and fanciful biography of Edgar, *The Dreamer,* published in New York in 1909, from which it is worth quoting this extract:

> As the hours and days dragged by the patient grew steadily weaker and weaker. She seldom spoke, but lay quite silent and still save when shaken by the torturing cough. On a Sunday morning early in December she lay thus motionless, but wide-eyed, listening to the sounds of church-bells that broke the quiet air. As the voice of the last bell died away she stirred and requested, in faint accents, that a packet from the bottom of her trunk be brought to her. When this was done she asked for the children, and when Nurse Betty brought them to the bedside she gave into the hands of the wondering boy a miniature of herself, upon the back of which was written: 'For my dear little son Edgar, from his mother', and a small bundle of letters tied with blue ribbon. She clasped the baby fingers of the girl about an enamelled jewel-case, of artistic workmanship, but empty, for its contents had, alas, gone to pay for food. She then motioned that the little ones be raised up and allowed to kiss her, after which, a frail, white hand fluttered to the sunny head of each, as she murmured a few words of blessing, then with a gentle sigh, closed her eyes in her last, long sleep.

It is unlikely that there was any great, flower-bedecked, moving funeral such as Mrs Stanard went on to describe in imaginative detail. Probably it was a short, sad, dismal affair, for Elizabeth Arnold Hopkins Poe was buried in an unmarked grave and forgotten until America at last began to appreciate the gift of her son, many years after his own death. But it must have been a bewildering and frightening time for little Edgar, as he was taken away from everything he had known and into the family of John Allan, tobacco merchant. Rosalie, who was adopted by the Mackenzie family, was too young to know what was happening; William had already gone to his grandfather, David Poe Sr, in Baltimore. So it was upon Edgar that the heaviest emotional blow must have fallen. With the astonishing resilience of the child, he settled comfortably into his new life, but during the identity crisis of the teenage years the scar left by the loss of his mother began to reveal itself and he embarked upon the search for love and security that would finally drive him to despair and to his death. As he moved from a world of seedy boarding houses into the comfortable home of a successful businessman, who would later inherit great wealth, it seemed that Edgar's future was assured. He was a bright, attractive child and, with all the advantages that his new background could provide, he might have built himself a life blessed with happiness and fulfilment. But something went wrong; some mysterious force propelled Edgar Allan Poe towards disaster. As the long drawn-out tragedy of his life unfolds, we can only marvel at the fact that, in spite of it all, he managed to leave us some of the most unforgettable prose and verse ever written.

Chapter 2

The New World and the Old

The Richmond in which the little Edgar Poe found himself orphaned in the winter of 1811 was the capital of the wealthiest and most populous of the eighteen states then in the Union. The city had been built on a bend of the James River, where waterfalls had blocked the passage of the English explorers who in 1607 had founded the first permanent settlement in America, some sixty miles downriver at Jamestown. Virginia had played a prominent role in the War of Independence, becoming known as the 'Cradle of American Civilization' and the 'Mother of States', and providing three of the new nation's first four Presidents: George Washington, Thomas Jefferson and James Madison (the second President, John Adams, hailed from Massachusetts). Richmond had become the state capital in 1779, when British troops threatened the old seat of government at Williamsburg, and by the turn of the century it exerted a powerful influence on the political, social and economic life of the whole country. Its wealth was largely founded on tobacco, an industry that began in 1612 when John Rolfe planted some seeds brought from West Indies. Rolfe's success in growing and curing the new crop, and transporting it to England, encouraged many young men to leave the Old Country and try their luck in Virginia as planters, merchants and shippers. By the time Edgar Poe became an adopted citizen, Richmond's population had grown to about 6,000, roughly half of which was made up of black slaves and servants, and the city was characterized by the sweet, almost sickly smell of cured tobacco that still hangs over parts of it today.

John and Frances Allan, who replaced the missing father and the dead mother in Edgar's life, had been married for eight years and had no children. Mrs Allan was one of the sympathetic group of ladies who ministered to Elizabeth Poe in her sickroom and, always a prey to her emotions, she developed an affection for Edgar. When Mrs Poe died, Frances Allan took the little boy to her home over the store in which her husband was a partner, at the corner of Main and Thirteenth Streets, a few blocks east of the city centre. John Allan

loved children and, at the age of thirty-one, was no doubt anxious
for a son to whom he could pass on the business fortune he had
hopes of making. But he was not keen to adopt. One reason for this
reluctance was that he already had an illegitimate son, though he
could hardly use that as an excuse to his wife. Eventually, however,
the earnest entreaties of the highly-strung Frances, the fact that
Edgar was a bright and attractive child, and the assumption by his
friends that he was to be the lad's benefactor, persuaded Allan to
play the father officially. On 7 January 1812, he paid the firm of
Hobday and Seaton eight dollars for a crib.

It is important to take a close look at the man who was to be such
a great influence in the life of Edgar Poe. John Allan has been
pictured by Poe's more apologetic biographers as something of a
monster, hard and unfeeling, interested only in money, and completely out of sympathy with Edgar's ambition to be a writer. It is
true that he worked hard and that he tended to organize his private
affairs in much the same way as he ran his business, but there was
more to him than that — and if he was harsh with Edgar in later
years, perhaps he had good reason.

John Allan was born in Scotland, in the parish of Dundonald,
Ayrshire, in 1780. At the age of fourteen or fifteen he arrived in
America to work as a clerk for his uncle, William Galt, who during
twenty years had established himself as one of Richmond's leading
merchants. In 1800 Allan and another of William Galt's clerks,
Charles Ellis, went into business on their own, with working capital
of two thousand pounds; they were mainly interested in exporting
tobacco, but they also set up a general dealer's shop, which prospered as Richmond grew.

Three years after becoming his own man, Allan felt that he was
doing well enough to take a wife, and on Saturday, 5 February 1803,
he married Frances Keeling Valentine, of Princess Anne County, a
beauty apparently much sought-after by the eligible bachelors of
Richmond. John Allan must have been considered not only a handsome young fellow but also a businessman with good prospects. And
he was grateful for the blessings bestowed upon him by the new
country: on 4 June 1804, he became a naturalized American before
Chief Justice John Marshall. Thus it was with satisfaction at his
progress and confidence in the future that he settled down to married
life in an apartment above the Ellis and Allan store at Thirteenth and
Main, seeming not to resent the fact that he was obliged to share his
home with his sister-in-law, Ann Moore Valentine — indeed his letters
show that he took a great interest in his wife's family.

The Allans were also interested in the social life of Richmond,
mixing not only with their own merchant class but also with the

families of wealthy tobacco planters, the Virginian 'aristocracy', some of whom claimed links with the English Cavaliers of the seventeenth century and carried on an outmoded tradition of chivalry associated with the noble and romantic supporters of Charles I. It was these people, rather than the hard-headed entrepreneurs of the Allan's closer circle, who were to influence the young Edgar Poe: their extreme sensitivity in the matter of honour, their flamboyant good manners and their losing battle against a world that seemed set on relegating them to history and turning their virtues into vices, combined to excite the dramatic sensibilities Poe had inherited from his parents and caused him, in later life, to regard the 'aristocracy' as his true ancestors. Not long before his death he would write to a woman he had hopes of marrying that 'my soul is incapable of dishonor' and that 'I can call to mind no act of my life which would bring a blush to my cheek — or to yours. If I have erred at all, in this regard, it has been on the side of what the world would call a Quixotic sense of the honorable — of the chivalrous. The indulgence of this sense has been the true voluptuousness of my life. It was for this species of luxury that, in early youth, I deliberately threw away a large fortune, rather than endure a trivial wrong.'

Such sentiments would hardly have endeared him to John Allan, who though he did become wealthy never appears to have suffered from delusions of grandeur. He was a product of the Jeffersonian democracy that promoted equal opportunity, a member of the rising middle class that prospered entirely by its own efforts without relying on background and breeding. But it is a mistake to infer from this that Allan was a man without imagination and out of sympathy with artistic ideals. He was well read, and his voluminous letters show that he both enjoyed writing and could use language with intelligence, delicacy and even wit. And though by his own admission he was 'not one of those much addicted to suffer by unavailing regrets', there was perhaps a nagging, unfulfilled ambition to write something more worthy than a well constructed, enjoyable family letter, for he once confessed that he would give anything to have a talent for writing, adding 'and what use would I not make of the raw material at my command!' This ambition of Allan's has been used to explain why he later turned against Edgar, the argument being that his jealousy would have been aroused when Poe announced his desire to be a writer. I believe it will become obvious that the reasons for Allan's behaviour were much more concrete.

But those early days in Richmond gave no hint of the storms to come. Little Edgar quickly settled into his new home and began to develop a deep affection for Frances Allan, from whom he received the love and care he needed while her husband provided the material benefits that had been so conspicuously lacking in the boy's earlier life. The Ellis and Allan company was doing well — dealing not only in tobacco but also in cloth, hardware, grain, tea, coffee, liquors, shipping, indeed almost anything that would turn a profit — and this, combined with the fact that John Allan knew he would inherit the large fortune of his uncle, William Galt, meant that life for the Allans was not marred by financial worries. They held frequent parties, visited great plantations, and often journeyed into the beautiful heartland of Virginia. Edgar played a full part in this life; John Allan's reservations about taking him in seem to have disappeared, and although he did not actually adopt the boy this should not be seen as being of great significance, for legal adoptions were rare in those days. In every respect Edgar was one of the family. He was, in the words of his aunt, Elizabeth Poe of Baltimore, 'truly the child of fortune to be placed under the fostering care of the amiable Mr and Mrs Allen [sic], Oh how few meet with such a lot — the Almighty Father of the Universe grant that he may never abuse the kindness he has received and *that* from those who were not bound by any ties except those that the feeling and humane heart dictates.'

At the age of four Edgar, a bright, attractive child with large eyes and dark curly hair, was sent to a dame school run by one Clotilda Fisher, and the following year he was enrolled in the academy of William Ewing, which John Allan knew was a good school because his illegitimate son, Edward Collier, had attended it, and because Mr Ewing's discretion was probably as valuable as his schoolmasterly skills. According to Ewing, Edgar was 'a charming boy' who quickly got used to school, liked it, and did well at his lessons. But the boy was heading for a second fundamental change in his background. Having just become accustomed to the well-regulated life of the Virginian middle class, he found another great upheaval before him. He was going to England.

The business of Ellis and Allan had been expanding rapidly. John Allan had made a trip to Lisbon in 1811 with a shipload of provisions for the British army which was then fighting the Peninsular War, and he had formed plans to set up an office in London, but the European conflict intervened. It would later have disastrous consequences for John Allan and the firm.

Under Napoleon, France had become the master of central and western Europe; Britain's only way of checking her territorial ambitions was through sea power, and the British fleet established a tight blockade of the sea routes to Europe. Unfortunately this damaged not only the French but also the Americans, who previously had been able to make large profits on European sales of grain, tobacco and so on. President Thomas Jefferson tried to retaliate by pushing through Congress the Embargo Act, designed to deprive the world of American goods. Among enraged United States merchants, however, this rapidly became turned round into the 'O-grab-me' Act or the 'Damnbargo', and Jefferson was forced to replace it with the Non-intercourse Act, which permitted trade with any country other than France and Britain. This was not much help either, since both the British and the French simply seized American cargoes on the high seas. But the main fury of the American people was reserved for the British, who had also been 'arresting' United States naval vessels and taking from them crew members claimed to be British deserters. Cries for war with Britain grew steadily louder, and in 1812 Jefferson's successor, James Madison, was forced by the so-called 'War Hawks' of Congress to declare hostilities, in spite of a British undertaking to stop harassing American shipping.

The outbreak of war, of course, put an end to the expansion plans of Ellis and Allan. John Allan offered his services to the army, making it clear that he was not a military man. Charles Ellis enlisted in the Nineteenth Richmond Regiment. Even old David Poe, Edgar's grandfather, emerged from retirement to do his bit: when the British attacked Baltimore in 1814, the 'General' was active among the city's defenders. Frances Allan retired to Staunton, Virginia, in the safety of the beautiful Shenandoah Valley, presumably taking Edgar with her. In September 1814 she wrote to her husband that she was 'pleased to heare [sic] that my dear friends were well and also that our City is safe from the enemy'. She trusted in God that Richmond would remain unharmed but was alarmed by a report that the British had landed at York and pointed out 'how badly my trembling hands perform'.

Neither side gained much from the War of 1812. The Americans were lucky that the British army was fully occupied in Europe, though the United States navy of sixteen ships did dent the myth of Britain's invincibility at sea with a number of daring and brilliant actions, while on land General Andrew Jackson wiped out a large British force at the Battle of New Orleans. On the other hand, the British badly wounded American pride by landing at Chesapeake Bay and marching to occupy Washington, withdrawing only when they were defeated at Baltimore. By 1814 it was clear than any military victory was impossible; the Americans realized that Napoleon's imminent defeat would end their trading difficulties, while Britain recognized that its former colony had grown into a nation worthy of respect. In December 1814, a peace treaty was signed at Ghent, in Belgium.

Back in Richmond, John Allan revived his plans to establish a branch of the partnership in London, and by June 1815 the whole family, including Ann Valentine (who was always known as Nancy), was waiting to embark at Norfolk. On 22 June Allan wrote to Charles Ellis asking him to sell one of the Allan slaves for six hundred dollars and to arrange for others to be hired out at fifty dollars a year. He added that at nine o'clock the following morning they would go to Hampton Roads, in the estuary of the James River, to join their ship: 'Frances and Nancey [sic] evince much fortitude; it has been a severe trial to them, their Spirit is good, Ned cared but little about it, poor fellow.' By half past three in the afternoon of the 23rd they were on their way — 'Frances & Nancy rather qualmish Edgar and myself well'.

The journey to England was far from comfortable. The ship's captain appears to have been quite a tyrant, and in order to increase his profits on the voyage he kept his passengers short of accommodation and facilities. John Allan had to sleep on the floor of the cabin into which the whole family was crammed, and although they had brought a good stock of provisions these were of limited use because the captain denied them cooking facilities, saying that wood was in short supply. Allan later wrote a letter of protest to the owners of the ship, but by that time, of course, the privations were over.

They arrived off Liverpool at five o'clock in the evening of 28 July, to the great relief of the two women, who had proved to be very poor sailors, and docked the following morning, after which they made their way to Lillyman's Hotel. Edgar, who had quickly overcome seasickness and enjoyed the voyage, began to absorb the images of the Old World that were always to remain in his mind.

The first-time reader of Edgar Allan Poe's more popular works could perhaps be forgiven for thinking that he was an English writer: his elaborate, even luxuriant style, his backdrops of ruined castles and palaces with their rich but tasteful draperies, his damp and misty landscapes, his obsession with ancestry and tradition — all have the feel, almost the smell of England. Much of this is derivative, borrowed from English and other European authors, but there is no doubting the influence of four-and-a-half boyhood years in England.

For an intelligent and observant six-year-old, the sights and sounds of the bustling city of Liverpool, its narrow streets and stone buildings in sharp contrast to the open spaces and wooden mansions of Virginia, would have been exciting enough, but they were followed by an even greater adventure — a coach journey to Scotland to visit the Allan relatives. They travelled up the west coast of England and crossed the border into Scotland north of Carlisle, making their way through the counties of Dumfriesshire and Ayrshire to Irvine, a village a few miles inland from the beautiful Firth of Clyde. It may have been memories of the English Lakeland or the Scottish glens through which they passed that prompted Poe to write, many years later, in a poem called 'The Lake':

> In the spring of youth it was my lot
> To haunt of the wide world a spot
> The which I could not love the less —
> So lovely was the loneliness
> Of a wild lake, with black rock bound,
> And the tall pines that towered around.

After a few days in Irvine staying with John Allan's sisters, Mary and Jane, the visitors moved east to the town of Kilmarnock, which lies about twenty miles south-west of Glasgow and which was the home of Allan Fowlds, who had married Nancy Allan, John's third sister. The good-hearted Scots must have received their long-lost relative with a show of traditional hospitality, for Frances Allan was, in her husband's words, 'so bewildered with wonder' that she could not bring herself to write home to the Ellises. By this time, though, the northern autumn was far advanced and the damp atmosphere did not agree with the Virginians; when they arrived in London on 10 October 1815, after what must have been an arduous and uncomfortable journey via Glasgow, Edinburgh, Newcastle and Sheffield, Frances was obliged to retire to bed with a bad cold and sore throat, while the rest of the family felt 'cursedly dissatisfied', as John Allan told Charles Ellis in a letter.

They took furnished lodgings at 47 Southampton Row, Bloomsbury — pleasant and comfortable, but inconvenient for Allan's work since there was no room to set up an office, and expensive at six guineas a week. Indeed, the high price of everything in England at that time dismayed and alarmed the visitors, and Frances kept a sharp eye on the budget. The French war had ended in the summer of 1815, but it had cost Britain dearly: by 1816 the annual interest payments on the National Debt totalled more than thirty million pounds, and the Tory Government led by the Earl of Liverpool pushed taxation up to a crippling level. Tea, sugar, tobacco, beer, soap, candles, paper — the excise man, it seemed, could not keep his grasping hands off anything, and prices soared (bread cost a shilling a loaf, an enormous sum in those days). Mass unemployment hit every industry from manufacturing to agriculture; food riots broke out; factories were sacked by desperate workers; savagely repressive laws were introduced to crush what the Government saw as the spirit of rebellion.

In short, it was the worst possible time to set up a new business, but John Allan was a stubborn man and wrote to Ellis: 'I told you I should stay here three years . . . You may count upon five years without an accident — the expense of making an establishment is too heavy for a shorter period.' Ellis, however, was plainly worried. He wrote back:

> As bad off as we are, God preserve us in anything worse . . .
> Tobacco down; down . . . that is a state I am afraid you will
> be caught in when your consignments reach you. But let me
> suggest again I think you had better come down in the price
> so as to induce buyers to come forward . . . As great as the
> losses will be they will be small in comparison to those who
> hold . . .

Allan said, 'If I get through the year I hope I shall not see such another.' He was not only thinking about his business. Frances was now continually ill, though the nature of the sickness remains a mystery (it may have been simply 'nerves', which afflicted her from time to time and in this case may have been brought on by the family's difficulties), and Nancy Valentine wrote home to say they were all miserably dissatisfied in London.

Edgar was far too busy to be dissatisfied. He had been enrolled in a boarding school at 146 Sloane Street, Chelsea, run by two sisters named Dubourg — a name Poe recalled when he gave it to a character in 'The Murders in the Rue Morgue' — whose brother George worked as a clerk in the office John Allan had set up at 18 Basinghall Street, in the City of London. Difficult as things were, Allan spared no expense when it came to Edgar's education. 'Master Allan', as he was known in England, did not sleep in a dormitory at the Dubourgs' school but had the luxury of 'separate bed' at an extra guinea a term. The school bill to midsummer 1816 read as follows:

Board & Tuition ¼ year	7	17	6
Separate Bed	1	1	0
Washing	0	10	6
Seat in Church	0	3	0
Teachers & Servants	0	5	0
Writing	0	15	0
Do. Entrance	0	10	6
Copy Book, Pen &c	0	3	0
Medicine, School Expenses	0	5	0
Repairing Linen, Shoe-strings &c	0	3	0

Mavor's Spelling	0	2	0
Fresnoy's Geography	0	2	0
Prayer Book	0	3	0
Church Catechism explained	0	0	9
Catechism of Hist. of England	0	0	9
	£12	2	0

In December of that year, Allan paid the Misses Dubourg another twenty-three pounds sixteen shillings, and at the end of August 1817 a further twenty-four pounds sixteen shillings.

At this point, against all the odds, John Allan did something which many writers have taken as an indication that he really had Edgar's best interests at heart and that, during this period at least, he may have truly regarded him as his son: he sent him to a better and more expensive school. On the face of it, this seems to have been a brave step — his financial insecurity was increasing with England's troubles, and only blind optimism would have suggested that there was any sign of improvement on the horizon. (Allan himself wrote of 'Taxes heavy, debt large, People discontented & desperate, Revenue falling off & scarcely a hope left of relieving the one or providing for the other'.) Allan was having personal difficulties as well as business ones, however. Frances had continued in poor health and Nancy remained unhappy in London, which cannot have made Allan's life any easier. He dealt with the two women by taking them to Cheltenham Spa, the famous Gloucestershire health resort, and leaving them there. Perhaps he felt that the expense of sending Edgar away to school in the country was equally worthwhile, for with Frances, Nancy and the boy out of the way he could devote all his attention to his work, if not to other women, with whom he seems to have been involved so often, as we shall see. John Allan was nothing if not a pragmatist.

So, whether concern or selfishness lay behind Allan's decision, Edgar was sent to the Manor House School, run by the Reverend John Bransby, Master of Arts, at Stoke Newington, which was then a village a few miles north of London. Bransby was an august gentleman and a scholar in the best traditions of late eighteenth-century England — well versed in classics, an amateur botanist and a horticulturist, an energetic sportsman, and a man with a magpie instinct for collecting scraps of information on all manner of subjects. Poe, looking back twenty years later, described him well in one of his finest tales, 'William Wilson':

With how deep a spirit of wonder and perplexity was I
wont to regard him from our remote pew in the gallery, as,
with step solemn and slow, he ascended the pulpit! This
reverend man, with countenance so demurely benign, with
robes so glossy and so clerically flowing, with wig so
minutely powdered, so rigid and so vast, — could this be he
who, of late, with sour visage, and in snuffy habiliments,
administered, ferule in hand, the Draconian laws of the
academy?

For his part, Bransby, questioned long afterwards by a Poe
admirer and former pupil of the Manor House, classified Edgar Allan
as 'wayward and wilful', though the reverend gentleman did admit
that he was 'a quick and clever boy' who, by the time he left the
school, could speak French, had a working knowledge of Latin, and
'was far better acquainted with history and literature than many
boys of a more advanced age who had had greater advantages than he
had had'.

But it is Poe himself who gives us the clearest picture of his school-
days in England, even though it is somewhat distorted through
embellishment necessary to the substance of the story. 'William
Wilson' is a classic study of the *doppelgänger*, the ghostly 'double'
that can haunt the troubled mind; in this case the 'double' is the
personification of William Wilson's conscience which first manifests
itself at school:

> . . . a large, rambling, Elizabethan house, in a misty-looking
> village of England, where were a vast number of gigantic
> and gnarled trees, and where all the houses were exces-
> sively ancient. In truth, it was a dream-like and spirit-
> soothing place, that venerable old town. At this moment,
> in fancy, I feel the refreshing chilliness of its deeply-
> shadowed avenues, inhale the fragrance of its thousand
> shrubberies, and thrill anew with undefinable delight, at
> the deep hollow note of the church-bell, breaking, each
> hour, with sullen and sudden roar, upon the stillness of the
> dusky atmosphere in which the fretted Gothic steeple lay
> imbedded and asleep.

In fact the Manor House was no such thing; the school took its
name from the real manor house, which stood across the road, and
the building inhabited by Mr Bransby's boys was rather plain, if not
ugly. Gothic intricacies ascribed to it by Poe in his tale were necessary
to his creation of an air of indefinable menace. His description

of the classroom and the life of the school, however, is likely to be
more factual:

> The school-room was the largest in the house — I could not
> help thinking, in the world. It was very long, narrow and
> dismally low, with pointed Gothic windows and a ceiling
> of oak. In a remote and terror-inspiring angle was a square
> enclosure of eight or ten feet, comprising the *sanctum,*
> 'during hours', of our principal, the Reverend Dr Bransby.
> It was a solid structure, with massy door, sooner than open
> which in the absence of the 'Dominie', we would all have
> willingly perished by the *peine forte et dure.* In other
> angles were two other similar boxes, far less reverenced,
> indeed, but still greatly matters of awe. One of these was
> the pulpit of the 'classical' usher, one of the 'English and
> mathematical'. Interspersed about the room, crossing and
> recrossing in endless irregularity, were innumerable
> benches and desks, black, ancient, and time-worn, piled
> desperately with much-bethumbed books, and so beseamed
> with initial letters, names at full length, grotesque figures,
> and other multiplied efforts of the knife, as to have
> entirely lost what little of original form might have been
> their portion in days long departed. A huge bucket with
> water stood at one extremity of the room, and a clock of
> stupendous dimensions at the other.
>
> The grounds were extensive, and a high and solid brick
> wall, topped with a bed of mortar and broken glass,
> encompassed the whole. This prison-like rampart formed
> the limit of our domain; beyond it we saw but thrice a
> week — once every Saturday afternoon, when, attended by
> two ushers, we were permitted to take brief walks in a
> body through some of the neighbouring fields — and twice
> during Sunday, when we were paraded in the same formal
> manner to the morning and evening service in the one church
> of the village.
>
> The morning's awakening, the nightly summons to bed;
> the connings, the recitations; the periodical half-holidays,
> the perambulations; the play-ground, with its broils, its
> pastimes, its intrigues; — these, by a mental sorcery long
> forgotten, were made to involve a wilderness of sensation,
> a world of rich incident, an universe of varied emotion, of
> excitement the most passionate and spirit-stirring.

What was provided in terms of actual education and care can be
seen from the following bill, the only one in existence:

Manor House School.
Stoke Newington. Xmas 1818

J. Allan Esqr
  for Masr Allan

To the Revd John Bransby

	£	s	d
Board & Education	23	12	6
Washing £1:11:6 Single Bed £2:2:0	3	13	6
Allowance £0:5:0 Pew & Chary Sermon £0:3:6	—	8	6
Books, Stationary &c	—	14	11
French	—	—	—
Dancing £2:2:0 Drawing £— Music £—	2	2	—
Shoemaker £1:15:6 Taylor £ Hairdresser £0:2:0	1	17	6
Sundries	—	1	—
Apothecary	0	13	0

Please to pay to Messrs. Sikes Snaith & Co
                    Mansion House St   £33   2   11

The apothecary's bill apparently concerned an injury to Edgar's hand, for attached to Bransby's account was one from Thos. Smith & Son of Stoke Newington for 'Mas. Allen [sic] at Mr Bransby . . . Dress — Hand' on 31 August 1818, and 'Ointment & Lint' on 16 September. Also interesting is the shoemaker's bill, which seems to show that Edgar was pretty heavy on his feet — he had his shoes mended on 26 August and again on both 21 and 25 September.

In all, from the beginning of 1818 to the spring of 1820, John Allan paid out almost two hundred and fifty pounds for Edgar's education at the Manor House School, and he seems to have taken pride in the boy, writing to his uncle, William Galt, that 'Edgar is growing wonderfully and enjoys a good reputation as both willing and able to receive instruction' and 'he is a verry [sic] fine boy and a good scholar'. Even if there had been a little self-interest in his decision to send Edgar to the Manor House, it seems that Allan was genuinely trying to give his ward a good start in life and was pleased by the boy's progress. Yet he was not really being a father to Edgar, who was rarely mentioned in letters to Richmond, and with Frances completely wrapped up in her own state of health 'Master Allan' was left to get along by himself at school, going home only in the Christmas and summer vacations. Turning again to the autobiographical 'William Wilson', it may be that one can detect a hint of slight bitterness as well as pride in Edgar's statement that 'at the age when few children have abandoned their leading-strings, I was left to the guidance of my own will, and became, in all but name, the master of my own actions'.

Perhaps it should be said in Allan's defence that he had plenty of other things on his mind. Upon his return from Cheltenham, where he had left his wife and sister-in-law in the autumn of 1817, he took a house at 39 Southampton Row (another English memory that remained with Edgar, who used the address in his comic story 'Why the Little Frenchman Wears His Hand in a Sling') and settled down to try to fend off the financial collapse that would eventually overwhelm him. He also seems to have found time to enjoy himself, and this caused friction between him and Frances, if the half-humorous but barbed comments are anything to go by in the following letter written by Mrs Allan during a trip to Devonshire in 1818 (and with her execrable spelling and punctuation left intact):

Dawlish, Octr 15

My dear hubby

Your kind letter of the 13 was received this morning and you will perceive I have lost no time in replying to it, however pleasant a duty it may be I fear it will be long ere I shall write with any facility or ease to myself, as I fiend you are determined to think my health better contrary to all I say it will be needless for me to say more on that subject but be assured I embrace every opportunity that offers for takeing air and exercies but at this advanced seasons of the year we cant expect the weather to be very good I am this moment interrupted with a message from Mrs Dunlop requesting I would accompany her in a ride which I shall accept the Carriage is now at the door

Friday morning Octr 16

we had a very long and pleasant ride we started at two o'clock and did not return until six the day was remarkably fine we had a beautyfull view of the surrounding Cuntry we had a smart Beau with us who arrived here from London a few days ago I was very much pressed to go to the ball last night and nothing prevented me from going but the want of a little finery so you and the Doctr may lay aside some of your consequence for I really think you have a great deal of Vanity to immagien you are the cause of all my misery, I only wish my health would admit of entering into all the gaieties of this place I would soon let you see I could be as happy and contented without you as

you appear to be in my absence as I hear of nothing but
partyes at home and abroad but long may the Almighty
grant my dear husband health and spirits to enjoy them.

Plainly Allan thought little of his wife's illness, while she did not
much like the goings-on at Southampton Row, which no doubt had
been reported to her by Nancy, who was back in London by that
time. Frances returned to the city in November 1818, but she continued to yearn for the English countryside and made efforts to find
a retreat on the South Coast. Edgar came home that Christmas, and
it was probably quite a jolly time, for there were signs of better days
ahead as the country enjoyed something of a commercial boom. The
economic revival was short-lived, however. The year 1819 —
notorious for the 'Peterloo Massacre' of protesting workers in
Manchester — saw a return to financial crisis, and the Government's
decision to adhere to the gold standard (relating the value of
currency to the market value of gold) effectively lowered the
purchasing power of money. John Allan was within a whisker of
bankruptcy by the end of the year; he wrote to Charles Ellis, 'Please
to bear in mind that I have only about £100 here in the world.' He
had no choice but to wind up the English end of the business and go
home, but that in itself was no easy task. The company was heavily
in debt, and on the personal level Mrs Allan had 'the greatest aversion
to the sea and nothing but dire necessity' could entice her aboard
ship. It was not until the end of May 1820 that Allan managed to sell
his effects, settle the company's debt and Edgar's school bill, and get
the family north to Liverpool to await a passage to America.
At the beginning of June he wrote to Ellis: 'The Martha Capt
Sketchly will not sail before Wednesday next the 14th inst . . . Mrs
Allan is in better Health than usual Ann is quite well so is Edgar. I for
myself was never better.' The prospect of returning home had done
wonders for them all, and it must have been with great relief that
they watched the English coast fading away into the distance behind
their ship. Edgar, who loved sea travel and would later often describe
it in his stories, was probably in a state of high excitement over the
voyage, and there is no evidence that he had any regrets at leaving
England. Certainly, his writings betray no particular love or regard for
the mother country, though they were influenced by the thorough-
ness and discipline of an English education, albeit brief, and the more
subtle effects wrought by life in a part of the world so very different
in experience, tradition, appearance and atmosphere from the
America in which he was to spend the rest of his days. It remains a
matter for conjecture whether the stay in England contributed to
Poe's later restlessness in his native land — his failure to settle down

at university, for instance, and his lifelong impatience with a society which, it is fair to say, was less cultured and in some respects less civilized, perhaps, than the England of the early nineteenth century. Edgar Allan Poe was never very impressed by the democracy on which his fellow-countrymen so prided themselves. He compared it to mob rule and wrote that, 'They started with the queerest idea: that all men are born free and equal.' It may well be that he formed such attitudes while enjoying the advantages of the class-ridden society of Georgian England.

These thoughts were for the future, however. As the 'Martha' beat out into the Atlantic there was a month-long sea trip to look forward to, and it turned out to be a great deal more comfortable than the previous voyage. When the ship docked in New York on 21 July 1820 there was the excitement of the homecoming, though the full pleasure of that had to be delayed while Mrs Allan recovered from the journey and it was not until 2 August that the family reached Richmond, having travelled to Norfolk by steamboat and from there by coach. They moved into the Ellises' home at the south-west corner of Franklin and Second Streets, 'an unpretentious residence', according to the historian Mordecai, with a garden 'embellished by a row of fine linden trees along its front'. It was to be some time before the Allans regained their former comforts and status, but at least Edgar got something back immediately — his name. He was no longer 'Master Allan', he was Edgar Allan Poe.

Chapter 3

Birth of a Poet

The years immediately following the return to Richmond saw the nadir of John Allan's fortunes; paradoxically, they also formed the happiest period in the early part of Edgar Poe's life. At the end of 1820 the family moved into a cottage on Fifth Street, between Marshall and Clay Streets, at the north-west limit of the fashionable district surrounding the Capitol. Edgar was enrolled in one of Richmond's best schools, run by Joseph H. Clarke on Broad Street, only a few blocks from the Allans' home. Clarke later recalled that Edgar was as 'playful as most boys', though 'his general deportment differed in some respects from others. He was remarkable for self-respect, without haughtiness, strictly just in his demeanor with his fellow playmates, which rendered him a favorite even with those above his years.' He was also stubborn, never giving way in an argument until faced with irrefutable evidence, and such tenacity helped him to do well at his lessons. He was intellectually advanced for his age, for a school bill covering the summer term of 1822 — when he was thirteen — shows that he was studying Horace and Cicero, and Clarke added that at the same time he was reading the works of Homer in Greek.

This schooling cost John Allan about sixty dollars a year, which was considerably cheaper than the annual fee he had paid in England, but in the parlous state of his finances he still had difficulty in meeting the bills and was obliged to pay some of them by instalment. Nevertheless he was able to pay thirty dollars in advance when, in April 1823, Edgar's education was entrusted to William Burke. Joseph Clarke was leaving Richmond, and Burke either took over his school or was running one of his own.

It was at this time that Edgar began to write poetry. Clarke remembered the boy's highly developed powers of imagination and 'sensitive and tender heart', which showed in 'juvenile compositions addressed to his young female friends'. The young ladies in question were the inmates of a smart boarding school run by Miss Jane Mackenzie, sister of the Mr Mackenzie who had adopted Rosalie Poe.

Edgar would make pencil sketches of the girls who took his fancy and send them to the subjects, with accompanying verses, via Rosalie, who naturally had access to the establishment. Both he and his sister got into serious trouble when Miss Jane discovered the clandestine correspondence and took steps to protect the innocence of her charges. Rosalie was very close to Edgar during this period, spending much time playing with him and Tom Ellis, the son of John Allan's partner. Soon, however, she became something of an embarrassment. She seemed to be a perfectly normal, healthy child, with blue eyes, rosy cheeks and a cheerful nature, but when she was twelve some quirk of heredity produced in her abnormal retardation: her mental development ceased, and the rest of her life was spent in childish dependence on other people.

It would be wrong to picture Edgar at this time as a pale, mooning, rather soppy young poet. He was big for his age, could box well, was good at bandy (a form of tennis) and was a strong swimmer — the story is told of how at about the age of fifteen he swam six miles against the tide in the James River. Such a boy might justly expect to be regarded as a leader among his classmates, but Edgar had one great drawback: he was the child of common play actors who, no matter how much they might have been appreciated by theatre audiences, could never have been socially acceptable in Virginia, with its aristocratic pretensions. The sympathy which had surrounded Elizabeth Poe on her deathbed had evaporated; she lay in an unmarked plot in St John's churchyard, remembered only occasionally by those who had applauded her performances, and recalled woundingly by the snobbish schoolfellows of her son, who was probably an object of envy because of his academic ability and athletic prowess. The point is reinforced by one of Edgar's classmates at the Burke school, John Preston: 'It was known that his parents had been players, and that he was dependent upon the bounty that is bestowed upon an adopted son. All this had the effect of making the boys decline his leadership; and on looking back on it since, I fancy it gave him a fierceness he would otherwise not have had.' There is a legend that while Edgar was at Burke's he was insulted by an older boy, promptly challenged him and, using guile as much as strength, soundly thrashed him.

Edgar was not without firm friends, however. One, Thomas Sully, came from a home where Elizabeth Poe was remembered with affection, for his father had known and acted with her and would have been able to answer many of the questions that must have occupied her son's mind. Thomas Sully was struck by Edgar's loyalty to and concern for his friends: 'Edgar when he knew that I had an unusually hard lesson would help me with it. He would never allow the big boys to tease me, and was kind to me in every way. I used to admire and envy him, he was so bright, clever and handsome.'

Then there was Tom Ellis, who after Edgar's death paid tribute to him in the *Richmond Standard* in 1881: 'No boy ever had a greater influence over me than he had . . . He was very beautiful, yet brave and manly for one so young . . . He was trained in all the habits of the most polished society. There was not a brighter, more graceful, or more attractive boy in the city than Edgar Allan Poe . . . Talent for declamation was one of his gifts. I well remember a public exhibition at the close of a course of instruction in elocution which he had attended . . . and my delight when he bore off the prize in competition with . . . others who were regarded as among the most promising of the Richmond boys.'

Not that Edgar was always the perfect little gentleman. He had a great sense of fun and adventure like any other healthy boy of his age, and often led Tom Ellis into trouble for doing 'many a forbidden thing . . . He taught me to shoot, to swim, and to skate, to play bandy &c; and I ought to mention that he once saved me from drowning — for having thrown me into the falls headlong, that I might strike out for myself, he presently found it necessary to come to my help, or it would have been too late.' Other evidence of boyish high spirits comes from Jack Mackenzie, Rosalie's stepbrother, who remembered joining Edgar on raiding expeditions to local orchards and turnip patches. This sense of adventure remained with Poe all his life, giving rise to stories like 'The Gold Bug', which concerns buried treasure, the nautical *Narrative of Arthur Gordon Pym,* and others. In an article for the *Southern Literary Messenger* in 1836 he was to write: 'How fondly do we recur in memory to those enchanted days when we first learned to grow serious over Robinson Crusoe! — when we first found the spirit of wild adventure enkindling within us, as by the dim firelight we labored out, line by line, the marvelous import of those pages, and hung breathless and trembling with eagerness over their absorbing — over their enchanting interest. Alas! the days of desolate islands are no more.'

The proud, adventurous boy must have been thrilled, then, towards the end of 1824 when Richmond prepared to receive a visit from General LaFayette, hero of the War of Independence, and a military cadet company was formed with one John Lyle as its captain and Edgar A. Poe as his lieutenant. The company, known as the Richmond Junior Volunteers or the Junior Morgan Riflemen, was decked out in frontier-style fringed shirts, provided with real guns and swords, and detailed to act as guard of honour for the victor of Yorktown as he attended a service at the Memorial Church. Legend has it that Captain Lyle and Lieutenant Poe, swords drawn in salute, accompanied the great man up the aisle to the pew occupied by

Chief Justice Marshall. It is interesting to speculate on whether Edgar made himself known to LaFayette as the grandson of the Baltimore patriot who was to draw such a warm tribute from his old commander a few weeks later. Be that as it may, Edgar seems to have acquired a taste for things military, because he joined Lyle in appealing to the Governor of Virginia, a month after LaFayette's visit, for permission to retain the weapons issued to the Junior Volunteers, promising that 'each individual will not only pledge himself to take proper care of them, but we ourselves will promise to attend strictly to the order in which they are kept by the company'. Whether the Governor granted the request is not known, but what is certain is that experience with the cadets was to stand Edgar in good stead when he later found himself obliged to join the United States Army.

In the meantime, the situation in the Allan household was not particularly happy for Edgar. He still adored and was adored by Frances, his 'Mama', but she was in poor health, as well as being rather neurotic and inclined to dwell upon her own difficulties. As for John Allan, there is an interesting insight in the recollection of Jack Mackenzie: 'Mr Allan was a good man in his way, but Edgar was not fond of him. He was sharp and exacting, and with his long, hooked nose and small keen eyes looking from under his shaggy eyebrows, he always reminded me of a hawk. I know that often when angry with Edgar he would threaten to turn him adrift, and that he never allowed him to lose sight of his dependence on his charity.' Towards the end of 1824 Allan certainly had cause to be anxious and irritable. Weakened by the English debacle and also by economic crisis at home, the firm of Ellis and Allan had fallen ever deeper into debt, and by 1822 Allan had been obliged to seek permission from creditors to retain his property in return for a personal guarantee that his debts would be discharged. His uncle, William Galt, came to his aid by giving the family a house at the corner of Fourteenth Street and Tobacco Alley, but in 1824 Allan had to agree to the winding up of the partnership.

It was against this background that Allan wrote to Henry Poe, Edgar's elder brother, on 1 November 1824:

> I have just seen your letter of the 25th ult. to Edgar and am much afflicted that he has not written to you. He has had little else to do, for me he does nothing & seems quite miserable, sulky & ill-tempered to all the Family. How we have acted to produce this is beyond my conception — why I have put up so long with his conduct is little less wonderful. The boy possesses not a Spark of affection for us not a particle of gratitude for all my care and kindness

towards him. I have given a much superior Education than
ever I received myself. If Rosalie has to relie on any affection from him God in his mercy preserve her — I fear his
associates have led him to adopt a line of thinking & acting
very contrary to what he possessed when in England. I feel
proudly the difference between your principles & his &
have my desire to Stand as I ought to do in your Estimation. Had I done my duty as faithfully to my God as I
have to Edgar, then had Death come when he will he had
no terrors for me, but I must end this with a devout wish
that God may yet bless him & you and that Success may
crown all your endeavors & between you your poor Sister
Rosalie may not suffer. At least She is half your Sister &
God forbid my dear Henry that We should visit upon the
living the Errors & frailties of the dead . . .

This is an astonishing letter for John Allan to have written, lacking
all the balance and style of his usual epistles, and one can only
wonder at his reason for sending it and at the effect it must have had
on its seventeen-year-old recipient. It is an angry, bitter and rather
vicious outburst from a man who yet seems to be seeking approval.
Why he should have wanted to ingratiate himself with Henry is a
mystery, but he went a very strange way about it, casting a slur on
his dead mother and throwing doubt upon the paternity of his sister.
As far as the references to Edgar are concerned, such sentiments will
sound familiar to many a teenager: often parents cannot accept the
mental development and growing independence of an adolescent
whose search for identity and truth, the nature of which is only
half-comprehended, may call into question the beliefs and standards
on which the parents have based their lives, perhaps even raising
embarrassing uncertainties in their own minds. When the child is
adopted, the situation can be much worse. Any reaction against the
adoptive parents can be viewed as base ingratitude or, in extreme
cases, as the result of inferior breeding. Clearly, John Allan had
adopted these defensive positions, for which there were probably
several reasons.

Allan was a businessman by inclination as well as by profession,
and a boy like Edgar Poe was not likely to be any friend of com-
merce and those who operated it. Indeed his attitude is forcefully
expressed in his satires 'The Business Man' (published in 1840) and
'The Literary Life of Thingum Bob' (1844), the second of which is
mainly an attack on literary charlatans but contains the following
sideswipe: 'My father, Thomas Bob, Esq., stood for many years at
the summit of his profession, which was that of a merchant-barber, in

the city of Smug. His warehouse was the resort of all the principal people of the place . . .' The narrator also refers to having 'been christened Thingum after a wealthy relative so surnamed', an obvious reference to Poe's own middle name.

The knives really come out in 'The Business Man', however:

> I am a business man. I am a methodical man. Method is *the* thing after all . . . If there is anything on earth I hate it is a genius. Your geniuses are all arrant asses — the greater the genius the greater the ass — and to this rule there is no exception whatever . . . The Assault and Battery business . . . was somewhat ill-adapted to the delicate nature of my constitution; but I went to work in it with a good heart, and found my account, here as heretofore, in those stern habits of methodical accuracy . . . The truth is that few individuals in any line did a snugger little business than I. I will just copy a page or so out of my Day-Book; and this will save me the necessity of blowing my own trumpet — a contemptible practice, of which no high-minded man will be guilty. Now, the Day-Book is a thing that don't lie . . .

Attitudes like these are deep-rooted, and John Allan — who appears to have found his most regular reading matter in day-books and ledgers, and who kept careful account of every penny — must have been deeply disappointed to see that young Edgar showed no inclination towards pursuing some worthwhile career which would have made him financially independent. The remark in Allan's letter to Henry about the boy's associates leading him into a 'contrary' way of thinking is significant: those friends belonged to some of the best families in Richmond; they were proud, aristocratic, wealthy — and idle. A life such as theirs would not only have appealed to the romantic side of Edgar's nature, concerned as it was with the glories of tradition and the mystique of 'a good name', but it would also have attracted his inherited sense of the histrionic. As an imaginative teenager he would have seen the nobility of Virginia as great heroic characters striding across the stage of history before an audience of gawping and envious peasants, as representatives of a well-founded past threatened by the encroachments of an uncertain and somehow less worthy future.

Apart from all this, there was Edgar's passion for reading and his developing interest in poetry. With adolescent fervour, he may even have expressed a desire to devote his life to literature, which would not have endeared him to his guardian. Although it is difficult to accept the conventional picture of John Allan as the complete counting-house philistine — as we have seen, he was not un-acquainted with literature and he indulged his pleasure in writing through his extensive correspondence — in his world literature could be no more than a diversion, or perhaps a social accomplishment. Like many Americans in a hard-headed age when economic growth was the prime concern of an emergent nation, Allan could not accept art as a way of life, even though he might appreciate the fruits of the artists' labours. Art was something other people produced; it was not like working for one's living. 'If there is anything on earth I hate it is a genius. Your geniuses are all arrant asses . . .'

Unfortunately, Allan was not the only one to hold such views, as Edgar was to discover to his cost. The very Southern nobility young Poe admired so much turned its back on him almost as soon as he first began to be successful at making his living by writing. The planter aristocrats appreciated art well enough, but they could not stand a professional artist. It was ungentlemanly, they thought, to apply professional standards to writing poetry, for instance. It was a pursuit for the gifted amateur. Edgar, whose creed it was that the true artist must be a professional in the sense that he lived by and for his art, was completely bewildered by this attitude, which would eventually cause him to turn his back on the South.

However, it was not just Edgar's views about writing which produced the friction that seems to have arisen between John Allan and him. There was, from Allan's point of view, a more pressing reason. Allan had been unfaithful to his wife even before the family had gone to England, and had at least one illegitimate child, Edward Collier. After the return to Richmond he appears to have made quite a hobby of adultery — his mistress Mrs Elizabeth Wills and her children, all three of whom seem to have been Allan's, would figure in Edgar's life at a later stage. Richmond was a fairly small place and word of Allan's gallivantings would certainly have got around. Edgar, with his ever-widening circle of acquaintances, would almost certainly have heard rumours, and that was worrying to his guardian. It is impossible to tell whether Frances knew that her husband was unfaithful, but if she did know she must have decided to do nothing about it, for there is no record of any rift between the couple. Allan obviously wanted to keep his marriage going (with his business problems, a scandal would have been fatal — quite apart from whatever feelings he had for Frances), and he must have realized that if Edgar had heard gossip his position was threatened. The boy was very fond of his 'Ma' and, as Allan knew, he suffered from an overdeveloped sense of honour. Perhaps, then, it was to discredit in advance anything Edgar might say that Allan began to try to blacken his charac-

ter, as he did in the infamous letter to Henry. Later on, Edgar would
do much of his guardian's work for him in this respect, by telling lies
about Allan.

There is no saying how bad things were at home for Edgar at this
time, but if he needed something to take his mind off his troubles, he
found it sometime in 1823 when Rob Stanard, a younger boy who
had fallen under the spell of Poe's heroic personality, took him home
to show him off to his mother. Jane Craig Stanard, who was thirty,
was a rare beauty, proud and statuesque, with large dark eyes, a fine
straight nose, full sensuous lips, and a complexion 'which was pale,
with the radiant and warm palor of a tea-rose or a pearl'. In the
flowing, flattering dress of the period, and against the noble, almost
palatial background of her elegant home overlooking Capitol Square,
she reminded Edgar of what must have been for him one of the joys
of his Greek lessons, the *Iliad* — for who was she but Helen, and what
could he do but worship her as the Greeks had worshipped Zeus's
daughter. He wrote a poem for her, calling it simply 'To Helen':

> Helen, thy beauty is to me
>   Like those Nicéan barks of yore,
> That gently, o'er a perfumed sea,
>   The weary, wayworn wanderer bore
>   To his own native shore.
>
> On desperate seas long wont to roam,
>   Thy hyacinth hair, thy classic face,
> Thy Naiad airs have brought me home
>   To the glory that was Greece,
> And the grandeur that was Rome.
>
> Lo! in yon brilliant window niche
>   How statue-like I see thee stand,
> The agate lamp within thy hand!
> Ah, Psyche, from the regions which
>   Are Holy Land!

'To the glory that was Greece, And the grandeur that was Rome'
Those are the most famous words Edgar Allan Poe ever wrote, an
undying memorial to the woman who inspired them.

When 'To Helen' appeared in a volume of Poe's poems in 1845,
the author noted: 'Private reasons — some of which have reference to
the sin of plagiarism, and others to the date of Tennyson's first
poems — have induced me, after some hesitation, to republish these,
the crude compositions of my earliest boyhood. They are printed
verbatim — without alteration from the original edition — the date of

which is too remote to be judiciously acknowledged.' In fact, the original edition was published in 1831: 'To Helen' was not among the poems in his first two collections — 1827 and 1829 — but that is not to say it had not been written in 'earliest boyhood', for Poe constantly polished and revised his poems and may not have considered that one properly finished until 1831. On the other hand, when the 1845 volume was published Poe was defending himself against charges of imitating Tennyson (the subject of plagiarism became quite an obsession with him towards the end of his life), so he had good reason for dating his poems as early as possible. None the less, that Mrs Stanard was the poem's inspiration is hardly to be doubted, since Poe later spoke of 'the lines I had written, in my passionate boyhood, to the first, purely ideal love of my soul . . . Helen Stannard [sic] '.

Mrs Stanard, who was married to a judge, became Edgar's friend and confidante, his refuge when things were uncomfortable at home, his spiritual guide and temporal adviser, his mother-figure and his symbol of perfect womanhood. She was the first resurrection of Elizabeth Arnold Poe: she had all the beauty Edgar remembered (and no doubt embellished) in his mother, and all the maternal tenderness that lived on in his mind. True, he had already found a second mother in Frances Allan, but she was not the mother he really wanted, perhaps not the mother he felt he deserved. Jane Stanard, by comparison, was a goddess, as intelligent as she was beautiful, and hers was the image with which Edgar replaced his mother's, the image he would revere for the rest of his life.

The joy Edgar found in Mrs Stanard, however, was to be short-lived. She had a brain tumour and, after a period of insanity, she died in April 1824. Edgar was shattered. He had experienced at first hand one of the abiding themes of romantic literature, the death of a beautiful woman, and the horror of it was to figure in some of his greatest stories and in most of his best poetry. Many years later he would meet a second Helen, who turned out to be rather less ideal than the first, and he would confess to her that throughout the spring of 1824 he had haunted Mrs Stanard's grave. It was, perhaps, his first attempt to understand the relationship between love and death, a purpose he would pursue mercilessly in his work. More immediately, the death of Jane Stanard may have been another reason why John Allan, when he wrote to Henry Poe in the autumn of 1824, found Edgar 'quite miserable, sulky & ill-tempered'.

Allan himself, though, was not in the best of tempers towards the end of 1824. He was facing total financial ruin. His business had collapsed, and he was provided with a roof over his head only through the charity of his uncle. It must have been a very worrying time. As the year turned, however, there was a sudden and dramatic change of circumstances. William Galt became ill, and in March 1825 he died, having named John Allan as his main beneficiary, and thus one of the wealthiest men in Richmond: 'I give, devise and bequeath to the said John Allan my three landed estates named the "Byrd" . . . with the slaves stocks and property of all kinds there belonging to . . .' That little parcel was six thousand acres or more of fertile land by the James River some fifty miles west of Richmond. And there was more: land and tenements on E Street in Richmond, a vacant lot at the corner of F Street and Second Street, some property Galt had bought from Ellis and Allan when the firm was going into liquidation, and the house at Fourteenth Street and Tobacco Alley in which the Allan family was then living. John Allan had suddenly become a man of substance, a man of property, a man of leisure. His situation had been completely reversed. No longer need he worry about the price of tobacco, indeed about where the next dollar was coming from. He was, by virtue of his wealth if not his background, a gentleman. It might be thought that this stroke of good fortune would have made him more indulgent towards Edgar, but as things turned out he became meaner than he had ever been, forcing the boy to take actions that would blight his entire future. In the spring of 1825, however, the excitement of new-found wealth at least made Allan forget for a while about the boy, no kin of his, whom he had come to regard as being so troublesome.

The first thing was to move into a house better fitted to the Allans' new station in life, and they found it at the corner of Fifth and Main Streets, almost within the precincts of the Capitol. It was a splendid and rather exotic building of two storeys, each of which was fronted by a spacious verandah, and it was surrounded by an extensive landscaped garden filled with fig trees, vines, shrubs and flowers. In short, it was a veritable mansion, and John Allan paid fifteen thousand dollars for it. Through this house passed some of the leading families of Virginia as Mrs Allan indulged her taste for entertaining and for social climbing, and from these guests Edgar learnt the courtly and rather affected Southern manners that were to remain with him throughout his life (impressing some people, particularly women, but causing amusement among members of New York society with whom he later mixed during an ill-fated attempt to establish himself as a literary personality in the North).

Another visitor was Henry Poe, who spent some time in Richmond in 1825; by then he was a midshipman in the United States Navy. He brought news of the family in Baltimore, whom Edgar had never met. Grandmother Poe, widowed in 1816 and unable to manage on the 'General's' pension of two hundred and forty dollars a year, had gone to live with her daughter, Maria Clemm, a move that was to have important implications for Edgar in later years.

Edgar had news for Henry, too. He was in love, really properly in love, with fifteen-year-old Sarah Elmira Royster. This was not the pure, chaste passion of the poet for his Helen of Troy (Elmira later confessed that Edgar never wrote verses to her), but the strong, physical, unbounded love of the teenager. They had met shortly after the removal to Fifth Street — the Roysters lived across the road from the Allans' new house — and must have been attracted to each other almost immediately, for it was only a few months before they were to be parted and in that time they had become unofficially engaged. According to her contemporaries, Elmira was a beautiful girl, with a pale, china-doll face, large dark eyes, and a crown of ringlets. Her description of Edgar as a teenager, recorded in a conversation with Edward V. Valentine in 1875 and now in the Valentine Museum, Richmond, is as follows:

> He was a beautiful boy — Not very talkative. When he did talk though he was pleasant but his general manner was sad — He was devoted to . . . Mrs Allan and she to him . . . He was very generous . . . He had strong prejudices. Hated anything coarse and unrefined. Never spoke of his parents. He was kind to his sister as far as in his power. He was as warm and zealous in any cause he was interested in, very enthusiastic and impulsive. I was about 15 or 16 when he first addressed me and I engaged myself to him . . .

To illustrate her point about Poe's hatred of anything unrefined, Elmira told how she and a girl friend met Edgar on Church Hill in Richmond, and when the friend made some coarse remark, young Poe chided Elmira for associating with such a person. The bond between them grew steadily throughout the summer of 1825, and as Edgar prepared to leave Richmond to attend the University of Virginia they swore to be true to each other. But it was to be more than twenty years before they were able to contemplate marriage.

Chapter 4

Learning the Hard Way

Edgar's departure for the brand new University of Virginia at Charlottesville, seventy miles to the west of Richmond, was to prove a turning point in his life, and may even be seen as the very beginning of his decline into misery and despair. There were brief periods of happiness and hope to come, it is true, but Poe never recovered from the traumatic experiences that were in store for him when he left home early in 1825. For one thing, he did not know as the coach rattled out of Richmond, that his romance with Elmira Royster was over: her parents had other plans for her. Nor did he know that John Allan, whose reasons for sending Edgar to Charlottesville in the first place will be discussed later, would set out to completely discredit him, indeed to crush him. And he could not know that for the first time his own weakness of character — and perhaps his physical deficiency — was to be exposed.

His name, date of birth, place of residence, and the name of his guardian were entered in the university matriculation book on 14 February 1826, and Edgar joined an exclusive group of 177 young men, mostly from the first families of Virginia, to enjoy what was then a novel form of higher education, arising out of the vision of Thomas Jefferson. The author of the Declaration of Independence had retired from the Presidency, after two terms, in 1808, and at the age of sixty-five he had settled down to establish a cultural, educational and philosophical tradition in the same way that he had laid the foundations for the peculiarly American political principles of democracy and individual liberty which still hold good today. Jefferson was an idealist, but that is not to say he was naive: he always sought practical applications for his theories, even if he never quite realized that not everyone could live up to his own high standards.

The University of Virginia was one practical result of Jefferson's reforming zeal. He believed not only that the provision of education was incumbent upon every state, but also that education was an essential part of the democratic process -- and what better place to demonstrate his theory than in his home state, whose higher education system at that time was modelled on the English public school system. Jefferson's aim in establishing the university was, he said, 'to develop the reasoning faculties of our youth, enlarge their minds, cultivate their morals, and instil into them the precepts of virtue and order – and generally to form them to habits of reflection and correct action, rendering them examples of virtue to others, and of happiness within themselves'.

The achievement of his ambition was no easy task, and it was nine years before he could persuade the Virginia State Legislature to allot fifteen thousand dollars annually from its Literary Fund to the new university. Jefferson chose the site at Charlottesville, drew up the plans for the buildings – which remain outstanding examples of the classical style of architecture – and supervised their construction; then he formulated the ground rules for the administration of the university and its academic endeavours; finally he persuaded the finest scholars he could find to join the staff. When the University of Virginia opened its doors to students early in 1825, it became the first institution of higher education to include music and the liberal arts in its curriculum and the first to allow students to choose their own courses of study.

Edgar Poe studied ancient and modern languages, the former under Professor George Long, a young English don, and the latter under Professor George Blaetterman, a bad tempered and sometimes violent German (he was finally sacked after protests from the students); but, according to a nineteenth-century biographer, George E. Woodberry, Poe 'being facile rather than studious, did not acquire a critical knowledge of these languages'. What he did acquire, however, was a reputation for hard drinking which not only dogged him for the rest of his life but also sullied his name after his death. Woodberry again:

> He was now seventeen years old, somewhat short in stature, thick-set, compact, bow-legged, with the rapid and jerky gait of an English boy [presumably in contrast to the easy, loping stride of the all-American boy]; his natural shyness had become a fixed reserve; his face, clustered about by dark, curly hair, wore usually a grave and melancholy expression, the look that comes rather from the habit of reverie than any actual sadness, but his features would kindle with lively animation when, as frequently happened, he grew warm in his cause. He divided his time, after the custom of the undergraduates, between the recitation room, the punch bowl, the card table, athletic

sports, and pedestrianism ... he moved in a jolly set. At
first he roomed with a chum, one Miles George, of
Richmond, on the lawn, to adopt the local description, but
after a quarrel and pugilistic duel in correct form between
them (the combatants shook hands at the end of it) Poe
settled in No 13 West Range, decorated the walls with
charcoal sketches of Byron, and there gathered the fellows
to enjoy peach and honey, as the delectable old-time
Southern punch was called, and to play at loo or seven-up
[card games]. Both in drinking and in card-playing Poe
acted capriciously, and either was or affected to be the
creature of impulse.

There is the classic statement of one of the Poe legends, that
university turned him into a drunken waster. It was a legend that
people were only too ready to believe after Poe's death, in view of
the gossip which circulated about him towards the end of his life and
of the lies told about him by his very first biographer, Rufus
Griswold, who felt he had good reason to dislike Poe, as will become
clear. Woodberry was in fact trying to write a sympathetic
biography, and he did recognize Poe's literary worth, but he was
writing at a time when the puritan attitudes which Edgar was to
offend were still prevalent, so he did not examine the gossip too
closely.

Fortunately, there is plenty of evidence available to help to build
up a more balanced picture of Poe. Some of it in this particular case
comes from the 'one Miles George, of Richmond', who in a letter to
Edward Valentine dated 18 May 1888 pointed out that he and Edgar
had never been room mates, and had certainly not quarrelled. The
'pugilistic duel', he said, had been no more than boyish high spirits.
George also disagreed with Woodberry's physical description of Poe,
saying that he recalled him as being rather delicate and slender —
weighing between a hundred and thirty and a hundred and forty
pounds — and that if his legs were bowed the malformation must
have been so slight as to be unnoticeable.

Miles George's insight into Poe's personality is revealing. He went
on to say that Edgar was fond of gathering together his friends and
reading poetry to them, often his own work; sometimes for their
entertainment he would seize a piece of charcoal and sketch
whimsical figures on the walls of his room with such skill that his
fellows found themselves wondering whether in later life he would
become a painter rather than a poet; he was restless and easily
excited, occasionally wild, at other times melancholic and morose,

but generally a spirited and agreeable companion. George also spoke of Poe labouring under excessive nervous excitability, but concluded that when he drank, it was more to calm himself than for artificial stimulation.

Another fellow-student, Thomas Goode Tucker, wrote of the young Poe's drinking habits: 'Poe's passion for strong drink was as marked and as peculiar as that for cards. It was not the *taste* of the beverage that influenced him; without a sip or a smack of the mouth he would seize a full glass, without water or sugar, and send it home at a single gulp. This frequently used him up; but if not, he rarely returned to the charge.' Highly suggestive, that — but not in the way Woodberry assumed when he used it to illustrate Poe's 'capricious' behaviour. What it suggests is that Poe did not actually like the potent brew of peach brandy and honey, which was surely drunk for its taste as much as for its intoxicating effect, and that he drank it with such bravado purely to cover up his dislike, fearing that he would become the butt of his companions' jokes if they knew his secret. He was, after all, 'in a jolly set', indeed the jolliest set that was likely to be found in Virginia: his companions belonged to the plantation aristocracy and had been brought up to believe in their own superiority, unused to restraint and caring more for horses than for history, more for cards than for classics, more for liquid delights than for literature. The orphaned son of poor actors could not hope to match his fellow-students, in spite of his guardian's newfound wealth and status — as many a would-be social climber has learnt, money is no substitute for pedigree; earned wealth creates a class of its own which does not easily merge with an established aristocracy. Indeed, a serious social split was developing in the Old South as the landed gentry battled for survival in the face of a growing mercantile class. Edgar, rather ungratefully it might be thought, remained sympathetic towards the old ruling class, and if he could never become part of it, his time at university at least gave him the opportunity of joining in the life of the young aristocrats. Unfortunately for him, that way of life attracted a great deal of critical attention: Professor Long, who left the university in 1828 and returned to England, later recalled: 'There were some excellent young men, and some of the worst that I ever knew.'

The university was not running quite as Jefferson had intended. The great revolutionary's concept of democracy decreed that the student body should be self-governing, but those proud under-graduates were not the best subjects for discipline of any kind, much less for self-control, and by the end of the first year there was such chaos that the administration of college law had to be placed in the hands of the staff. The immediate result was the imposition of strict rules, which brought a violent reaction from the students. In May 1826, Edgar wrote home:

> You have heard no doubt about the disturbances in college — Soon after you left here the Grand Jury met and put the students in a terrible fright — so much so that the lectures were unattended — and those whose names were upon the Sheriff's list — travelled off into the woods and mountains — taking their beds and provisions along with them — there were about 50 on the list — so you may suppose the college was very well thinn'd — this was the first day of the fright — the second day 'A proclamation' was issued by the faculty forbidding 'any student under pain of a major punishment to leave his dormitory between the hours of 8 & 10 AM — (at which time the sheriffs would be about) or in any way resist the lawful authority of the sheriffs' — This order was very little attended to — as the fear of the faculty could not counterbalance that of the Grand Jury — most of the 'indicted' ran off a second time into the woods — and upon the examination the next morning by the Faculty — some were reprimanded — some suspended — and one expelled — James Albert Clarke from Manchester (I went to school with him at Burke's) was suspended for two months. Armstead Carter from this neighbourhood, for the remainder of the session — And Thomas Barclay for ever — There have been several fights since you were here — One between Turner Dixon, and Blow from Norfolk excited more interest than any I have seen, for a common fight is so trifling an occurrence that no notice is taken of it — Blow got much the advantage in the scuffle — but Dixon posted him in very indecent terms — upon which the whole Norfolk party rose in arms — and nothing was talked of for a week — but Dixon's charge and Blow's explanation — every pillar in the University was white with scratched paper — Dixon made a physical attack upon Arthur Smith one of Blow's Norfolk friends — and a 'very fine fellow' — he struck him with a very large stone on the side of his head — whereupon Smith drew a pistol (which are all the fashion here) and had it not missed fire — would have put an end to the controversy — but so it was — it did miss fire — and the matter has since been more peaceably settled — as the Proctor engaged a Magistrate to bind the whole forces on both sides — over to the peace . . .

Such incidents would be repeated a hundred times, and on occasion there were serious riots, but Edgar seems never to have been involved in the violence, though on one occasion he was summoned to appear before a Faculty inquiry into 'information that certain Hotel Keepers . . . had been in the habit of playing at games of chance with the students in their Dormitories'. The hotel keepers did not fulfil the function that their title implies today; they were leading citizens appointed to provide the undergraduates with food, furniture, laundry and other services — and also, Jefferson fondly hoped, to act as spiritual guides and advisers. Of course, commercial interest was a powerful influence on the actions of these men, and they were not about to endanger their catering concessions by trying to prevent the students from dissipating their energies in drinking and gambling, two vices which, in any case, were considered proper for a Southern gentleman. Poe, with his pretensions towards gentility and a perfectly natural desire to be accepted into the group, threw himself into both these activities with gusto, but if he was hampered by a dislike of alcohol, his position as a gambler put him at even more of a disadvantage: he provided an excellent justification for the old admonition that you shouldn't gamble if you cannot afford to lose.

John Allan had sent his ward off to university with one hundred and ten dollars in his pocket. Before the end of his first week at Charlottesville, Edgar was, through no fault of his own, thirty-nine dollars in debt. Several years later he would explain:

> The expenses of the institution at the lowest estimate were $350 per annum . . . Of this $50 were to be paid immediately for board — $60 for attendance upon 2 professors . . . Then $15 more were to be paid for room-rent — remember that all this was to be paid in *advance*, with $110. — $12 more for a bed — and $12 more for room furniture . . .

All that came to a hundred and forty-nine dollars, so Edgar was at once obliged to seek credit from an hotel keeper, George Spotswood (which was, in fact, against the rules of the university). He wrote to Allan for more money, and was rewarded with forty dollars, which covered his debt and left him with a dollar in his pocket. Poe recalled bitterly:

> I was obliged to hire a servant, to pay for wood, for washing, and a thousand other necessaries . . . Books must be had, if I intended to remain at the institution — and they were bought accordingly *upon credit*. In this manner

debts were accumulated, and money borrowed of Jews in Charlottesville at extravagant interest . . .

There is ample evidence that Poe was telling the truth: a year later George Spotswood was still trying to get money out of Allan for the provision of Edgar's college servant, and as late as 1828 a bill for sixty-eight dollars owed to a gentleman's outfitter called Samuel Leitch remained unpaid. Spotswood told Allan in a letter that he presumed 'when you sent Mr Poe to the University of Virginia you felt yourself bound to pay all his necessary expenses', but this was obviously not the case. Allan must have had at least a rough idea of what the university would cost, and there is no doubt that he was in a position to pay — he simply refused to do so. But if he was not prepared to foot the bill, why did he send Edgar to college? There are two possible explanations. First, that he was anxious to get the boy out of Richmond because Edgar knew too much about his guardian's extra-marital activities and might have told Frances about them; second that Allan's inheritance had made him one of Richmond's premier citizens and as such he would have been expected to live up to certain standards, among which would have been the kind of education he provided for his 'son and heir' (which no one at the time doubted that Edgar was). The obvious course would have been for him to have enrolled Edgar at William and Mary College in Williamsburg, one of the greatest of the old colonial seats of learning and Jefferson's own alma mater, but Allan was almost certainly persuaded to choose Charlottesville by a close friend, General John H. Cocke, who had been one of Jefferson's warmest supporters in the university project. One can imagine the attraction from the point of view of the newly-rich Allan. Here was something unique in education, something devised by one of the fathers of the nation, and supported by the local aristocracy. There were social points, to back up the financial ones, to be gained from sending one's 'heir' to such an institution.

But if these two thoughts did influence Allan, in the end he seems to have had but one purpose in view. That aim, as we shall see, was to humiliate, degrade and discredit Edgar Poe, and ultimately to be able to banish him from the Allan family. John Allan was a man who cared about his public prestige, as he would later prove when he drew up his will, and that meant he had not only to protect his reputation by keeping his marriage intact despite his passion for other women, but also to make provision for the fruits of this passion. There was Edward Collier to think about, apparently his first illegitimate child, and by 1826 there may have been a second, a daughter by Mrs Wills to whom Allan would attempt to bequeath an allowance (this child's date of birth is unknown). If Edgar were to be accepted as his heir, these offspring would be left out in the cold, and then what would people say about their father? To make matters worse, it seemed that Edgar was not going to be a suitable caretaker for the Allan fortune. In John Allan's eyes he was turning into an idler, interested only in writing poetry and reading books, and Allan was not a man to throw away good money. Somehow he had to 'fix' Edgar: there seems to be no other reasonable explanation for his conduct.

Not that there was, during those exciting early months of 1826, any sign of the drama to come in Edgar's life. Shortage of money was a problem, but he soon found that he could easily obtain credit because his guardian was widely known as a wealthy and respectable citizen — and in any case there were far more important things on the mind of a seventeen-year-old boy with new worlds to conquer. His academic schedule was not exactly demanding: two hours' teaching daily, six days a week, beginning at seven o'clock in the morning. The rest of the time was his own, to be divided between study and pleasure. Studying was not so easy. In those early days the university library was open only one day a week and requests for books had to be delivered in writing twenty-four hours beforehand; Poe borrowed only about a dozen books during his time at university, and none at all during the first four months. He bought what books he could on credit and wrote home for others (with little success — Allan sent him the Cambridge Mathematics and *Gil Blas*, neither of which had any bearing on his course of study). He was not the most diligent student in the world anyway: his success in class — he was numbered among the top students in both Latin and French — depended more upon a natural facility of the mental process than upon any capacity for sustained effort in learning. Indeed, throughout his life Poe always pretended far greater erudition than he ever possessed. His intellectual range was impressive, but he was never the scholar that he would have so loved to have been.

The pleasurable side of Poe's life at the university leads, as I have suggested, into the realm of legend. The charges of excessive drinking and gambling were answered by Edgar in a letter to John Allan from which I have already quoted details of his college expenses. He went on to say that he was

> . . . regarded in the light of a beggar . . . I became dissolute, for how could it be otherwise? I could associate with no students, except those who were in a similar situation with myself — altho' from different causes — They from drunkenness, and extravagance — I, because it was my crime to have no one on Earth who cared for me, or loved

me. I call God to witness that I have never loved
dissipation. — Those who know me know that my pursuits
and habits are very far from anything of the kind. But I
was drawn into it by my companions. Even their profes-
sions of friendship — hollow as they were — were a
relief . . . I then became desperate and gambled — until I
finally involved myself irretrievably . . .

Such snivelling self-pity and self-justification does Poe no credit. He
blamed his companions, he blamed John Allan, he blamed anyone
but himself for his misfortunes, and that reaction was to become a
habit with him. In later years he would rail against the literary
establishment to disguise his own failure — or at least, since he was
partly right in his attacks, that aspect of his failure which was his
alone.

And yet Edgar's weakness of character was not the root cause of
his difficulties at Charlottesville. His excesses were brought on in
large measure by John Allan's calculated parsimony rather than by
any love of the dissolute life. In his most easily identifiable piece of
autobiography, 'William Wilson', Poe, on mature reflection, charted
the horrific downfall of a liar, gambler, cheat and drunkard against
the background of what he called 'the most dissolute university in
Europe' (it would have been foolish to place it in its true location).
He was not entirely a lost cause, and he never would be.

There is another, stranger aspect of the Poe myth which is worth
considering because it leads to further illumination of Poe's character
and attitudes as they are expressed through his work. This part of the
legend concerns one of the outdoor pleasures afforded by the
University of Virginia, what Woodberry called 'pedestrianism'.
Charlottesville is situated in the beautiful valley of the Rivanna River
with mountains on three sides — the fabled Blue Ridge, the Southwest
Mountains, and the Ragged Mountains. Poe, the disciple of Beauty,
has often been pictured wandering lonely as a cloud among those
mountains, spellbound by the natural wonders he saw; yet this
comforting portrait ill accords with Poe's own description of 'the
chain of wild and dreary hills that lie westward and southward of
Charlottesville, and are dignified by the title of the Ragged
Mountains', and his use of them as the scene of a story of mystery,
violence and horror. His hero in 'A Tale of the Ragged Mountains',
Augustus Bedloe, out walking among the hills, finds himself in:

. . . a gorge which was entirely new to me . . . The scenery
which presented itself on all sides, although scarcely
entitled to be called grand, had about it an indescribable

and to me a delicious aspect of dreary desolation . . . The
thick and peculiar mist, or smoke, which distinguishes the
Indian summer, and which now hung heavily over all
objects, served, no doubt, to deepen the vague impressions
which these objects created.

. . . I walked on for several hours, during which the mist
deepened around me to so great an extent that at length I
was reduced to an absolute groping of the way. And now
an indescribable uneasiness possessed me — a species of
nervous hesitation and tremor. I feared to tread, lest I
should be precipitated into some abyss. I remembered,
too, strange stories told about these Ragged Hills, and of
the uncouth and fierce races of men who tenanted their
groves and caverns. A thousand vague fancies oppressed
and disconcerted me — fancies the more distressing
because vague . . .

This affords an interesting insight into Poe's conception of beauty,
which is not at all what might have been expected from a self-
proclaimed Romantic of the nineteenth century and is, in fact, closer
to the view expressed in 1753 by Oliver Goldsmith when he
pronounced himself disgusted by the dismal landscape and hideous
wilderness of the Scottish Highlands. The delight in mountain
scenery which we take for granted today is actually a comparatively
modern development, dating from around the end of the eighteenth
century. Before that, as Lord Macaulay pointed out in his monu-
mental *History of England*, 'the crags and glens . . . were indeed the
same that now swarm . . . with admiring gazers . . . Yet none of these
sights had power, till a recent period, to attract a single poet or
painter from more opulent and more tranquil regions'. The poet
Thomas Gray, visiting the Alps in 1739, described one peak as
carrying 'the permission mountains have of being frightful rather too
far', and an earlier traveller saw the mountains of Scotland as 'part of
the creation left undressed; rubbish thrown aside when the
magnificent fabric of the world was created . . .' Such is the feeling
Poe conveyed in 'A Tale of the Ragged Mountains', and it adds force
to the impression of a man out of his time, someone who longed for
the glories of the past and never quite came to terms with the
demands and attitudes of the present: he leaned towards the mores
of an old aristocracy, deplored the rise of commercialism, and his
ideas of Art and Beauty were rooted more in the eighteenth century
than in his own.

His joy in the classical concept of order is neatly illustrated by two
of his less popularly regarded tales, 'The Domain of Arnheim', first

published in 1847, two years before his death, and 'Landor's Cottage', described by the author as 'a pendant' to the former. In 'Arnheim' Poe introduced a man named Ellison, who used his vast wealth to do 'much toward solving what has always seemed to me an enigma:— I mean the fact (which none but the ignorant dispute) that no such combination of scenery exists in nature as the painter of genius may produce . . . In the most enchanting of natural landscapes there will always be found a defect or an excess — many excesses and defects . . . no position can be attained on the wide surface of the *natural* earth, from which an artistical eye, looking steadily, will not find matter of offence in what is termed the "composition" of the landscape . . .' Ellison's solution is to suppose the 'sense of the Almighty creation to be *one step depressed* — to be brought into harmony or consistency with the sense of human art . . .' and produce a nature 'which is not God, nor an emanation from God, but which is still nature in the sense of the handiwork of the angels that hover between man and God' (with the additional attraction that this earthly paradise should be created 'not far from a populous city' — there is no love of wild and remote regions in this ideal).

The point is reinforced in 'Landor's cottage', when the wandering narrator happens upon a 'fairy-like avenue' with grass resembling Genoese velvet, clumps of wild flowers growing luxuriantly, and 'stones that once obstructed the way had been carefully *placed* — not thrown — along the sides of the lane, so as to define its boundaries at bottom with a kind of half-precise, half-negligent, and wholly picturesque definition . . . One thing became more and more evident the longer I gazed: an artist, and one with a most scrupulous eye for form, had superintended all these arrangements. The greatest care had been taken to preserve a due medium between the neat and graceful on the one hand, and the *pittoresco,* in the true sense of the Italian term, on the other . . . It was a piece of "composition", in which the most fastidiously critical taste could scarcely have suggested an emendation.'

Such were the visions that began to form in Poe's mind as he surveyed the classical splendour of Jefferson's university buildings in their setting of neat lawns and landscaped gardens. If he delighted in the surrounding scenery, it was most probably the rolling, open, fertile country — an eighteenth-century landscape painter's dream — to the north of Charlottesville that attracted him, rather than what would now be considered the rugged beauty of the mountains.

But there was more on his mind than beauty. As the year progressed, he sank ever more deeply into debt, and as well as his everyday expenses there were increasing losses at cards to be taken into account: according to a contemporary, William Burwell, Poe threw himself into gaming with a recklessness of nature which acknowledged no restraint, and by the end of the year his debts had soared to somewhere between two thousand and two thousand five hundred dollars (though how much of that sum he ran up at the card table is impossible to estimate). The curious thing is that Allan apparently knew nothing of all this, for in the two surviving letters to him that Poe wrote during this period, there is no mention of money troubles. The first of these letters, dated May 1826, has already been quoted. The second, written on September 21, gives no hint of trouble, other than that,

> . . . the whole college has been put in great consternation by the prospect of an examination — there is to be a general one on the first of December, which will occupy the time of the students till the fifteenth — the time for breaking up — It has not yet been determined whether there will be any diplomas, or doctors degrees given — but I should hardly think there will be any such thing, as this is only the second year of the institution and in other colleges three or four years are required in order to take a degree — that is, that time is supposed to be necessary — altho they sometimes confer them before — if the applicants are qualified.
>
> Tho' it will hardly be fair to examine those who have only been here one session, with those who have been here two — and some of them have come from other colleges — still I suppose I shall have to stand my examination with the rest—
>
> I have been studying a great deal in order to be prepared, and dare say I shall come off as well as the rest of them, that is — if I don't get frightened — Perhaps you will have some business up here about that time, and then you can judge for yourself —
>
> They have nearly finished the Rotunda — The pillars of the Portico are completed and it greatly improves the appearance of the whole — The books are removed into the library — and we have a fine collection.
>
> We have had a great many fights up here lately — The faculty expelled Wickliffe last night for general bad conduct — but more especially for biting one of the student's arms with whom he had been fighting — I saw the whole affair — it took place before my door — Wickliffe was much the stronger but not content with that — after getting the other completely in his power, he began

to bite — I saw the arm afterwards — and it was really a serious matter — It was bitten from the shoulder to the elbow — and it is likely that pieces of flesh as large as my hand will be obliged to be cut out — He is from Kentucky — the same one that was in suspension when you were up here some time ago — Give my love to Ma and Miss Nancy — I remain,

Yours affectionately,
Edgar A. Poe

It is not clear whether Edgar, when he writes 'you were up here some time ago', is referring to the same visit mentioned in the May letter, or whether Allan had made a second journey to Charlottesville. At all events, Allan sent Edgar a hundred dollars towards the end of the university session, but that was a mere drop in the ocean of debts threatening to overwhelm the boy. So it seems that if Allan did make a second trip to see his ward he did not pay much attention to what was going on, and was not approached — as might have been expected — by any of the business people to whom Poe owed money. There is, however, no doubt about Allan having been in Charlottesville in December 1826, for it was then that the floodtide struck, sweeping away all Edgar's hopes. The hard-headed Scot was appalled by the extent of the boy's debts and more particularly by the fact that gambling was responsible for a large part of them, but at the same time he took full advantage of the situation his meanness had helped to create. Now he could show Edgar to the world, and especially to the doting Frances, in 'his true colours'; now he had the ultimate weapon to combat possible exposure by Edgar of his own sins, for who was going to take the word of an ungrateful wretch guilty of throwing away his benefactor's money on drink and cards?

Allan played his own cards well. He paid off the most pressing debts, leaving enough outstanding to be of embarrassment to Edgar, as witness the bills from Spotswood and Leitch already mentioned, and a letter to Poe, dated 25 March 1827, from 'Your friend Edward G. Crump', asking whether he was able to repay money he had borrowed. Then Allan charged the boy with idleness because he had not taken the mathematics course at the university (Edgar had played into Allan's hands by concealing this fact from him), though he must have been aware that on the money he had provided Edgar could not have afforded the tuition fee. Finally he took his ward back to Richmond, letting it be known that Edgar had so besmirched his honour at Charlottesville that he could not possibly return there.

As if all this were not bad enough, there was a further blow awaiting Edgar on his return home. Elmira Royster's parents had sent her out of town, and he was coldly turned away when he called at her home. He had wondered why she had not replied to his letters from Charlottesville. It was many years before he learnt that they had not reached her, since her parents had intercepted and destroyed them. Another precious female had been wrenched from Edgar's grasp — first his mother, then Jane Stanard, and now Elmira. The pattern was beginning to establish itself. But Elmira, who would be married a few months later to a man called A. Barrett Shelton, still had an important role to play in Edgar's life.

The months following Poe's return from university must have been hell for him. His creditors were threatening to swear out warrants against him, raising the fearful prospect of the debtors' prison; his disgrace meant that he could not face his friends; and John Allan lost no chance of showing him up, even in front of the servants, as Edgar makes clear in the following letter, written in March 1827. He may have received some secret comfort from Frances, but the constant abuse from Allan was more than he could bear — and eventually he was provoked into answering back. What happened next is best told in his own words:

Richmond, Monday.

Sir,
  After my treatment on yesterday and what passed between us this morning, I can hardly think you will be surprised at the contents of this letter. My determination is at length taken to leave your house and endeavour to find some place in this wide world, where I will be treated — not as *you* have treated me — This is not a hurried determination, but one on which I have long considered — and having so considered my resolution is unalterable — You may perhaps think that I have flown off in a passion, & that I am already wishing to return. But not so — I will give you the reasons which have activated me, and then judge —
  Since I have been able to think on any subject, my thoughts have aspired, and they have been taught by you to aspire, to eminence in public life — this cannot be attained without a good Education, such a one I cannot obtain at a Primary school — A collegiate Education therefore was what I most ardently desired, and I had been led to expect that it would at some future time be granted — but in a moment of caprice you have blasted my hope — because forsooth I disagree with you in an opinion, which opinion I was forced to express—

Again, I have heard you say (when you little thought I was listening and therefore must have said it in earnest) that you had no affection for me —

You have moreover ordered me to quit your house, and are continually upbraiding me with eating the bread of Idleness, when you yourself were the only person to remedy the evil by placing me to some business — You take delight in exposing me before those whom you think likely to advance my interests in this world —

You suffer me to be subjected to the whims & caprice, not only of your white family, but the complete authority of the blacks — these grievances I could not submit to, and I am gone. I request that you will send me my trunk containing my clothes & books — and if you still have the least affection for me, as the last call I shall make on your bounty to prevent the fulfillment of the Prediction you this morning expressed, send me as much money as will defray the expenses of my passage to some of the Northern cities & then support me for one month, by which time I shall be enabled to place myself in some situation where I may not only obtain a livelihood, but lay by a sum which one day or another will support me at the University — Send my trunk &c to the Court-house Tavern, send me I entreat you some money immediately — as I am in the greatest necessity — If you fail to comply with my request — I tremble for the consequence.

Yours &c

Edgar A. Poe

It depends on yourself if hereafter you see or hear from me.

It is not difficult to read between the lines of this letter, though what 'opinion I was forced to express' must remain a mystery. 'Your white family' no doubt refers to Nancy Valentine, who seems to have had some attachment to her brother-in-law (she remained a member of his household even after the death of Frances) and may have supported his campaign against Edgar, perhaps also with an eye on a future legacy. And 'the Prediction you this morning expressed' was no doubt to the effect that such an ungrateful, reckless and dissolute character as Edgar would end up in jail. What is also clear is that the creditors were pressing hard — a note among John Allan's papers says Poe had given his name at the Court House Tavern as Henri Le Rennet — which explains why, in spite of his bold postcript, Poe was writing to Allan again the following day, 20 March 1827:

I am in the greatest necessity, not having tasted food since
yesterday morning. I have no where to sleep at night, but
roam about the Streets — I am nearly exhausted — I
beseech you as you wish not your prediction concerning
me to be fulfilled, to send me without delay my trunk
containing my clothes, and to lend me if you will not give
me as much money as will defray the expense of my
passage to Boston ($12) and a little to support me there
until I shall be enabled to engage in some business . . . I sail
on Saturday . . .

Whatever gaps may have been left in Poe's education by his
untimely removal from the University of Virginia, he had learnt one
lesson that he would never forget: how to beg for money.

In that year at college, too, lay many of the seeds of Edgar's
future misery and of the black reputation he would acquire. For one
thing, he began to develop a sense of grievance, a feeling that the
world was against him, in which he would often wallow later, and for
another there was the start of his drinking, which was to do so much
harm not only to his image but also to his mind and body. The
recollection of Thomas Goode Tucker, that one drink frequently
'used up' Edgar, is significant. It suggests that Poe's metabolism
reacted badly to alcohol and may mark the earliest indication of a
chronic illness that contributed to his death. Yet in spite of the fact
that he could not take liquor, Poe continued to drink, and this also
formed a pattern: in alcohol, though it made him ill, he thought he
had found a prop and a sort of anaesthetic to see him through the
bad times, of which he had more than his fair share. The drinking,
the self-pity, the illness, the conviction that he was badly done by —
Poe was beginning to gather in his fingers the strands of a rope that
would eventually strangle him.

Chapter 5

The Good Soldier Perry

It was a bewildered and frightened young man who fled from Richmond at the end of March 1827. He was smarting under the disgrace of his discharge from the university; he was shocked by his guardian's behaviour; and he felt himself in imminent danger of arrest for debt. Somehow he raised the money (perhaps by appealing secretly to Frances Allan) to pay the boat fare to Boston, the city of which Elizabeth Poe had made a sketch, inscribing it: 'For my little son Edgar, who should ever love Boston, the city of his birth, and where his mother found her best and most sympathetic friends.' But being down and out in Boston was better than being ostracized in Richmond only in the sense that Edgar's creditors were not at hand to seize him. How he survived in the smart, snobbish and rather unsympathetic Northern city is a mystery — it has been suggested that he followed his father onto the stage, with equal lack of success, or he may have used what education he had acquired to obtain work as a clerk. Both suggestions are unlikely to have been true, for on 26 May, less than two months after his arrival in Boston, Edgar Poe enlisted in the United States Army. Name, Edgar A. Perry; age, twenty-two; height, five feet eight inches; colour of eyes, grey; colour of hair, brown; complexion, fair; term of enlistment, five years.

This was an act of panic. There can be no other explanation for the would-be Southern gentleman's decision to share the life of the licentious soldiery. He lied about his name and age to cover both his tracks and his shame, and the ploy worked. John Allan came to the conclusion that his ward had run away to sea to seek his fortune. In fact, Edgar was undergoing initial training with H Battery, First Artillery, at Fort Independence, on Boston Harbour. His experiences in the Richmond Junior Volunteers enabled him quickly to master military drill and his native intelligence ensured that he was not slow to learn the intricacies of loading and firing a field gun. What must have been more difficult for the new recruit was adjusting to the rough-and-ready life of the barrack room: true, it cannot have been any more violent and dissolute than what he had seen during his year at Charlottesville, but his companions were hardly the sort of people with whom he was used to associating. Nevertheless, Edgar was grateful for the anonymity of the uniform and for the home provided for him by the government, which — added to the simple camaraderie of private soldiers — no doubt helped him to make the best of things. Like many another unfortunate before and since, he found that the army can be a safe haven.

Even as 'Private Perry' was embarking on military life, he was in his other persona beginning a career as a poet. In the early summer of 1827 there appeared a slim volume entitled *Tamerlane and Other Poems*, 'by a Bostonian'. The book was published by one Calvin Thomas, who later became well known as an editor and publisher but was at that time no more than an obscure printer, and how he came to undertake the publication is unknown. But whatever the background, and in spite of the fact that the forty-page booklet made no money and was not reviewed, Poe was grateful to see his first printed work. 'Tamerlane' is Byronic in flavour and lacks the power of some of Poe's later verse, though it displays a lyricism unusual in American poetry of the day. From the biographer's point of view, one of the 'other poems' is more interesting:

> I saw thee on thy bridal day —
>   When a burning blush came o'er thee,
> Though happiness around thee lay,
>   The world all love before thee:
>
> And in thine eye a kindling light
>   (Whatever it might be)
> Was all on Earth my aching sight
>   Of Loveliness could see.
>
> That blush, perhaps, was maiden shame —
>   As such it well may pass —
> Though its glow hath raised a fiercer flame
>   In the breast of him, alas!
>
> Who saw thee on that bridal day,
>   When that deep blush *would* come o'er thee,
> Though happiness around thee lay,
>   The world all love before thee.

Elmira Royster had been getting married at about the time Edgar was enlisting in the army, so he could not have seen her on her wedding day. That poem, called simply 'Song', proves, however, that Elmira was still on his mind.

For the time being, though, Poe was wedded to the army, and he proved himself to be an efficient soldier. It soon became obvious to his officers that he had more intelligence and education than the usual run of recruits, and by the autumn of 1827 he had been given clerking duties in the company stores, with the promise of early promotion. In November, the regiment was transferred from Boston to Fort Moultrie, South Carolina. After an eleven-day sea voyage, Poe found himself in the South once more, and in the responsible position of company clerk. Within six months he was promoted to the rank of artificer, with attendant increases in pay and free time. The military life was turning out to be not so bad.

Indeed, life at Fort Moultrie was positively pleasant. The fort was situated on Sullivan's Island, with before it the Atlantic and behind it the subtropical lowlands of the South Carolina coast. Not far away, where the Cooper and Ashley rivers flow into the sea, is the beautiful city of Charleston, renowned then as now for its aristocratic grace and Southern hospitality and good manners. Since Poe had grown up as a Southerner, he naturally fitted into Charleston society, and in spite of his humble position as an enlisted man he rapidly made friends, among them the influential Colonel William Drayton, a rising politician who had hopes of being given a place in a Democratic Administration if Andrew Jackson won the presidential election of 1828. Another friend was Dr Edmund Ravenel, a naturalist who lived on Sullivan's Island: he was the inspiration for one of Poe's most popular stories, 'The Gold Bug', first published in *The Dollar Newspaper* of Philadelphia in 1843.

The hero of 'The Gold Bug', William Legrand, is, like Ravenel, a naturalist 'of an ancient Huguenot family', and he lives on Sullivan's Island:

> This Island is a very singular one. It consists of little else than sea sand, and is about three miles long. Its breadth at no point exceeds a quarter of a mile. It is separated from the main land by a scarcely perceptible creek, oozing its way through a wilderness of reeds and slime, a favorite resort of the marsh-hen. The vegetation, as might have been supposed, is scant, or at least dwarfish. No trees of any magnitude are to be seen. Near the western extremity, where Fort Moultrie stands, and where are some miserable frame buildings, tenanted during the summer by the fugitives from Charleston dust and fever, may be found, indeed, the bristly palmetto; but the whole island, with the exception of this western point, and a line of hard, white beach on the seacoast, is covered with a dense under-

growth of the sweet myrtle, so much prized by the horticulturists of England. The shrub often here attains the height of fifteen or twenty feet, and forms an almost impenetrable coppice, burthening the air with its fragrance.

That is how Poe described the island in 'The Gold Bug'. The whole of that coast was rich in stories about the pirates who frequented it in colonial days — Charleston had once been menaced by the infamous Black Beard, and the equally notorious Steede Bonnet had been hanged there in 1718. This naturally led to tales of buried treasure, which Poe took as the theme for his story, selecting for his pirate the most famous buccaneer of them all, Captain Kidd, who in fact never visited Charleston as far as anyone knows. 'The Gold Bug' revolves around a cryptogram discovered by William Legrand on a piece of old parchment on which he had drawn a sketch of an unknown *scarabaeus* beetle he had found. Much of the story hangs on the fact that the beetle resembles a human skull, since that is what marks the site of the buried treasure, and it has been convincingly stated that Poe constructed his mythical bug from the characteristics of two beetles common on Sullivan's Island, no doubt shown to him by Dr Ravenel. That was not all he learnt from the doctor — information he gleaned about seashells was to be put to a much less reputable use later on.

There is one piece of Charleston folklore that concerns Edgar himself: local Poe buffs have suggested that Sullivan's Island may have been the setting for the famous poem 'Annabel Lee'.

It was many and many a year ago,
    In a kingdom by the sea,
That a maiden there lived whom you may know
    By the name of Annabel Lee;
And this maiden she lived with no other thought
    Than to love and be loved by me.

I was a child and *she* was a child,
    In this kingdom by the sea:
But we loved with a love that was more than love —
    I and my Annabel Lee;
With a love that the winged seraphs of heaven
    Coveted her and me.

And this was the reason that, long ago,
    In this kingdom by the sea,
A wind blew out of a cloud, chilling

> My beautiful Annabel Lee;
> So that her highborn kinsmen came
> And bore her away from me,
> To shut her up in a sepulchre
> In this kingdom by the sea.
>
> . . .
>
> For the moon never beams, without bringing me dreams
> Of the beautiful Annabel Lee;
> And the stars never rise, but I feel the bright eyes
> Of the beautiful Annabel Lee;
> And so, all the night-tide, I lie down by the side
> Of my darling — my darling — my life and my bride,
> In her sepulchre there by the sea,
> In her tomb by the side of the sea.

This beautiful and brilliantly constructed poem was Poe's last, written in the spring of 1849, and there has been much speculation about who might have been its subject. There are those in Charleston who think they may have the answer, following the discovery a few years ago in a local cemetery of a tombstone bearing the initials A.L.R. One theory is that those letters stand for 'Annabel Lee Requiescat'; another — fastening on to the idea that the 'highborn kinsmen' mentioned in the poem might refer to aristocratic Huguenots — fits the initials to the name Annabel Lee Ravenel! This is the kind of charming association that appeals to romantic Poe devotees, though in fact the likelihood is that 'Annabel Lee' was written for Edgar's wife after her death.

Meanwhile, in his real kingdom by the sea, 'Artificer Perry' was beginning to tire of life as an enlisted man. He was once again on the fringes of Southern society, to which he felt he rightly belonged, and it is possible that he revealed his true identity to the friends he made. Certainly Colonel Drayton was to keep in touch with him later and, given that Edgar felt he had been badly treated, it seems likely that Drayton would have heard the whole sorry story of Poe's breach with Allan. The tale of the boy who had been so insulted that he had run away from home to join the army would have appealed to the romantic side of the Southern character, particularly if Edgar had revealed that he was a published poet. But he was still in the army and since he was not an officer his social style was cramped, no matter how appealing his personal qualities might be. Towards the end of 1828, Edgar decided to make a clean breast of things to one of his officers, Lieutenant Howard, and asked for his help. Howard took pity on the unhappy nineteen-year-old and sent a message to

John Allan, who until that time had been unaware of Edgar's where-abouts. Early biographers have assumed that Poe wrote to Allan before making his confession to Howard, but careful reading of the exchange of letters which followed makes it clear that this was not the case.

Allan, who was ill when he received Howard's message, wrote back not to Edgar but to the lieutenant, expressing little sympathy for his ward, as the following letter from Poe to Allan, written on 1 December 1828, makes clear:

Dear Sir,
The letter of Lieut. I. Howard left by Mr John O. Lay for your perusal will explain the cause of my writing from Fort Moultrie.

Your note addressed to Mr Lay and inclosed by him to Lieut. Howard was handed over by the latter to myself. In that note what chiefly gave me concern was hearing of your indisposition — I can readily see & forgive the sugges-tion which prompted you to write 'he had better remain as he is until the termination of his enlistment'. It was perhaps under the impression that a *military* life was one after my own heart and that it might be possible (although contrary to the Regulation of our Army) to obtain a commission for one who had not received his education at West Point, & who, from his age, was excluded that Academy; but I could not help thinking that you believed me degraded & disgraced and that any thing were prefer-able to my returning home & entailing on yourself a portion of my infamy: But at no period of my life have I regarded myself with a deeper satisfaction — or did my heart swell with more honourable pride — The time may come (if at all it will come speedily) when much that appears of a doubtful nature will be explained away and I shall have no hesitation in appearing among my former connections — at the present I have no such intentions, and nothing, short of your absolute commands, should deter me from my purpose.

I have been in the American army as long as suits my ends or my inclination, and it is now time that I should leave it — To this effect I made known my circumstances to Lieut. Howard who promised me my discharge solely upon a re-conciliation with yourself — In vain I told him that your wishes for me (as your letter assured me) were, and had always been those of a father & that you were ready to forgive even the worst offence — He insisted upon my writing you & that if a re-conciliation could be effected he would grant me my wish — This was advised in the goodness of his heart & with a view of serving me in a double sense — He has always been kind to me, and, in many respects reminds me forcibly of yourself.

The period of Enlistment is five years — the prime of my life would be wasted — I shall be driven to more decided measures if you refuse to assist me. You need not fear for my future prosperity — I am altered from what you knew me, & am no longer a boy tossing about on the world without aim or consistency — I feel that within me which will make me fulfil your highest wishes & only beg you to suspend your judgment until you hear *of* me again.

You will perceive that I speak confidently — but when did ever Ambition exist or Talent prosper without prior conviction of success? I have thrown myself on the world like the Norman Conqueror on the shores of Britain & by my avowed assurance of victory, have destroyed the fleet which could alone cover my retreat — I must either conquer or die — succeed or be disgraced.

A letter addressed to Lieut. Howard assuring him of your re-conciliation with myself (which you have never yet refused) & desiring my discharge would be all that is necessary — He is already acquainted with you from report & the high character given of you by Mr Lay.

Write me once more if you do really forgive me, let me know how my Ma preserves her health, and the concerns of the family since my departure. Pecuniary assistance I do not desire — unless of your own free & unbiased choice — I can struggle with any difficulty. My dearest love to Ma — it is only when absent that we can tell the value of such a friend — I hope she will not let my wayward disposition wear away the love she used to have for me.

Yours respectfully & affectionately

Edgar A. Poe

This was a fairly unpleasant and unprincipled letter, at once cajoling and threatening, displaying a strange degree of arrogance in one who was seeking help, and ending with a sentimental appeal to the woman who had no doubt protected Edgar many times before. It is hardly surprising that Allan did not reply to it — but Edgar was not to be put off. On 22 December he wrote again, this time from Fort Monroe at Old Point Comfort, on Hampton Roads, the estuary of the James River, about seventy-five miles south-east of Richmond, where the regiment had been posted.

> Dear Sir,
> I wrote to you shortly before leaving Fort Moultrie & am much hurt at receiving no answer — Perhaps my letter has not reached you & under that supposition I will recapitulate its contents . . .

Which he proceeded to do, in rather humbler form than the original, adding that since he asked so little he was hurt that Allan should decline to answer. (He really did not doubt that the letter had been received, but merely used that thought as an excuse to have another go.) But humility was not Poe's natural feeling. He went on:

> Since arriving at Fort Moultrie, Lieut. Howard has given me an introduction to Col. James House of the 1st Arty. to whom I was before personally known only as a soldier of his regiment. He spoke kindly to me, told me that he was personally acquainted with my Grandfather Gen. Poe, with yourself & family, & reassured me of my immediate discharge upon your consent. It must have been a matter of regret to me, that when those who were strangers took such deep interest in my welfare, you who called me your son should refuse me even the common civility of answering a letter. If it is your wish to forget that I have been your son I am too proud to remind you of it again — I only beg you to remember that you yourself cherished the cause of my leaving your family — Ambition — If it has not taken the channel you wished it, it is not the less certain of its object. Richmond, the U. States were too narrow a sphere & the world shall be my theatre.
> As I observed in the letter which you have not received — (you would have answered it if you had) you believe me degraded — but do not believe it — There is that within my heart which has no connection with degradation — I can walk among infection & be uncontaminated. There never was any period of my life when my bosom swelled with a deeper satisfaction of myself & (except in the injury which I may have done to your feeling) — of my conduct — My father do not throw me aside as *degraded*. I will be an honor to your name.

Give my best love to Ma & to all friends — If you deter-
mine to abandon me — here take our farewell — Neglected
— I will be doubly ambitious, & the world shall
hear of the son whom you have thought unworthy of your
notice. But if you let the love you bear me outweigh the
offence which I have given — then write me my father,
quickly. My desire is for the present to be freed from the
Army — Since I have been in my character is one that will
bear scrutiny & has merited the esteem of my officers . . .

His last point, at least, was justified. On 1 January 1829 he was
promoted to sergeant-major, the army's highest non-commissioned
rank — and he was still three weeks short of his twentieth birthday.
Obviously he was a good soldier, and as his letters to Allan show, he
was proud of his success: so when Lieutenant Howard, and perhaps
the colonel as well, suggested that he might further his military
career by applying for an officer-cadetship, Edgar was inclined to
listen. This could be his salvation. He would be a 'gentleman' again,
with status obvious to all, acceptable in society, and provided with
the income and the freedom to allow him to write. Not only that,
but such an ambition would surely find favour with John Allan. On 4
February he wrote to Richmond yet again:

Dear Sir:
I wrote to you some time ago from this place but have as
yet received no reply. Since that time I wrote to John
McKenzie desiring him to see you personally & desire for
me, of you, that you would interest yourself in procuring
me a cadet's appointment at the Military Academy. To this
likewise I have received no answer, for which I can in no
manner account, as he wrote me before I wrote to him &
seemed to take an interest in my welfare. I made a request
to obtain a cadet's appointment partly because I know
that (if my age should prove no obstacle as I have since
ascertained it will not) the appointment could easily be
obtained either by your personal acquaintance with Mr
Wirt [Attorney General of the United States, whom Poe
had met at the University of Virginia] or by the recommendation of General Scott, or even of the officers
residing at Fort Monroe, & partly because in making the
request you would at once see to what direction my
'future views & expectations' were inclined.
You can have no idea of the immense advantages which
my present station in the army would give me in the

appointment of a cadet — it would be an unprecedented case in the American army, & having already passed thro the practical part even of the higher portion of the Artillery arm, my cadet-ship would only be considered as a necessary form which I am positive I could run thro' in 6 months.

This is the view of the case which many at this place have taken in regard to myself. If you are willing to assist me it can now be effectually done — if not (as late circumstances have induced me to believe) I must remain contented until chance or other friends shall render me that assistance.

Under the expectation of kind news from home I have been led into expenses which my present income will not support. I hinted as much in my former letter, and am at present in an uncomfortable situation. I have known the time when you would not have suffered me long to remain so. Whatever fault you may find with me I have not been ungrateful for past services but you blame me for the path which I have taken without considering the powerful influences which actuated me — You will remember how much I had to suffer upon my return from the University. I never meant to offer a shadow of excuse for the infamous conduct of others & myself at that place. It was however at the commencement of that year that I got deeply entangled in difficulty which all my after good conduct in the close of the session (to which all there can testify) could not clear away. I had never been from home before for any length of time. I say again I have no excuse to offer for my conduct except that common one of youth — folly — but I repeat that I was unable if my life had depended upon it to bear the consequences of that conduct in the taunts & abuse that followed it even from those who had been my warmest friends.

I shall wait with impatience for an answer to this letter for upon it depend a great many of the circumstances of my future life — the assurance of an honourable & highly successful course in my own country — or the prospect — no *certainty* of an exile forever to another.

> Give my love to Ma
> I am
> > Yours affectionately
> > Edgar A. Poe

I have quoted in full this one-sided correspondence because it shows Edgar in a rather bad light, and also serves to delineate very clearly the split between the boy and his guardian. It would be easy to portray John Allan as a selfish brute who callously cut off his ward without a penny, and certainly he does not appear to deserve much sympathy, particularly in view of his meanness to and harsh treatment of Edgar during the year at Charlottesville and immediately afterwards. On the other hand, Edgar had not exactly covered himself with glory (though, to be fair, his action in joining the army and the success he made of it show admirable spirit and determination). From Allan's point of view, the boy had thrown away all the opportunities with which his guardian had presented him, had bitten the hand that fed him, had wilfully followed his own course in the blithe expectation that someone else would foot the bill — he even admitted, in the letter above, that he had got into debt 'under the expectation of kind news from home'. Of course, we can see now that Allan pushed the boy into his folly, and that he had reasons for doing so, but Edgar's behaviour and attitude towards his adoptive family do him little credit. He appears to have shown scant regard for the family except when he wanted something and, even more infuriating for Allan, he repeatedly laid the blame for his actions and resulting difficulties on someone other than himself, or at best on circumstances beyond his control (a technique which, it will be recalled, Edgar's father had employed).

The letters from Fort Moultrie and Fort Monroe show that Edgar was always ready to play the dutiful son when he needed help — and that he expected to be received like the returning prodigal. At the same time, he was not above using threats and bitter reproaches in the attempt to achieve his objective, or resorting to low appeals to sentiment. It might be said in his defence that life had played him false, that nothing had turned out as he might have expected it to, and yet it is hardly to be doubted that his own attitudes contributed largely to the misfortunes which overtook him — a state of affairs for which John Allan must take some of the blame (not to mention the indulgent Frances), but which is also partly explained, as I have already said, by inherited personality traits.

Edgar probably knew nothing of his father's character, but in later life he saw in himself the kind of impulse which had led David Poe Jr to disaster. In his tale 'The Imp of the Perverse', Edgar wrote: 'I am not more sure that I breathe, than that the assurance of the wrong or error of any action is often the one unconquerable *force* which impels us, and alone impels us to its prosecution. Nor will this overwhelming tendency to do wrong for the wrong's sake, admit of analysis, or resolution into ulterior elements. It is a radical, a primitive impulse — elementary.'

So it was with those letters to Allan at the end of 1828 and the beginning of 1829. Edgar wanted help, he needed a reconciliation, and yet he could not resist adding touches of arrogance and recrimination almost guaranteed to produce an effect exactly opposite to the one he desired.

It is quite likely that Allan would not have come to Poe's aid had it not been for an event which altered the whole situation — the death of Frances Allan on 28 February 1829. Edgar did not see 'Ma' before she died (he did not arrive in Richmond until after she had been buried), but it may be supposed that on her deathbed she remembered the little orphan who had won her heart almost twenty years before, and it requires only a little imagination to picture her begging her husband to let her die happy by taking the opportunity of reconciling himself with Edgar, and by giving him the help he needed. Something of the sort must have happened, for when Edgar did reach Richmond on compassionate leave he was welcomed courteously, if not exactly warmly, and given a new suit of clothes. Allan was a man with a conscience, as will become obvious, and a last appeal from his wife would have stirred him to action. He agreed to help Edgar to gain a discharge from the army, which was necessary before he could apply to West Point, and to support an application for a cadetship. When Poe returned to Fort Monroe on 10 March, he wrote to his guardian in affectionate terms: 'My dear Pa, I arrived on the point [Old Point Comfort] this morning in good health and if it were not for late occurrences should feel much happier than I have for a long time . . .'

By the end of March, Colonel House was writing to his commanding general requesting 'your permission to discharge from the service Edgar A. Perry, at present the Sergeant-Major of the Ist Reg't of Artillery, on his procuring a substitute'. Army regulations laid down that if an enlisted man wished to be discharged before his term of enlistment had expired, he had to get someone else to complete that term. Colonel House went on to give a garbled account of 'Sergeant-Major Perry's' history, compiled from various pieces of misinformation given to him by Poe and Allan:

> The said Perry is one of a family of orphans whose unfortunate parents were the victims of the conflagration of the Richmond theatre, in 1809. The subject of this letter was taken under the protection of a Mr Allen [sic], a gentleman of wealth and respectability, of that city, who, as I understand, adopted his protégé as his son and heir;

with the intention of giving him a liberal education, he had placed him at the University of Virginia from which, after considerable progress in his studies, in a moment of youthful indiscretion he absconded, and was not heard from by his Patron for several years; in the mean time he became reduced to the necessity of enlisting into the service and accordingly entered as a soldier in my Regiment, at Fort Independence in 1827. — Since the arrival of his company at this place, he has made his situation known to his Patron at whose request, the young man has been permitted to visit him; the result is, an entire reconciliation on the part of Mr Allen, who reinstates him into his family and favor, and who in a letter I have received from him requests that his son may be discharged on procuring a substitute; an experienced soldier and approved sergeant is ready to take the place of Perry so soon as his discharge can be obtained. The good of the service, therefore cannot be materially injured by the discharge . . .

Poe had been under a misapprehension about his substitute. Normally, the enlisted man who wished to be discharged could provide his company commander with twelve dollars (the usual sum paid by the army as bounty) and the officer could then put up as substitute the first recruit who offered himself. Poe assumed this would apply in his case, and told Allan that the substitution would cost him a mere twelve dollars. Unfortunately, things again did not work out as he expected, and he found himself having to promise a fellow non-commissioned officer, Sergeant Samuel 'Bully' Graves, seventy-five dollars to sign on for a further term of enlistment. (Perhaps Colonel House had suggested that the army might look with more favour on his request for discharge if he had another NCO to replace him.) Edgar did not see fit to inform Allan of the change in circumstances, but gave 'Bully' Graves twenty-five dollars in cash and an IOU for the balance. It was yet another debt that would later come home to roost.

Anyway, the discharge went through, and on 15 April Poe was released from the army. He returned to Richmond with a pocketful of testimonials — making it clear that Poe and Perry were one and the same — from officers of the Ist Artillery, which he later delivered to the War Department in Washington. Lieutenant Howard wrote that Poe's conduct had been 'unexceptionable' and 'his habits are good and intirely free from drinking'. Colonel House's adjutant, Captain H. W. Griswold, added that Poe 'has been exemplary in his deportment, prompt and faithful in the discharge of his duties — and

is highly worthy of confidence'. Colonel House was away when Poe
left, so the commandant of Fort Monroe, Lieutenant-Colonel W. J.
Worth, added his own recommendation: 'His education is of a very
high order and he appears to be free from bad habits ... Understanding he is, thro' his friends, an applicant for cadet's warrant, I
unhesitatingly recommend him as promising to acquit himself of the
obligations of that station studiously and faithfully.'

One disappointment was that, although the Democrats had won
the election of 1828 and Andrew Jackson had become President,
Colonel Drayton of Charleston had failed to obtain his hoped-for
post as Secretary for War — that had gone to an old friend of
Jackson's, Major John Eaton. With Drayton in Washington, Poe's
acceptance at West Point would have been a foregone conclusion;
Eaton's presence there made things a little more difficult, but several
influential people in Richmond, who remembered Edgar as a boy,
wrote to the Secretary pleading his cause — among them James T.
Preston, a member of the House of Representatives and father of
Edgar's old classmate John Preston; Judge John Barber; and two
military men, Majors Campbell and Gibbon. Of course, John Allan
wrote, too — though his letter might be seen as more of a hindrance
than a help:

                                              Richmond, May 6, 1829
Dear Sir:
The youth who presents this, is the same alluded to by Lt.
Howard, Capt. Griswold, Colo Worth, our representative
[Preston] and the speaker, the Hon'ble Andrew Stevenson,
and my friend Major Jno Campbell.

    He left me in consequence of some gambling at the
University at Charlottesville, because (I presume) I refused
to sanction a rule that shopkeepers and others had adopted
there, making Debts of Honour of all indiscretions. I have
much pleasure in asserting that he stood his examination at
the close of the year with great credit to himself. His
history is short. He is the grandson of Quartermaster
General Poe, of Maryland, whose widow as I understand
still receives a pension for the services or disabilities of her
husband. Frankly Sir, do I declare that he is no relation to
me whatever; that I have many in whom I have taken an
active interest to promote theirs; with no other feeling
than that, every man is my care, if he be in distress. For
myself I ask nothing, but I do request your kindness to aid
this youth in the promotion of his future prospects. And it
will afford me great pleasure to reciprocate any kindness

you can show him. Pardon my frankness; but I address a
soldier.

Allan, then, was not prepared to commit himself too firmly; no
doubt Poe's record at Charlottesville had made his guardian feel that
he did not want to be too closely associated with any further pecca-
dilloes. But he could feel secure in the knowledge that he had done
his duty by Edgar, as Frances had probably asked him to, and there
seemed every reason to suppose that September would see Poe safely
ensconced at West Point, his future assured. Allan could afford to
be generous and forgiving: he gave Edgar money and sent him off to
Washington to deliver his testimonials.

Thus the military career of Edgar A. Perry came to an end, though
it remained a source of embarrassment to Poe. Asked to prepare
some biographical notes for a book entitled *Poets and Poetry of
America* in 1841, Edgar filled in his 'missing' years of soldiering by
inventing a Byronic legend for himself. After leaving the university,
he said, he had set off for Greece to join the struggle for liberation in
that country (Byron had died at Missolonghi during just such an
enterprise in 1824). Poe's 'biography' went on: 'Failed in reaching
Greece, but made my way to St Petersburg, in Russia. Got into many
difficulties, but was extricated by the kindness of Mr H. Middleton,
the American consul at St P. Came home safe in 1829, found Mrs
A[llan] dead, and immediately went to West Point as a cadet.'

This fable was accepted as the truth for many years, until Poe's
military record came to light to disprove it. There are still those who
fondly believe that Edgar must have had some connexion with St
Petersburg, even if not at the time he claimed, in order for him to
have known the name of the consular official there, which he gave
correctly (Middleton was consul from 1819 to 1830). But such
people forget that Poe spent his life picking up scraps of information
that others might overlook, and also that since he never earned a
living other than by journalism, he would have had easier access to
information than most.

The whole point of that biographical fantasy was that it would
never have done, in Poe's mind, for the world to have known that a
gentleman of letters such as himself had spent time as a common
soldier: that did not agree at all with his own image of himself. An
officer-cadet, now there was something entirely different. But in
spite of his high hopes in the spring of 1829, it was going to be a long
time before he achieved that status.

Chapter 6

Officer's Mess

The death of his 'Ma' had come as a great shock to Edgar. He told John Allan: 'I have had a fearful warning, and have hardly ever known before what distress was.' Both his natural mother and the idealized Jane Stanard had been taken from him before he really knew them, but Frances Allan had been part of his life for seventeen years, loving and protecting him through childhood and adolescence, always there when he needed her. Whatever the difficulties of his relationship with John Allan, he had regarded Frances as a constant source of comfort and reassurance, as someone he could rely on not to try to diminish him, someone who admired him as a man. With her limited education and understanding, her timidity and her nervous disposition, Frances was perhaps not the best of mothers for Edgar, but she was gentle and kind-hearted, and she was all he had. There are no letters from Edgar to Frances in existence, which may indicate either that he did not write to her or that she did not store letters in the way her methodical husband did, but there can be little doubt that Edgar rather took 'Ma' for granted (she must have been the kind of person one takes for granted, because John Allan appears to have done the same) and, as is so often the case, only realized her importance after her death.

There was now a great gap in his life. He was aware that John Allan did not really want him (though while Allan lived Edgar never gave up seeking his help and, more important perhaps, his approval), and he could not turn to Nancy Valentine, for she kept her eye on the main chance and firmly supported Allan — there has even been a suggestion that Allan proposed marriage and that Nancy turned him down, but this cannot be confirmed. So Edgar turned to his real family, the Poes of Baltimore, of whom he knew very little. Baltimore was in any case the first staging post in his journey from Richmond to Washington to deliver his testimonials, and it is probable that his own natural desire to become acquainted with the kinfolk he had never met was further encouraged by his guardian. John Allan was already getting over his grief with the help of Mrs

Elizabeth Wills — with whom he had evidently been having an affair before his wife's death, and who was later to bear him twin boys — and he sent Edgar off with fifty dollars in his pocket, to which he later added a bank draft for a hundred payable to the Union Bank of Maryland in Baltimore, as well as honouring a draft for a further fifty obtained by Edgar. On 18 May 1829 he wrote to Poe advising: 'While you are in Maryland ascertain and get a Certificate of the fact whether your Grandfather was in the service during the revol^y. war, where he served, Rank &c &c, it may be of service & cannot do you any harm.' It has been claimed that this constituted a slur on Poe's antecedents, but more likely it was a heavy-handed attempt by Allan to give his ward something to do that would keep him in Baltimore for as long as possible. If such was the case, it failed, for Edgar replied rather haughtily that 'the fact of my Grand-father's having been Quarter Master General of the whole US Army during the Revolutionary war is clearly established — but its being a well-known fact at Washington, obviates the necessity of obtaining the certificates you mentioned'. Nevertheless, there were good reasons for Poe to stay on.

It was not simply that Baltimore was a thriving, bustling seaport with a sense of urgency and excitement missing from the measured, class-ridden life of Richmond, but also that the name Poe meant something there. Edgar wrote: 'I have been introduced to many gentlemen of high standing in the city, who were formerly acquainted with my grandfather, and have altogether treated me handsomely.' But a good reputation alone will not pay for bread, and the Poes were in anything but comfortable circumstances: Edgar's grandmother was suffering from paralysis and adding her niggardly pension to the household in Mechanics Row, Wilkes Street, presided over by her widowed daughter, Maria Clemm, who had two children to support — Henry, aged eleven, and Virginia, aged six — as well as Edgar's brother, William Henry, who had left the sea and was, according to Edgar, 'entirely given up to drink and unable to help himself'. How they lived is a mystery (Mrs Clemm was apparently employed as a teacher at one point) but one thing is certain — they were in no position to take in their long-lost relative.

Not that Edgar needed any help at first. He had a couple of hundred dollars which enabled him to set himself up in a boarding house and, taking full advantage of his name, to enter Baltimore society. One man he called on was William Wirt, who had been offered and had declined the law professorship at the University of Virginia, had served as United States Attorney General, and who in 1829 was a political leader in Baltimore. From Poe's point of view, however, Wirt was important as the biographer of Patrick Henry and author of the well-known *Letters of a British Spy,* and the aspiring young poet presented him with his latest work, a long poem entitled 'Al Aaraaf'. Wirt was frankly mystified by this extraordinary poem, but for this he tactfully blamed his own unfamiliarity with modern fashions in verse, adding that the work might find favour with the contemporary reader and advising Poe to submit it personally to Robert Walsh, editor of the influential *American Quarterly Review* in Philadelphia.

Wirt's bewilderment is not hard to understand and sympathize with. 'Al Aaraaf' is obscure and almost entirely lacking in the simple charm of many of Poe's shorter poems: at times it seems as if its author used it as a showcase for a large proportion of the miscellaneous information he had harvested from his reading. It appears to be a consciously 'intellectual' poem, and as such is difficult to absorb. In its final form, the second part begins:

High on a mountain of enamelled head —
Such as the drowsy shepherd on his bed
Of giant pasturage lying at his ease,
Raising his heavy eyelid, starts and sees
With many a muttered 'hope to be forgiven'
What time the moon is quadrated in Heaven —
Of rosy head that, towering far away
Into the sunlit ether, caught the ray
Of sunken suns at eve — at noon of night,
While the moon danced with the fair stranger light —
Unprepared upon such height arose a pile
Of gorgeous columns of th' unburthened air,
Flashing from Parian marble that twin smile
Far down upon the wave that sparkled there,
And nursled the young mountain in its lair.
Of molten stars their pavement, such as fall
Thro' the ebon air, besilvering the pall
Of their own dissolution, while they die —
Adorning then the dwellings of the sky.
A dome, by linked light from Heaven let down,
Sat gently on these columns as a crown —
A window of one circular diamond, there,
Looked out above into the purple air,
And rays from God shot down that meteor chain
And hallowed all the beauty twice again,
Save when, between th' Empyrean and that ring,
Some eager spirit flapped his dusky wing . . .

And so on . . . and on . . . and on. Not, perhaps, among the most memorable verse in the English language — and Poe felt obliged to add copious notes. For example, his explanation of the poem's inspiration: ' "Al Aaraaf". A star was discovered by Tycho Brahe which appeared suddenly in the heavens — attained, in a few days, a brilliancy surpassing that of Jupiter — then as suddenly disappeared, and has never been seen since.' And then, the key to the whole thing: 'With the Arabians there is a medium between Heaven and Hell, where men suffer no punishment, but yet do not attain that tranquil and even happiness which they suppose to be characteristic of heavenly enjoyment . . . Sorrow is not excluded from "Al Aaraaf ", but it is that sorrow which the living love to cherish for the dead, and which, in some minds, resembles the delirium of opium. The passionate excitement of Love and the buoyancy of spirit attendant upon intoxication are its less holy pleasures — the price of which, to those souls who make choice of "Al Aaraaf " as their residence after life, is final death and annihilation.' Poe was obviously not too confident that his meaning would be apparent in the poem itself, and his doubts were well founded.

And yet there are signs in 'Al Aaraaf' of some fine verse that would come later. Take this beautiful lyric:

> Ligeia! wherever
>   Thy image may be,
> No magic shall sever
>   Thy music from thee.
> Thou hast bound many eyes
>   In a dreamy sleep —
> But the strains still arise
>   Which *thy* vigilance keep —
> The sound of the rain,
>   Which leaps down to the flower
> And dances again
>   In the rhythm of the shower —
> The murmur that springs
>   From the growing of grass —
> Are the music of things —
>   But are modell'd, alas! —
> Away, then, my dearest,
>   O! hie thee away
> To springs that lie clearest
>   Beneath the moon-ray —

> To the lone lake that smiles,
>   In its dream of deep rest,
> At the many star-isles
>   That enjewel its breast . . .

Taken as a whole, however 'Al Aaraaf' is not a successful poem, even allowing for the fact that at least one part of Poe's original is missing — indeed he never submitted it to the publishers. But the joy of the lyrics contained within it, its experimental use of the sound of words in the way that a composer uses musical sounds to express his thoughts and feelings, and the fact that it *seemed* important (the obscure is often mistaken for the profound) all combined to make William Wirt, and others, think it worthy of merit. Poe took Wirt's advice and journeyed to Philadelphia where, no doubt encouraged by the prospect of a literary success, he felt bold enough, and rich enough, to stay at Heiskill's Indian Queen Hotel on South Fourth Street. Robert Walsh apparently endorsed Wirt's opinion of 'Al Aaraaf', and Poe submitted the poem to the publishers Carey, Lea and Carey, pointing out in his covering letter that he had the support of Wirt and Walsh and explaining the purpose of the work. He was, he said, sending parts one, two and three of the poem and had reasons for not wishing to publish part four at that time — and to provide enough material for a volume he enclosed a selection of shorter pieces. He had high hopes, but this did not blind him to the realities of the publishing business, as he explained in a letter to John Allan from Baltimore on 29 May 1829:

> I am aware of the difficulty of getting a poem published in this country — Mr Wirt & Mr Walsh have advised me of that — but the *difficulty* should be no object with a proper aim in view. If Messrs Carey, Lea & Carey, should decline publishing (as I have no reason to think they will not — they having invariably declined it with all our American poets) that is upon their *own risk* the request I have to make is this — that you will give me a letter to Messrs Carey, Lea & Carey saying that if in publishing the poem 'Al Aaraaf' they shall incur any *loss* you will make it good to them. The cost of publishing the work, in a style equal to any of our American publications, will at the extent be $100. This then of course, must be the limit of any loss supposing not a single copy of the work to be sold — It is more than probable that the work will be profitable & that I may gain instead of lose, even in a pecuniary way.

Anxious to please, and perhaps bearing in mind past insults from his guardian, he added that he had 'long given up *Byron* as a model, for which, I think, I deserve some credit' and he pointed out that, 'At my time of life there is much in being *before the eye of the world* — if once noticed I can easily cut a path to reputation', though this, of course, would not 'interfere with other objects which I have in view'. In other words, he would still be off Allan's hands by going to West Point, but his guardian could in a sense take out extra insurance by merely signing a guarantee for no more than a hundred dollars which would allow Edgar to generate an income of his own. In the mind of the twenty-year-old would-be poet it was all so straightforward. Allan thought otherwise: always a hard man to impress, he wrote back on 8 June reprimanding Edgar for his conduct and refusing help — in his eyes, it had been just another begging letter.

So once more high hopes came to naught, and misfortune began to close its grip on Edgar Poe. By the end of June he was almost broke, and since his relatives could not help out he wrote to Allan again: 'I am afraid you will think that I am trying to impose on your good nature & would not except under peculiar circumstances have applied to you for any more money — but it is only a little that I now want.' He explained that a cousin of his, James Mosher Poe, had robbed him of forty-six dollars while sharing his room at Beltzhoover's Hotel and that he had recovered only ten dollars by going through his cousin's pockets the following night: Mosher had admitted the theft and begged not to be exposed. Furthermore, '$50 of the money which you sent me I applied in paying a debt contracted at Old Point for my substitute, for which I gave my note — the money necessary if Lt. Howard had not gone on furlough would have been only $12 — but when he & Col. House left I had to scuffle for myself — I paid $25 & gave my note for $50 — in all $75.' (That explanation would return to haunt him, for he had not in fact paid his debt.)

In the same letter, Poe said that he had 'left untried no efforts to enter at W. Point & if I fail I can give you evidence that it is no fault of mine'. He also indicated that he wanted to return to Richmond, calling at Washington on the way to 'ascertain the fate of my application — which I am induced to think has succeeded'. Still John Allan was immovable: no money was forthcoming, not even a letter. On 15 July, Edgar wrote yet again:

> Dear Pa,
>   I have written you twice lately & have received no
> answer — I would not trouble you so often with my

letters, but I am afraid that being up at the Byrd [Allan's country estate] you might probably not have received them.

I am very anxious to return home thro' Washington where I have every hope of being appointed for Sept. & besides by being detained at Baltimore I am incurring unnecessary expense as Grandmother is not in a situation to give me any accommodation —

I sometimes am afraid that you are angry & perhaps you have reason to be — but if you will but put a little more confidence in me — I will endeavor to deserve it — I am sure no one can be more anxious, or would do more towards helping myself than I would — if I had any means of doing it — Without your assistance, I have none — I am anxious to abide by your directions, if I knew what they were.

You would relieve me from a great deal of anxiety by writing me soon — I think I have already had my share of trouble for one so young —

I am

Dear Pa

Yours affectionately

Edgar A. Poe

This cringing letter seems to have been designed to touch Allan's heart, but although he sent his ward some money there can be little doubt that his motive was to keep Edgar out of Richmond, and the letter accompanying the money was anything but friendly, as Edgar's reply on 26 July makes clear:

Dear Pa,

I received yours of the 19th on the 22d ult — I am truly thankful for the money which you sent me, notwithstanding the taunt with which it was given 'that men of genius ought not to apply to your aid' — It is too often their necessity to want that little timely assistance which would prevent such applications —

I did not answer your letter by return of mail on account of my departure for Washington the next morning — but before I proceed to tell you the event of my application I think it my duty to say something concerning the accusations & suspicions which are contained in your letter —

Allan apparently did not believe Edgar's story about the debt he owed Sergeant Graves, since at the time of the substitution Poe had not seen fit to inform his guardian of the extra money he had been obliged to pay — as far as Allan knew, it had been a matter of twelve dollars for the army bounty. 'As I had told you it would only cost me $12 I did not wish to make you think me imposing on you', Poe said in his 26 July letter by way of explanation, recounting the whole story about the officers being absent, his promissory note, and adding that 'when you remitted me $100 — thinking I had more than I should want — I thought it my best opportunity of taking up my note — which I did'. It was the second time he felt obliged to justify his conduct in this matter, and it served to drag him deeper into trouble.

The letter went on:

> If you take into consideration the length of time I have been from home, which was occasioned by my not hearing from you (& I was unwilling to leave the city without your answer, expecting it every day) & other expenses, you will find that it has been impossible for me to enter into any extravagancies or improper expense — even supposing I had not lost the $46 — the time which intervened between my letter & your answer in the first instance was 22 days — in the latter one month & 4 days — as I had no reason to suppose you would not reply to my letter as I was unconscious of having offended, it would have been imprudent to leave without your answer — this expense was unavoidable —
>
> As regards the money which was stolen I have sent you the only proof in my possession a letter from Mosher in which there is an acknowledgement of the theft — I have no other.

Poe then told of his journey to Washington, which he had made on foot (a round trip of about eighty miles) because he needed the money Allan had sent him to support himself in Baltimore.

> I saw Mr Eaton — he addressed me by name, & in reply to my questions told me — that of the 47 surplus on the roll ... 19 were rejected 9 dismissed & 8 resigned — consequently there was yet a surplus of 10 before me on the roll. On asking for my papers of recommendation, which might be of service elsewhere — he told me that in that case my application would be considered as withdrawn,

which he strongly advised me not to do — saying that there were still hopes of my obtaining the appointment in Sepr. as during the encampment every year there were numerous resignations — if the number exceeded 10 I should be sure of the appt. without further application in Sepr. if not I would at least be among the first on the next roll for the ensuing year — when of course my appointment was certain — when I mentioned that I feared my age would interfere he replied that 21 was the limit — that many entered at that time — & that I might call myself 21 until I was 22 — On leaving the office he called me back to endorse on my papers the name of my P. Office — I wrote Richmond. He said that I should certainly hear from him & that he regretted my useless trip to Washington — These are his precise words.

Edgar was now at a loss: if he stayed in Baltimore, he would shortly be reduced to begging again for money which Allan was reluctant to provide, and yet he could not immediately return to Richmond because Allan was equally unwilling to have him there. He wrote:

Having now explained every circumstance that seemed to require an explanation & shown that I have spared no exertions in the pursuit of my object, I write to you for information as to what course I must pursue — I would have returned home immediately but for the words in your letter 'I am not particularly anxious to see you' I know not how to interpret them — I could not help thinking that they amounted to a prohibition of return — if I had any means of support until I could obtain an appointment, I would not trouble you again — I am conscious of having offended you formerly — greatly — but I thought *that had been forgiven*, at least you told me so — I know I have done nothing since to deserve your displeasure —

As regards the poem, I have offended you only in asking your approbation — I can publish it upon the terms you mentioned — but will have no more to do with it without your entire approbation — I will wait with great anxiety for your answer — you must be aware how important it is that I should hear from you soon — as I do not know how to act.

> I am yours affectionately
> Edgar A. Poe

That last statement about the poem was no more than window-dressing, for within two days of writing to Allan, Edgar had sent a letter to Carey, Lea and Carey asking for the return of his manuscript of 'Al Aaraaf' and seeking advice on how to go about offering it to magazines for publication. He said he was unfamiliar with such procedures owing to a recent absence abroad, a subterfuge which has been seen as an attempt to cover up his army service, though why he should bother to conceal something that the publishers would have had no way of knowing or discovering is beyond comprehension; more likely his pride made him unwilling to admit that he was a novice so he invented the absence to disguise his ignorance.

At the same time, he knew that he would shortly run out of money again, and on 4 August he wrote to Allan once more, gently chiding him for failing to make greater efforts on his behalf in the matter of the West Point cadetship, and suggesting that 'I have many enemies at home who fancy it in their interest to injure me in your estimation' (possibly a dig at Nancy Valentine). He repeated that he was anxious to return home — strange that after so many tribulations he still regarded Allan's house as his home — and that he needed his guardian's advice as to his future conduct. He concluded:

> If you are determined to do nothing more on my behalf —
> you will at least do me the common justice to tell me so —
> I am almost sure of getting the appt. in Sepr. & certain at
> any rate of getting it in June. If I could manage until that
> time I would be no longer a trouble to you . . . Perhaps the
> time may come when you will find that I have not
> deserved ½ the misfortunes which have happened to me &
> that you suspected me unworthily.

The sight of Edgar cajoling, complaining and threatening in order to extract money from Allan, as shown by letters like the one above, is rather unpleasant. He wanted to be independent, to be free of the burden of having to justify himself to his guardian, but he was not prepared to earn his independence. Apparently he still saw himself as a 'gentleman' and did not feel inclined to lower himself sufficiently to take a job. His persistent entreaties, however, must have touched some nerve in John Allan, even if it was only the fear that Edgar would turn up unannounced on his doorstep, and he quickly sent some money, for which his ward was duly grateful, writing back on 10 August:

> I received yours this morning which relieved me from more
> trouble than you can well imagine — I was afraid that you

were offended & although I knew that I had done nothing
to deserve your anger, I was in a most uncomfortable situation — without one cent of money & so quickly engaged
in difficulties after the serious misfortunes which I have
just escaped . . .

I am unwilling to appear obstinate as regards the
substitute [evidently Allan was still not satisfied with the
explanation] so will say nothing more concerning it —
only remarking that they will no longer enlist men for the
residue of another's enlistment as formerly, consequently
my substitute was enlisted for 5 years not 3 —

I stated in my last letter (to which I refer you) that Mr
Eaton gave me strong hopes for Sepr. at any rate that the
appt. could be obtained for June next — I can obtain
decent board lodging & washing with other expenses of
mending &c for 5 & perhaps even for 4½$ per week —

If I obtain the appt. by the last of Sepr. the amt of
expense would be at most $30 — If I should be unfortunate and not obtain it until June I will not desire you to
allow as much as that per week because by engaging for a
longer period at a cheap boarding house I can do with
much less — say even 10 even 8$ per month — any thing
with which you think it possible to exist — I am not so
anxious of obtaining money from your good nature as of
preserving your good will —

I am extremely anxious that you should believe that I
have not attempted to impose upon you — I will in the
meantime (if you wish it) write you often, but pledge
myself to apply for no other assistance than what you shall
think proper to allow —

I left behind me in Richmond a small trunk containing
books & some letters — will you forward it on to Baltimore to the care of *H. W. Bool Jr* & if you think I may ask
too much perhaps you will put in it for me some few
clothes as I am nearly without —

Give my love to Miss Valentine —

I remain

Dear Pa

Yours affectionately

Edgar A. Poe

Edgar judged Allan's mood correctly this time and a little more
than a week later received fifty dollars to ensure his continued
absence from Richmond. With the financial pressure temporarily

relieved, he could get on with the business of publishing his poetry. And now, for once, he was blessed with instant recognition: John Neal, editor of *The Yankee and Boston Literary Gazette*, printed in the September 1829 issue of his magazine an extract from the poem we now know as 'Fairyland', but to which Poe had at the time given the title of 'Heaven':

> Dim vales — and shadowy floods —
> And cloudy-looking woods,
> Whose forms we can't discover
> For the tears that drip all over!
> Huge moons there wax and wane —
> Again — again — again —
> Every moment of the night —
> For ever changing places —
> And they put out the star-light
> With the breath from their pale faces . . .

Neal, a New Englander who had enjoyed a large measure of success with his poetry and novels and had become a powerful literary force throughout the land, suggested that if 'E.A.P. of Baltimore . . . would but do himself justice' he might make a beautiful and perhaps magnificent poem — 'There is a good deal here to justify such a hope' and although the poem was nonsense it was 'rather exquisite nonsense'. Poe described these as 'the very first words of encouragement I ever remember to have heard'. But perhaps they were more than that. Neal may have summed up in those words the appeal of Poe's entire verse output — nonsense, but rather exquisite nonsense.

Literary criticism at that time bore all the characteristics of civil war, with attacks, counter-attacks, advances, retreats, sallies, bridge-heads and full-scale battles. As one of the multiplicity of literary magazines would praise and support a particular poet or author, so another would condemn and ridicule him in a welter of verbal sectarian violence. Thus Neal, who had fond memories of Baltimore and was anxious to establish its literary credentials, gave Poe his desperately needed encouragement — while the rival *American Monthly Magazine* dismissed 'Heaven' as no more than a collection of 'sickly rhymes'. All publicity, they say, is good publicity, and Edgar Poe was beginning to get his share. But recognition alone would not fill his belly or pay his board, and poetry did not look like a career, at least to John Allan, who sent another highly critical letter towards the end of October. Edgar replied:

Dear Pa —

I received your letter this evening and am grieved that I can give you no positive evidence of my industry & zeal as regards the appt. at W. Point: unless you will write to Mr Eaton himself who well remembers me & the earnestness of my application. But you are labouring under a mistake which I beg you to correct by reference to all my former letters — I stated that Mr Eaton told me that an appt. could be obtained by Sepr. *provided* there were a sufficient number *rejected* at the June examination & regretted that I had not made an earlier application — that *at all events* with the strong recommendations I had brought that I should have an appt. at the next term which is in June next — So far from having doubts about my appt. at that time, I am as certain of obtaining it as I am of being alive — If you find this statement to be incorrect then condemn me — otherwise acquit me of any intention to practise upon your good nature — which I now feel myself to be above.

It is my intention upon the receipt of your letter to go again to Washington &, tho' contrary to the usual practice, I will get Mr Eaton to give me my letter of appt. *now* — it will consist of an order to repair to W.P. in June for examination &c — & forward it to you that all doubts may be removed — I will tell him why I want it at present & I think he will give it.

He ended the letter: 'I am sorry that your letters to me have still with them a tone of anger as if my former errors were not forgiven — if I knew how to regain your affection God knows I would do any thing I could.' But if he expected that to touch Allan's heart (not to mention his pocket) he was disappointed, and on 12 November had to make a more direct appeal: 'I wrote you about a fortnight ago and as I have not heard from you, I was afraid you had forgotten me — I would not trouble you so often if I was not extraordinarily pinched — I am almost without clothes — and, as I board by the month, the lady with whom I board is anxious for money — I have not had any (you know) since the middle of August . . .' This time he was rewarded, with a cheque for eighty dollars; apparently Allan was not prepared to cast him adrift while there was still the possibility of his going to West Point. There was more good news, too, as Edgar reported in a letter home on 18 November: 'The Poems will be printed by Hatch & Dunning of this city upon terms advantageous to me — they printing it & giving me 250 copies of the book . . .'

Publicity had cast if not its glare then at least some candlelight over Edgar Allan Poe, and with two publications to his credit he began to think that he could call himself a poet. Neal puffed the new volume, *Al Aaraaf, Tamerlane and Minor Poems* in the December issue of his magazine, together with a letter from Poe in which he said that he had written 'the greater part' of the poems before he was fifteen years old — and, recalling the earlier words of Neal, he said he was sure he had not yet written 'a beautiful if not a magnificent poem' but swore that he could do so if the public and the critics were prepared to be patient. To which the editor of *The Yankee* added the pertinent comment that the 'young author' needed considerable determination to endure the present in the firm belief that recognition would be his in the future.

The present at this particular time, however, was being rather kinder to Poe than he might have expected. The publication of his seventy-two page book in December 1829 might have persuaded John Allan that there was something in this literary business after all, and Edgar was apparently welcomed home to Richmond and furnished with new clothes and equipment against his expected departure for West Point. Edgar almost certainly spent his time writing more verse (it is generally believed that 'To Helen', his hymn to Jane Stanard, was composed during the early months of 1830 rather than, as Poe claimed, 'in earliest boyhood') and dreaming of the success to come. Towards the end of March his West Point papers finally came through and Allan gave formal permission for his ward to spend the next five years of his life as an officer cadet. It looked as if everyone was going to be satisfied, but, as always in the life of Edgar Allan Poe, disaster was just around the corner: the first warning shot came in the form of a letter from Sergeant 'Bully' Graves, Edgar's army substitute, asking when he was going to receive the money Edgar owed him. Poe's reply, dated 3 May 1830, makes it clear that the sergeant had spent some time and effort in trying to contact Edgar and had also appealed to John Allan. In view of Poe's earlier statement to Allan that he was short of money because he had paid Graves the fifty dollars owed for the substitution, it would be generous to suppose that the sergeant's appeal referred to some other debt, but Poe's reply to him leaves no room for doubt:

> I have tried to get the money for you from Mr A a dozen times — but he always shuffles me off — I have been very sorry that *I have never had it in my power as yet to pay you or St. Griffith* [my italics] — but altho' appearances are very much against me I think you know me sufficiently well to believe that I have no intention of keeping you out of your money . . .

Perhaps it was true that he had no intention of keeping Graves and Sergeant Griffith out of their money, but he had certainly not done much about paying them. Admittedly, Allan had kept him short of money during his stay in Baltimore, but then Edgar had, at least as far as we know, never asked for money to pay his army debts; what he did do was lie about the disposal of the cash Allan had sent by saying he had paid Graves the fifty dollars. It was, therefore, defamatory to claim that Allan 'always shuffles me off', but even that was not the end of it: in order to defend himself, Edgar became downright vicious. Allan had apparently responded to Graves's inquiry to him by repeating Edgar's claim that the money had been dispatched from Baltimore. In the letter of 3 May, however, Poe stated: 'Mr A very evidently misunderstood me, and I wish you to understand that I never sent any money . . . Mr A is not very often sober — which accounts for it . . .' This was not only a vicious remark, in view of the truth of the matter, but also a stupid one, and it was not to be very long before it rebounded, and finally convinced John Allan that Edgar was a hopeless case.

Edgar left Richmond about the middle of May 1830, taking the steamboat to Baltimore on the first leg of his long journey to West Point, which lies on the Hudson River some fifty miles north of New York. He arrived at the academy towards the end of June, and found twenty dollars from John Allan waiting for him. On 28 June he wrote home, thanking his guardian for the money and expressing hopes that he would do well as an officer cadet. It was certainly not going to be easy: West Point had been a strategic military post during the Revolutionary War, when it was associated with the name of the notorious American traitor Benedict Arnold, who tried to sell it to the British, and as if to erase the memory of this shameful act it had in 1802 been turned into a breeding ground for super-soldiers. Only the fittest, both mentally and physically, survived this assault course — of 130 cadets accepted each year, only a little over a third ever graduated, the rest, in Poe's own words, 'being dismissed for bad conduct or deficiency . . . a great many cadets of good family &c have been rejected . . .'

The regulations stated that each cadet 'previous to his being admitted into the military academy, must be able to read and write well, and to perform with facility and accuracy, the various operations of the four ground rules of arithmetic — of reduction — of simple and compound proportion, — and vulgar and decimal fractions'. Each cadet had to report between 1 and 20 June and 'shall be examined in the last week of that month'. Before the examination there was a period of drill and instruction in simple arithmetic, and after it the cadets went into summer encampment, where they practised foot and gun drill, including the use of artillery pieces, and learnt how to construct fieldworks and make munitions. The days were long, with marching before breakfast, then classes interspersed between more drill periods, and finally spells of guard duty. Of course, Poe had been through all this before — indeed, as a former non-commissioned officer in the artillery, he probably knew as much as the instructors about cannon, mortars and howitzers, and he certainly would not have forgotten his foot drill. Furthermore, as an ex-university student, he would not have had too much difficulty with the academic side of West Point life. He told John Allan modestly: 'I find that I will possess many advantages . . .'

Thus broken in, the new cadets went into barracks at the end of August, and though there was no let-up in the pace, the emphasis now was on academic rather than purely military achievement. Reveille was at 5 am and breakfast at 7 am — between the two the cadets were expected to study, and after breakfast the fourth classmen (or first-year cadets) were orally tested in mathematics. There was then further time for study and a break for lunch, and at 2 pm there was an hour of French. Drill took place every evening except Saturday and Sunday from 4.10 until 5.30 pm and at 6.15 there was parade followed by supper and a further study period until 9.30, when the cadets went to bed. On Sundays there were corps inspection and church parade, and in the afternoons one hour of recreation. It was, you might say, a full life, and one which at first Poe seemed to take to: the military side was easy for him and on the academic side he was rated seventeenth in his year for mathematics (which consisted of algebra and geometry) and third in French. He wrote home on 6 November 1830:

> I have a very excellent standing in my class — in the first section in every thing and have great hopes of doing well . . . I have spent my time very pleasantly hitherto — but the study requisite is incessant, and the discipline exceedingly rigid . . . I am very much pleased with Col. Thayer [the superintendent], and indeed with every thing at the institution.

However, the letter also contained a paragraph with a distinct sense of *déjà vu:* 'If you would be so kind as to send me on a Box of Mathematical Instruments, and a copy of the Cambridge Mathematics, you would confer a great favor upon me and render my situation much more comfortable, or forward to Col. Thayer the means of obtaining them; for as I have no deposit, my more necessary expenditures have run me into debt.' It was beginning to look like Charlottesville all over again. The cadets were paid at the rate of sixteen dollars a month (they also received two rations a day) from which four dollars was subtracted for books and they also had to pay for their uniforms, other clothing and supplies outside of their rations. Most of the young men were of good family, and it was customary for them to receive allowances from home. Poe's 'allowance' appears to have consisted of only the twenty dollars Allan had sent in advance of his arrival at West Point.

There was one further significant comment in the letter to Allan, though the event that prompted it is not referred to: 'I was greatly in hopes you would have come on to W. Point while you were in N. York, and was very much disappointed when I heard you had gone on home without letting me hear from you.' The reason for Allan's journey north had been a wedding — his own. At the age of fifty, and in spite of the fact that his paramour, Mrs Wills, had recently given birth to twins, he married Louisa Gabriella Patterson, daughter of a family prominent in New York and New Jersey. The wedding took place at the Pattersons' New York house, and shortly afterwards Allan conveyed his bride to her new home in Virginia. How Edgar got to know about it, we cannot tell, for it seems clear that John Allan did not inform him, but it seems equally clear that Poe did not approve, since he did not mention the happy event in his November letter (though he did include 'my respects to Mrs A'). For her part, the new Mrs Allan was to make it quite obvious that on the basis of what her husband told her, she certainly did not approve of Edgar Allan Poe. It has been assumed by earlier biographers that Allan had confessed his various indiscretions to his new bride before the marriage, but in view of the scandalous fuss she was to create over her husband's will I believe this was not the case. What is beyond doubt, however, is that Louisa's entry into the Allan family signalled Edgar's exit from it.

But for the time being, Edgar had life at West Point to wrestle with. Discipline was very strict, with three hundred and four regulations covering every aspect of the cadets' lives, particularly the little time they had to themselves. Naturally enough, drinking was forbidden, as was smoking, and card playing was banned, along with games like chess and backgammon (presumably on the ground that it is possible to gamble on any game, whether it involves skill or depends entirely upon chance). On top of that, no cadet was allowed to keep in his room any book that did not concern his studies, unless he had the permission of the superintendent. Early biographers assumed that this last rule must have been irksome to an avid reader like Poe, but once again they may be accused of jumping to conclusions. In 1830, the West Point library contained almost three thousand books, of which more than seven hundred covered subjects not related to the course of study — travel, history, biography, philosophy, natural sciences and so on. Poe would almost certainly have been able to find something in that collection which interested him, yet his name does not appear in the library circulation records. He could have applied for permission to borrow non-course books, but, as he had done at university, he seems not to have taken advantage of the facilities offered. He might have spent some time in the library — which was open for reading for seven hours every day except Sunday — but it seems that he did not go out of his way to pursue his avowed interest in literature.

So what did Poe do with his free time? We know that he roomed at No. 28 South Barracks with Thomas W. Gibson and Timothy Pickering Jones, both of whom, in reminiscences published many years later, testified to Poe's liking for drink and spoke of expeditions after 'lights out' to a place called 'Benny's', where they bought brandy. There is no doubt that a good deal of illicit drinking went on among the cadets, but if Poe took much part in it he must have been cleverer or luckier than his fellows, for his name does not appear on any charge-sheet in connexion with such offences. Jones and Gibson added that Edgar was pretty well liked and admired for his scholastic ability and his talent for writing satirical verses, chiefly aimed at the tutors. But, as Gibson put it in an article for *Harper's* in 1867, Poe 'had a worn, weary discontented look, not easily forgotten by those who were intimate with him'. To which another classmate, Allan B. Magruder, added: 'He was very shy and reserved in his intercourse with his fellow-cadets — his associates being confined almost exclusively to Virginians.' No recollection has come to light which puts Poe among the activists of the famous West Point group, the Dialectic Society (formed in 1824 and still going strong), where members presented anonymous papers which were delivered to the assembly by an official known as the Reader; it may be, however, that Poe employed the good offices of the Dialectic to raise a subscription list which allowed him to publish a volume of poems in 1831, and possibly he did attend some of the society's meetings, which were popular.

The general picture that emerges from the sketchy accounts we have is of a moody, rather melancholy and often withdrawn Poe, who perhaps indulged in drinking but not frequently or excessively enough to engage the attention of the authorities; who sometimes felt lively enough to sharpen his wit at the expense of others (but, on the evidence of Gibson, did not like jokes directed against himself); and who gave the impression of being somewhat bowed down by worry. He certainly had a number of things to occupy his mind: for a start, any hopes he nursed of receiving a legacy from John Allan had suffered a setback with the arrival on the scene of Louisa, who at the age of thirty was almost certain to bear children; then there was life at West Point itself, which presented difficulties from two points of view, though they were related. In the first place there were the money problems arising from Allan's refusal to support him, and in the second the organization of the academy. Poe had boasted that he would complete the course within six months, implying that at the end of that time he would be in a position to take a commission with its accompanying salary and thus cease to be a drain on his guardian's pocket. But there was no express passage through West Point — every detail of the course as laid down had to be followed. So even though Poe had been comparatively well educated, and in spite of the fact that he had already undergone military training, there were no short cuts, and that meant it would be at least four years before he could begin to feel free. No doubt it was the realization of this that gave Edgar his 'weary discontented look'.

His decision to leave West Point resulted from a combination of all these factors — touched off, in the first days of 1831, by a furious letter from John Allan, to whom 'Bully' Graves, still trying to get his money, had sent Poe's defamatory communication of May 1830. It is not hard to imagine Allan's fury as he realized Edgar had lied all the way about the payment for his substitute, and even more as he read those damning words 'Mr A is not very often sober'. He immediately fired off a broadside, telling Edgar that their relationship was at an end; as far as we know, it was the last letter Poe ever received from him.

Edgar was shattered. On 3 January 1831 (making a common mistake by forgetting that it was a new year and dating his letter 1830) he wrote back in defiant mood:

> Sir,
>
> I suppose, (altho' you desire no further communication with yourself, on my part) that your restriction does not extend to my answering your final letter.
>
> Did I, when an infant, sollicit [sic] your charity and protection, or was it of your own free will, that you volunteered your services in my behalf ? It is well known to respectable individuals in Baltimore, and elsewhere, that my Grandfather (my natural protector at the time you interposed) was wealthy, and that I was his favorite grand-child. But the promises of adoption, and liberal education which you held forth to him in a letter which is

now in possession of my family, induced him to resign all care of me into your hands. Under such circumstances, can it be said that I have no right to expect anything at your hands? You may probably urge that you have given me a liberal education. I will leave the decision of that question to those who know how far liberal educations can be obtained in 8 months at the University of Va. Here you will say that it was my own fault that I did not return. You would not let me return because bills were presented to you for payment which I never wished or desired you to pay. Had you let me return, my reformation had been sure — as my conduct the last 3 months gave every reason to believe — and you would never have heard more of my extravagances. But I am not about to proclaim myself guilty of all that has been alleged against me, and which I have hitherto endured, simply because I was too proud to reply. I will boldly say that it was wholly and entirely your own mistaken parsimony that caused all the difficulties in which I was involved while at Charlottesville . . .

He went on to describe his financial arrangements and resultant difficulties at the university, which we have already noted, then returned to the attack:

Every day, threatened with a warrant &c, I left home — and after nearly 2 years conduct with which no fault could be found — in the army as a common soldier — I earned myself, by the most humiliating privations — a Cadet's warrant which you could have obtained at any time for asking. It was then that I thought I might venture to sollicit your assistance in giving me an outfit. I came home, you will remember, the night after the burial. If she had not died while I was away there would have been nothing for me to regret. Your love I never valued — but she I believe loved me as her own child. You promised me to forgive all — but you soon forgot your promise. You sent me to W. Point like a beggar. The same difficulties are threatening me as before at Charlottesville — and I must resign.

As to your injunction not to trouble you with further communication, rest assured, Sir, that I will most religiously observe it. When I parted from you — at the steam-boat — I knew that I should never see you again. As regards Sergt. Graves — I did write him that letter. As to the truth of its contents, I leave it to God, and your own conscience. — The Time in which I wrote it was within a half hour after you had embittered every feeling of my heart against you by your abuse of my family, and myself, under your own roof — and at a time when you knew that my heart was almost breaking.

I have no more to say — except that my future life (which thank God will not endure long) must be passed in indigence and sickness. I have no energy left, nor health. If it was possible to put up with the fatigues of this place, and the inconveniences which my absolute want of necessaries subject me to, and as I mentioned before it is my intention to resign — For this end it will be necessary that you (as my nominal guardian) enclose me your written permission. It will be useless to refuse me this last request — for I can leave the place without any permission — your refusal would only deprive me of the little pay which is now due as mileage.

From the time of this writing I shall neglect my studies and duties at the institution. If I do not receive your answer in 10 days, I will leave the Point without — for otherwise I should subject myself to dismission.

E. A. Poe

This strange mixture of recrimination and self-pity, of fact and fancy, was not likely to heal the breach. Indeed, the gulf between the two men was now so wide as to be unbridgeable. Allan noted on the letter: 'I recd. this on the 10th & did not from its conclusion deem it necessary to reply. I make this note on the 13th & can see no good Reason to alter my opinion. I do not think the Boy has one good quality. He may do or act as he pleases, tho' I wd have saved him but on his own terms & conditions since I cannot believe a word he writes. His letter is the most barefaced one sided statement.'

But in one respect at least Poe was as good as his word: he began to absent himself from his duties and studies, and the fact that he did so only five days after writing to Allan indicates that he did not have much hope of receiving a reply. On 28 January he appeared before a court martial presided over by an engineer lieutenant, charged with the following offences:

Charge 1st . . . Gross neglect of duty. Specification 1st . . . In this, that he the said Cadet Poe did absent himself from the following parades and roll calls between the 7th of January and 27th January 1831 . . . [this covered evening

parades, reveille roll calls, class parades, guard duties and
one church parade]. Specification 2d . . . In this, that he
the said Cadet E. A. Poe, did absent himself from all
Academical duties between the 15th and 27 Jan'y
1831 . . .

Charge 2d . . . Disobedience of Orders. Specification 1st
. . . In this that he the said Cadet Poe, after having been
directed by the officer of the day to attend church on the
23d January 1831 did fail to obey such order . . . Specification 2d . . . In this, that he the said Cadet Poe did fail to
attend the Academy on the 25 Jany. 1831, after having
been directed to do so by the officer of the day . . .

Poe pleaded guilty to the second charge and to the second
specification of the first, and to make sure of receiving the full
disapproval of the court he pleaded not guilty to the first specification of the first charge, offering no defence. Of course, the charges
could easily be proved, and, 'The court after mature deliberation on
the testimony adduced find the prisoner "Guilty" of the 1st
specification of the 1st charge and confirm his plea to the remainder
of the charges and specifications, and adjudge that he Cadet E. A.
Poe be *dismissed* the service of the United States.' The sentence was
confirmed by the Secretary for War on 8 February, and shortly
afterwards Poe left West Point, although his dismissal did not become
official until 6 March. No doubt Edgar was glad to get away from the
academy, but one wonders what he thought his future prospects
might be. Throughout his life, periods of blind optimism alternated
with the blackest depressions, and often the promise of some upturn
in his fortunes was enough to convince him that the hoped-for event
had already occurred. He had been in touch with a New York
publisher, Elam Bliss, who had been persuaded to bring out a volume
of Poe's poems by subscriptions of seventy-five cents a copy Edgar
had obtained from many of his fellow cadets, so it is possible that
when he left West Point Poe was looking forward to success as a
poet. On the other hand, all that had happened between him and
John Allan cannot have given him much cause for hope, and it was
probably in a state of some bewilderment that he took his last look
at West Point on 19 February and set off for New York.

Two days later — incredible as it might seem — we find him once
more appealing to Allan for money. He had presumably settled into a
cheap boarding house in New York and had then discovered that
there would be little left of the cash he had raised at West Point once
the publication costs of his new book had been paid. Any optimism
he had felt had quickly vanished, and on top of that he had fallen ill.

His letter to Allan is desperate and pathetic:

> Dear Sir,
>
> In spite of all my resolution to the contrary I am obliged once more to recur to you for assistance — It will however be the last time that I ever trouble any human being — I feel that I am on a sick bed from which I never shall get up. I now make an appeal not to your affection because I have lost that but to your sense of justice — I wrote to you for permission to resign — because it was *impossible* that I could stay — my *ear* has been too shocking for any description — I am wearing away every day — even if my last sickness had not completed it. I wrote to you as I say for permission to resign because without your permission no resignation can be received — My reason for doing so was that I should obtain my mileage amounting to $30.35 — according to the rules of the institution — in my present circumstances a single dollar is of more importance to me than 10,000 are to you and you *deliberately* refused to answer my letter — I, as I told you, neglected my duty when I found it impossible to attend to it — and the consequences were inevitable — dismissal. I have been *dismissed* — when a single line from you would have saved it — the whole Academy have interested themselves in my behalf because my only crime was being *sick*, but it was of no use — I refer you to Col. Thayer to the public records, for my standing and reputation for talent — but it was all in vain if you had granted me permission to resign — all might have been avoided — I have not strength nor energy left to write half what I feel — you one day or other will *feel* how you have treated me. I left W. Point two days ago and travelling to N. York without a cloak or any other clothing of importance I have caught a most violent cold and am confined to bed — I have no money — no friends — I have written to my brother — but he cannot help me — I shall never rise from my bed — besides a most violent cold on my lungs my *ear* discharges blood and matter continually and my headache is distracting — I hardly know what I am writing — I will write no more — Please send me a little money quickly — and forget what I said about you.
>
> God bless you —
E. A. Poe
>
> do not say a word to my sister.
> I shall send to the P.O. every day.

What the mysterious sickness was that he claimed to have suffered at West Point, we do not know. Perhaps it was, like the effect of his drinking at university, an early warning of the illness which was to afflict him later, or perhaps he was merely trying to gain Allan's sympathy. If the latter was the case, he failed, for John Allan did not reply. A long time later he must have come across Edgar's letter when he was going through his papers, and he noted on it: 'Apr. 12, 1833. It is now upward of 2 years since I received the above precious relict of the Blackest Heart & deepest ingratitude alike destitute of honour & principle every day of his life has only served to confirm his debased nature — suffice it to say my only regret is in Pity for his failings — his Talents are of an order that can never prove a comfort to their possessor.' He never knew how right he was with that last comment.

Edgar's relationship with John Allan has been described by previous biographers as one of the great mysteries of Poe's life. The question has been, how, after such promising beginnings, everything went wrong. The answer, I think, is not so much a clash of wills as a clash of weaknesses. Allan was split between sexual desires (and perhaps a need to have children) and his conscience, as well as his concern with what other people thought of him. Edgar's opposing forces were his pride and urge towards independence, and his inability to achieve his 'freedom' by himself, which led him into rash actions. These difficulties of Poe and Allan proved to be conflicting, and the situation was aggravated by what appears to have been a complete lack of understanding and tolerance between them. They provoked each other in turn, as if playing some highly ritualized game, and in the end neither gained anything.

Poe would try to keep the relationship alive, partly for sentimental reasons, partly out of his need for money, but by the early months of 1831 it had virtually come to an end.

Chapter 7

All in the Family

The Superintendent of the United States Military Academy, Colonel Thayer, received a curious letter early in March 1831. 'Sir,' it read, 'Having no longer any ties which can bind me to my native country — no projects — nor any friends — I intend by the first opportunity to proceed to Paris with the view of obtaining through the interest of the Marquis de La Fayette an appointment (if possible) in the Polish Army. In the event of the interference of France in behalf of Poland this may easily be effected — at all events it will be my only feasible plan of procedure. The object of this letter is respectfully to request that you will give me such assistance as may be in your power in furtherance of my views. A certificate of "standing" in my class is all that I have any right to expect. Anything further — a letter to a friend in Paris — or to the Marquis — would be a kindness which I should never forget.' The letter was signed, 'Most respectfully, Yr. obt. s't., Edgar A. Poe.'

What the colonel made of this wild idea is not known, for he does not appear to have replied. However, from this distance in time it can clearly be seen that in spite of Poe's earlier assurance to John Allan that he had forsaken Byron as a model, the spirit of that great romantic was still very much alive in the heart of the young poet. The Polish rising of 1830 had excited many idealistic imaginations, and although the insurrection was doomed from the start because of factionalism and lack of discipline, it seemed in the spring of 1831 that, with a little help from their friends, the Poles might succeed in driving out their Russian masters for good. What Greece was to Byron, Poland might be to Poe. But the plan came to naught, and Edgar was left in the obscurity of New York while the Polish freedom fighters headed towards a bloodbath in Warsaw.

Still, there was his third book to look forward to, and by the end of the month he was able to read the proofs in the offices of Elam Bliss on Broadway. *Poems* (Second Edition), a slim volume of one hundred and twenty-four pages, 'respectfully dedicated to the U.S. Corps of Cadets', appeared in April, but it attracted little money and

equally scant critical attention: indeed the *New York Mirror* might
be said to have damned it with faint praise when its reviewer
commented, 'The poetry of this little volume has a plausible air of
imagination, inconsistent with the general indefiniteness of the ideas.
Everything in the language betokens poetic inspiration, but it rather
resembles the leaves of the sybil when scattered by the winds . . .'
Nevertheless, the new poems showed significant advances on Poe's
earlier work — for a start there was the first version of 'To Helen'
(quoted in its final form in Chapter 3), in which the magnificent lines
'To the glory that was Greece,/And the grandeur that was Rome' had
not yet appeared; originally Poe wrote, 'To the beauty of fair
Greece/And the grandeur of old Rome', but fortunately for the
English language he later chose to enrich it with the phrases for
which he is perhaps best known.

Another poem of note was 'The Doomed City', which later
became 'The City in the Sea' (and again the quotation is from the
last published version):

> Lo! Death has reared himself a throne
> In a strange city lying alone
> Far down within the dim West,
> Where the good and the bad and the worst and the best
> Have gone to their eternal rest.
> There shrines and palaces and towers
> (Time-eaten towers that tremble not!)
> Resemble nothing that is ours.
> Around, by lifting winds forgot,
> Resignedly beneath the sky
> The melancholy waters lie.
>
> No rays from the holy Heaven come down
> On the long night-time of that town;
> But light from out the lurid sea
> Streams up the turrets silently —
> Gleams up the pinnacles far and free —
> Up domes — up spires — up kingly halls —
> Up fanes — up Babylon-like walls —
> Up shadowy long-forgotten bowers
> Of sculptured ivy and stone flowers —
> Up many and many a marvellous shrine,
> Whose wreathed friezes intertwine
> The viol, the violet, and the vine.
>
> Resignedly beneath the sky
> The melancholy waters lie.

So blend the turrets and shadows there
That all seem pendulous in air,
While from a proud tower in the town
Death looks gigantically down.

The adventurous use of language and metre foreshadows later and greater poems like 'The Raven' and 'Annabel Lee'. Certainly in 1831 the American reader had seen nothing like it, and it was to be many years before verse of such quality appeared again. But perhaps the real success of this second edition was 'Israfel', which, though it owes something to Thomas Moore, is a splendid and original lyric:

In Heaven a spirit doth dwell
    'Whose heart-strings are a lute';
None sing so wildly well
As the angel Israfel,
And the giddy stars (so legends tell),
Ceasing their hymns, attend the spell
    Of his voice, all mute.

Tottering above
    In her highest noon,
    The enamoured moon
Blushes with love,
    While, to listen, the red levin
    (With the rapid Pleiads, even,
    Which were seven),
    Pauses in heaven.

The last two stanzas are an expression of the human (that is, Poe's) condition:

Yes, Heaven is thine; but this
    Is a world of sweets and sours;
    Our flowers are merely — flowers,
And the shadow of thy perfect bliss
    Is the sunshine of ours.

If I could dwell
Where Israfel
    Hath dwelt, and he where I,
He might not sing so wildly well
    A mortal melody,
While a bolder note than this might swell
    From my lyre within the sky.

Yet the most significant thing in the 1831 *Poems* is not verse, but prose — the introduction, entitled 'Letter to Mr — —', in which Poe sets out for the first time his approach to poetry. He begins by telling 'Dear B—' (possibly Mr Bliss, his publisher) that criticism of poetry is useless unless it comes from a poet, 'the less poetical the critic, the less just the critique, and the converse'. The opinion of the world is that of a fool whose neighbour ('a step higher on the Andes of the mind') tells him that Shakespeare is the greatest of poets: 'On this account, and because there are but few B——s in the world, I would be as much ashamed of the world's good opinion as proud of your own.' Having thus dismissed the majority of the reading public, Poe goes on to bemoan 'the great barrier in the path of an American writer', who is read, 'if at all, in preference to the combined and established wit of the world' — for in literature, 'as with law or empire, an established name is an estate in tenure or a throne in possession'. Yes, but the name has to become established in the first place. Ah, says Poe, 'one might suppose that books, like their authors, improve by travel — their having crossed the sea is, with us, so great a distinction . . . our very fops glance from the binding to the bottom of the title page, where the mystic characters which spell London, Paris, or Genoa, are precisely so many letters of recommendation'.

Poe is getting into deep water here. One may ask whether it matters what the 'very fops' read if their opinions are worthless anyway. On the one hand Poe dismisses public opinion, yet on the other he seems to be asking for public recognition. But he plunges in deeper still: 'I mentioned just now a vulgar error as regards criticism. I think the notion that no poet can form a correct estimate of his own writings is another . . . a bad poet would, I grant make a false critique, and his self-love would infallibly bias his little judgment in his favor; but a poet, who is indeed a poet, could not, I think fail of making a just critique . . .' At this point it is a kindness to recall that Poe was only twenty-two years old when *Poems* (Second Edition) was published and, perhaps more important, that he had received no serious academic training — a fact which goes a long way towards explaining the flaws in his work, particularly in his essays. While he was always reaching beyond himself, sometimes with breathtaking success, he never fully appreciated the pitfalls in his way, and often fell into them. The remainder of the 'Letter' consists of tributes to and cribs from Coleridge (mainly from *Biographia Litteraria*) and an attack on Wordsworth which does little more than restate critical opinion that was current at the time and had been so for a couple of decades previously. In sum, the 'Letter to B' was an immature and imperfectly conceived effort in which assertion carelessly — even arrogantly — took the place of argument. However, it was also the first blow in Poe's lifelong defence of art, and that was something America needed, though it took many years for the message to get through.

What America definitely did not seem to need in the spring of 1831 was an idealistic young poet, and when Edgar counted up the few dollars he received from the subscriptions to his new book, it became clear that he could not survive on his own in New York. Neither did it seem likely that he would obtain any help from John Allan, who had not replied to recent letters and who, whether Edgar knew it or not, was by that time preoccupied with the impending arrival of his first legitimate child, a boy born on 23 August 1831. There was only one place where he could seek aid, and accordingly he spent the little money he had on a steamboat ticket to Baltimore, via Trenton, New Jersey, and Philadelphia.

Things had not improved in Mechanics Row: Grandmother Poe was completely bedridden; Edgar's brother Henry was wasting away under the effects of drink and tuberculosis; Mrs Clemm's son, also called Henry, was by his mother's testimony 'of not much account'; and Virginia was too young to add much to the household. But Maria Clemm was a remarkable woman. A few years younger than her brother, Edgar's father, she had at the age of twenty-seven married William Clemm Jr, a widower who had property and five children. Nine years and three more children later, Clemm died, and his small legacy was divided among the offspring of his first wife, leaving Maria penniless to raise her two children (the third had died in infancy). She managed on hard work and charity, begging what she could from wherever she could, but it must have been touch-and-go as more and more people crammed into the little house — old Mrs Poe, Henry, and then Edgar. Almost as soon as he had settled into the attic room with his sick brother, Edgar began to look for work. Never afraid to ask a favour, he wrote first to William Gwynn, proprietor and editor of the *Federal Gazette*, whom he had apparently offended during his previous stay in Baltimore:

May 6, 1831

Dear Sir,
I am almost ashamed to ask any favour at your hands after my foolish conduct upon a former occasion — but I trust your good nature.
    I am very anxious to remain and settle myself in Baltimore as Mr Allan has married again and I no longer look upon Richmond as my place of residence.
    This wish of mine has also met with his approbation. I

> wish to request your influence in obtaining some situation
> or employment in this city. Salary would be a minor
> consideration, but I do not wish to be idle.
>
> Perhaps . . . you might be so kind as to employ me in
> your office in some capacity. If so, I will use every exer-
> tion to deserve your confidence.

Edgar knew there was a vacancy in Gwynn's office because his
cousin, Neilson Poe, had just left it, but whatever it was that had
upset the editor apparently still rankled, and Edgar did not get the
job — perhaps he would have done better if he had told the truth
instead of pretending that 'salary would be a minor consideration'. A
couple of weeks later he tried another acquaintance, Nathan C.
Brooks, a man on the fringes of the literary world who had opened a
school on the outskirts of Baltimore, but again he failed to get a job.
The pressure on the family budget was relieved to some extent on 1
August, when Henry died; he was just twenty-four years old. But
there were still five mouths to feed, and Edgar no doubt felt that he
ought to be the breadwinner — with three books behind him already,
surely he could make a living with his pen. It was obvious that poetry
was not going to be profitable, but in June a new opportunity had
presented itself; *The Philadelphia Saturday Courier* had announced a
short story competition with a prize of one hundred dollars, closing
date for entries 1 December, and the result to be announced at the
end of that month. Edgar set to work in the little attic room he now
had to himself, and entered five stories for the competition. Perhaps
this would be the turning point.

December was a long way off, however, and present circumstances
were depressing. The death of his brother and the daily struggle to
survive weighed down Edgar's spirits and set him off comparing the
happiness and security of his childhood with the misery and
uncertainties of his current existence. How many of us, in times of
trouble, wish that we could return to the protected world we knew
as children, in the common human illusion that the past is always
better than the present? Poe put some of his thoughts on paper when
he wrote to John Allan on 16 October 1831:

> It is a long time since I have written to you unless with an
> application for money or assistance. I am sorry that it is so
> seldom that I hear from you or even *of* you — for all
> communication seems to be at an end; and when I think of
> the long twenty one years that I have called you father,
> and you have called me son, I could cry like a child to
> think that it should all end in this. You know me too well

to think me interested — if so: why have I rejected your thousand offers of love and kindness? It is true that when I have been in great extremity, I have always applied to you — for I had no other friend, but it is only at such a time as the present when I can write to you with the consciousness of making no application for assistance, that I dare to open my heart, or speak one word of old affection. When I look back on the past and think of every thing — of how much you tried to do for me — of your forbearance and your generosity, in spite of the most flagrant ingratitude on my part, I can not help thinking myself the greatest fool in existence, — I am ready to curse the day when I was born.

But I am fully — truly conscious that all these better feelings have *come too late*. I am not the damned villain even to ask you to restore me to the twentieth part of those affections which I have so deservedly lost, and I am resigned to whatever fate is allotted me.

I write merely because I am by myself and have been thinking over old times, and my only friends, until my heart is full — At such a time the conversation of new acquaintance is like ice, and I prefer writing to you altho' I know that you care nothing about me, and perhaps will not even read my letter.

I have nothing more to say — and *this time* no favour to ask — Altho I am wretchedly poor, I have managed to get clear of the difficulty I spoke of in my last, and am *out of debt*, at any rate.

May God bless you —

E.A.P.

Will you not write one word to me?

Of course, we cannot know the exact state of Edgar's mind when he wrote that letter, and the cynic might think that, in the light of a long string of begging letters from Edgar's hand, it was no more than an attempt to soften up Allan for a request for money to follow. There is no doubt that the family in Mechanics Row could have used a donation. And yet, the letter has the ring of sincerity about it, even if Poe's continual assurances that he is not asking for money make it look as if he was protesting too much. The rest of his letters to Allan do not betray any great subtlety of approach; his hints are usually heavy-handed and obvious, and it may be supposed that if the intention of the October letter was to obtain money, Poe would have said so directly. Which he was, in fact, obliged to do a month later. He may have thought that he was 'out of debt, at any rate', but there

was a creditor just around the corner, anxious to collect a debt Edgar
had contracted in 1829, probably to pay medical bills for Henry. On
18 November 1831 he wrote to Allan again, and did not mince his
words saying that 'if you refuse to help me I know not what I shall
do'. He stated that he had been arrested on account of the debt, that
he was 'in bad health and unable to undergo as much hardships as
formerly', and that he must have eighty dollars by the following
Wednesday. No record of Poe's arrest at this time has come to light,
but he had every reason to fear going to jail since debt was only too
common a cause of incarceration in those days.

The eighty dollars was not forthcoming, and on 5 December Mrs
Clemm appealed to Allan, confessing her distress at Edgar's situation
and pointing out that 'I have with great difficulty procured $20
which I will reserve for him, with all my heart — but it is insufficient
to extricate him — I beg that you will assist him out of this difficulty
and I am sure that it will be a warning for him as long as he lives — to
involve himself no further in debt — I am satisfied that except in this
instance he does not owe one cent in the world, and would do well if
you would relieve him . . .'

Still Allan did not reply, and on 15 December Edgar wrote to
'Dear Pa' in terms of the utmost desperation:

> I am sure you could not refuse to assist me if you were
> aware of the distress I am in. How often have you relieved
> the distresses of a perfect stranger in circumstances less
> urgent than mine, and yet when I beg and intreat you in
> the name of God to send me succour you will still refuse
> to aid me. I know that I have offended you past all forgive-
> ness, and I know that I have no longer any hopes of being
> again received into your favour, but for the sake of Christ
> do not let me perish for a sum of money which you would
> never miss, and which would relieve me from the greatest
> earthly misery — especially as I promise by all that is
> sacred that I will never under any circumstances apply to
> you again. Oh! if you knew at this moment how wretched
> I am you would never forgive yourself for having refused
> me. You are enjoying yourself in all the blessings that
> wealth & happiness can bestow, and I am suffering every
> extremity of want and misery without even a chance of
> escape, or a friend to whom I can look up to for assistance.
> Think for one moment, and if your nature and former
> heart are not altogether changed you will no longer refuse
> me your assistance if not for my sake for the sake of
> humanity. I know you have never turned a beggar from

your door, and I apply to you in that light. I *beg* you for a little aid, and for the sake of all that was formerly dear to you I trust that you will relieve me.

If you wish me to humble myself before you I am humble — Sickness and misfortune have left me not a shadow of pride. I own that I am miserable and unworthy of your notice, but do not leave me to perish without leaving me still one resource. I feel at the very bottom of my heart that if I were in your situation and you in mine, how differently I would act.

Yours affect'y
E.A.P.

In fact, Allan had already responded to Mrs Clemm's appeal, according to a note he added to Edgar's letter of 15 December. He had written to a friend in Baltimore with instructions to give Edgar the eighty dollars he needed '& to give him $20 besides to keep him out of further difficulties & value on me for such account as might be required'. But, in his own words, he had 'neglected sending' the letter! Had he just forgotten about it, or was he trying to 'punish' Edgar? The latter explanation seems the more likely, since the 15 December letter from Baltimore did not produce any action, and neither did a further plea from Edgar on 29 December, when he asked 'for the sake of the love you bore me when I sat upon your knee and called you father do not forsake me this only time — and God will remember you accordingly'. It was not until the turn of the year, on 12 January, that the much-needed aid was dispatched from Richmond. As far as we know, these were the last dealings — and indirect ones at that — John Allan ever had with his 'adopted son', though Edgar did write to him again asking, in spite of his 'promise by all that is sacred', for money.

In the meantime, the results of the *Courier* competition were out: Edgar had not won, the six judges having chosen a sentimental tale entitled 'Love's Martyr' by one Delia S. Bacon. The judgment is not entirely surprising, because four of Poe's five tales were satires on contemporary literary taste — 'The Duke de L'Omelette' and 'The Bargain Lost', both about mortals doing battle with the Devil; 'A Decided Loss', concerning a man who literally loses his breath while abusing his wife; and 'A Tale of Jerusalem', which poked fun at the kind of stories then popular with *Blackwood's Magazine*. Nevertheless, all were published in the *Courier* during 1832, together with the best of Poe's competition entries, a gripping though unlikely tale of the supernatural called 'Metzengerstein'. This last was also intended to be satirical, imitating the Gothic horror of the German writer E.

T. A. Hoffman (1776-1822), with an absurd plot based on the theory of metempsychosis — the passage of the soul after death into some other body — and concerning the relationship between an evil young Hungarian baron and a ghostly horse which appears from a tapestry portraying an act of brutality by one of the nobleman's ancestors. Grotesque and gruesome stories such as Hoffman wrote had really caught the public imagination in Europe and America, and Poe — with his avowed contempt for popular taste — would have considered the Gothic style a worthy target for his wit. In fact, he learnt too much from his German model, and 'Metzengerstein', like so many of Poe's later horror stories, becomes totally convincing through its Hoffmannesque realism and vividness, as though the writer knows the characters he is describing and has even experienced the terrible events that overtake them.

'Metzengerstein' opens with a fairly abstract discussion of metempsychosis and a brief history of the enmity between the families of Berlifitzing and Metzengerstein, including the dark prophecy, 'A lofty name shall have a fearful fall when, as the rider over his horse, the mortality of Metzengerstein shall triumph over the immortality of Berlifitzing'. The suspense is carefully built up, until:

> One tempestuous night, Metzengerstein, awaking from a heavy slumber, descended like a maniac from his chamber, and, mounting in hot haste, bounded away into the mazes of the forest. An occurrence so common attracted no particular attention, but his return was looked for with intense anxiety on the part of his domestics, when, after some hours' absence, the stupendous and magnificent battlements of the Palace Metzengerstein were discovered crackling and rocking to their very foundation, under the influence of a dense and livid mass of ungovernable fire . . .

And then the young baron returns.

> Up the long avenue of aged oaks which led from the forest to the main entrance of the Palace Metzengerstein, a steed, bearing an unbonneted and disordered rider, was seen leaping with an impetuosity which outstripped the very Demon of the Tempest.
> The career of the horseman was indisputably, on his own part, uncontrollable. The agony of his countenance, the convulsive struggle of his frame, gave evidence of superhuman exertion; but no sound, save a solitary shriek, escaped from his lacerated lips, which were bitten through

and through in the intensity of terror. One instant, and the clattering hooves resounded sharply and shrilly above the roaring of the flames and the shrieking of the winds — another, and, clearing at a single plunge the gate-way and the moat, the steed bounded far up the tottering staircases of the palace, and, with its rider, disappeared amid the whirlwind of chaotic fire.

The fury of the tempest immediately died away, and a dead calm suddenly succeeded. A white flame still enveloped the building like a shroud, and, streaming far away into the quiet atmosphere, shot forth a glare of preternatural light; while a cloud of smoke settled heavily over the battlements in the distinct colossal figure of — *a horse.*

That Poe had little regard for the long, rambling Gothic tales so much sought after in his day is evident from his comment on Charles Robert Maturin's *Melmoth the Wanderer* in the introduction to his 1831 poems: '. . . the devil in Melmoth . . . labors indefatigably through three octavo volumes, to accomplish the destruction of one or two souls, while any common devil would have demolished one or two thousand . . .' In setting out to lampoon such stuff Edgar Allan Poe had, by condensing it into a few brief paragraphs and thus heightening the tension and reinforcing the shock, begun to be the master of it — though in 1832 he still believed it was his skill as a satirist that had induced the *Courier* to publish 'Metzengerstein'.

The fact that those five tales had been published, however, was no help to the family in Mechanics Row, though it must have been a source of pride, even hope, for them. Since competition entries usually became the property of the publication running the competition, it is extremely unlikely that Edgar received any payment for them. And that is about as much as can be said for him in 1832: how he lived, what he did, whom he saw can only be guessed at, for nothing is known. It is fairly safe to assume that he remained in Baltimore — in spite of dramatic rumours that he went to Richmond and forced his way into Allan's house, which were believed by some earlier biographers — because in August of that year the Baltimore *Saturday Visiter* printed a notice to the effect that Mr Edgar A. Poe had submitted some manuscript tales which the *Visiter* hoped to publish at a future date. The idea of the Richmond trip is further discredited by the last letter Edgar is known to have written to Allan, dated 12 April 1833, in which he says: 'It has now been more than two years since you have assisted me, and more than three since you have spoken to me. I feel little hope that you will pay any regard to this letter, but still I cannot refrain from making one more attempt to interest you in my behalf. If you will only consider in what a situation I am placed you will surely pity me — without friends, without any means, consequently of obtaining employment, I am perishing — absolutely perishing from want of aid. And yet I am not idle — nor addicted to any vice — nor have I committed any offence against society which would render me deserving of so hard a fate. For God's sake pity me, and save me from destruction.' This letter leaves little doubt that relations had been quite definitely broken off, and Allan, who by the time he received it was the father of a second legitimate son, did nothing to revive them.

Another tall tale concerning Poe's activities in 1832 deals with a 'romance' he is said to have carried on with one Mary Devereaux of Baltimore. This rumour, also widely accepted by early biographers, is based on an article written at second hand in *Harper's Magazine* in 1899. It pictures Poe carrying on a passionate affair with Miss Devereaux, trying to force his way into her bedroom after a quarrel, and attacking her uncle. Miss Devereaux is quoted as saying that Poe was an atheist, valuing the laws of neither God nor man, who would have been as happy to 'live in sin' with a woman as to marry her. The article is not worth quoting at any length, since it conflicts with all other evidence as to Poe's character, in particular that supplied by women who knew him, and is completely inaccurate in other respects. But it is possible that Mary Devereaux knew Edgar and that she was attracted to him, as so many other women were to be. What Edgar's relations with women were like at this particular time is not known, but in later life he could hardly resist flirting with attractive women, and it is possible that he flirted with Miss Devereaux, though not likely that he did so in the reckless and passionate way she was said to have described to the writer of the *Harper's* article. What is worth quoting is Mary's physical description of Edgar, which agrees not only with other verbal records but also with surviving portraits of him:

Mr Poe was about five feet eight inches tall, and had dark, almost black hair, which he wore long and brushed back in student style over his ears. It was as fine as silk. His eyes were large and full, gray and piercing. He was entirely clean shaven. His nose was long and straight, and his features finely cut. The expression about his mouth was beautiful. He was pale, and had no color. His skin was of a clear, beautiful olive. He had a sad, melancholy look. He was very slender . . . but had a fine figure, an erect military carriage, and a quick step. But it was his manner that most charmed. It was elegant. When he looked at you it seemed as if he could read your thoughts. His voice was pleasant and musical but not deep. He always wore a black frock-coat buttoned up, with a cadet or military collar, a low turned-over shirt collar, and a black cravat tied in a loose knot. He did not follow the fashions, but had a style of his own.

More reliable evidence suggesting that Poe stayed in Baltimore in 1832 comes from Lambert A. Wilmer, literary editor of the *Visiter* between January and October that year. The two had become friendly after the publication of Poe's work in the *Courier*, and Wilmer said they often had long discussions during walks they took together. He also recalled that Poe was working extremely hard, 'at all hours', and this presumably refers to his short stories, though it is possible that he helped to support his family by taking on hack writing for local newspapers. By the beginning of 1833 he had apparently written eleven stories of the group later known as *Tales of the Folio Club* but which Poe called 'Eleven Tales of the Arabesque' when he vainly attempted to get at least one of them published in the *New England Magazine* in May. The fact that these were all humorous or satirical pieces indicates that Edgar had not realized what he had achieved with 'Metzengerstein': he told the magazine that the tales were supposed to be read at table by members of a literary society, each one followed by remarks which were meant to be 'a burlesque upon criticism'. The example he sent was 'Epimanes', written by club member 'Chronologos Chronology, who admired Horace Smith and had a very big nose which had been in Asia Minor'. Smith (1779-1849) was a prolific and popular English historical novelist who had turned to writing after having made his fortune as a stockbroker; Poe had already satirized him with 'A Tale of Jerusalem', and 'Epimanes', which takes the reader on a journey back through time, was evidently based on Smith's latest work, *Tales of Early Ages*, published in 1832. (In fact, Poe must have been an avid reader of Smith's work, for it was from the Englishman's witty essay 'Address to the Mummy in Belzoni's Exhibition', published in 1826, that he got the inspiration for his own 'Some Words with a Mummy', a satire on the glib conclusions of historical research, which first appeared in the *American Review* in the spring of 1845.)

In 1833, however, the public — or at least magazine editors — were not ready for 'Epimanes', which in any case is one of the least admirable stories Poe ever wrote, though the reason for its rejection may have had less to do with its quality than with its harsh criticism of the idea of democracy so rampant in the United States of

President Andrew Jackson. Another of the 'Folio Club' tales was to prove more important. In June 1833, the *Saturday Visiter* announced a poetry and prose competition with 'a premium of 50 dollars for the best Tale and 25 dollars for the best Poem, not exceeding one hundred lines'. Poe submitted one poem and at least five stories. On 12 October the results were published: the poetry prize was won by a Mr Henry Wilton, but in the short story competition, 'we have . . . awarded the prize . . . to the tale bearing the title of "A MS Found in a Bottle" ' which was 'the production of Edgar A. Poe, of Baltimore'. It was the beginning of Poe's recognition as a writer of horror stories, though it was to be many years before the true worth of those stories was to be appreciated.

There were three judges for the *Visiter* competition, J. H. B. Latrobe, Dr James H. Miller, and John P. Kennedy. Latrobe later recalled what happened at the judging session:

> . . . the committee had about made up their minds that there was nothing before them to which they would award a prize, when I noticed a small quarto-bound book that had until then accidentally escaped attention, possibly because so unlike, externally, the bundles of manuscript that it had to compete with. Opening it, an envelope with a motto corresponding with the one in the book appeared, and we found that our prose examination was still incomplete. Instead of the common cursive manuscript, the writing was in Roman characters — an imitation of printing.

These were some of Edgar Poe's *Tales of the Folio Club*: 'Epimanes', 'Lionizing', 'The Visionary', 'Siope', 'MS Found in a Bottle', and possibly (although Latrobe's memory is not to be trusted here) 'A Descent into the Maelstrom'.

Having been attracted by the unique calligraphy, the judges 'settled themselves in their comfortable chairs' while Latrobe began to read aloud.

> I had not proceeded far before my colleagues became as much interested as myself. The first tale finished, I went on to the second, then to the next and did not stop till I had gone through the volume, interrupted only by such exclamations as 'Capital!' 'Excellent!' and the like from my companions. There was genius in everything they listened to; there was no uncertain grammar, no feeble phraseology, no ill-placed punctuation, no worn truisms,

1 'Ultima Thule' daguerreotype of Edgar Allan Poe. Taken
in Providence, Rhode Island,
November 1848. Owned by
the Poe Foundation, Inc.

2 Reproduction of a
miniature of Poe's real mother,
the actress Elizabeth Arnold
Poe. Whereabouts of the
original miniature unknown.
Poe Foundation, Inc.

3   Photograph of a portrait of Frances Valentine Allan. Original in the Valentine Museum, Richmond, Virginia. Attributed to Thomas Sully. *Poe Foundation, Inc.*

4   Photograph of a portrait of John Allan. Whereabouts of the original portrait unknown. *Poe Foundation, Inc.*

5 *Above left:* Photograph of a daguerreotype of Elmira Royster Shelton. *Poe Foundation, Inc.*

6 *Above right:* Reproduction of an etching of Virginia Clemm Poe by A. G. Learned. *Poe Foundation, Inc.*

7 Photograph of a daguerreotype of Maria Clemm. Whereabouts of the original unknown. *Poe Foundation, Inc.*

KNOW ALL MEN BY THESE PRESENTS, That we *Edgar A. Poe and Thomas W. Cleland*

and acting as governor

are held and firmly bound unto *Wyndham Robertson, Lieutenant* Governor of the Commonwealth of Virginia, in the just and full sum of ONE HUNDRED AND FIFTY DOLLARS, to the payment whereof, well and truly to be made to the said Governor, or his successors, for the use of the said Commonwealth, we bind ourselves and each of us, our and each of our heirs, executors and administrators, jointly and severally, firmly by these presents. Sealed with our seals, and dated this *16* day of *May* 183*6*.

THE CONDITION OF THE ABOVE OBLIGATION IS SUCH, That whereas a marriage is shortly intended to be had and solemnized between the above bound *Edgar A. Poe* and *Virginia E. Clemm* of the City of Richmond. Now if there is no lawful cause to obstruct said marriage, then the above obligation to be void, else to remain in full force and virtue.

Signed, sealed and delivered }
in the presence of   }

Tho. Howard

Edgar A Poe   [SEAL.]

Tho. W. Cleland   [SEAL.]

CITY OF RICHMOND, To wit :

This day *Thomas W. Cleland* above named, made oath before me, as *Deputy* Clerk of the Court of Hustings for the said City, that *Virginia E. Clemm* is of the full age of twenty-one years, and a resident of the said City. Given under my hand, this *16* day of *May* 183*6*

Tho. Howard

8   The marriage bond of Edgar Allan Poe and Virginia Clemm. *Virginia State Library*

9 'Once upon a midnight dreary . . .' Photograph of an illustration by James Carling for 'The Raven'. The drawing, in ink and wash on buff paper, was done in the 1880s and is now the property of the Poe Foundation, Inc., in Richmond, Virginia. © Poe Foundation, Inc.

10   Central Richmond in Poe's day. The map by Micajah Bates shows the city in 1835. Capitol Square can be seen on the right, and to the right of that (off 13th Street) is Tobacco Alley. *Virginia State Library*

Annabel Lee.

By Edgar A. Poe.

s many and many a year ago,
  In a kingdom by the sea,
a maiden there lived whom you may know
  By the name of Annabel Lee; —
this maiden she lived with no other thought
  Than to love and be loved by me.

was a child and I was a child,
  In this kingdom by the sea,
we loved with a love that was more than love —
  I and my Annabel Lee —
a love that the wingèd seraphs in Heaven
  Coveted her and me.

this was the reason that, long ago,
  In this kingdom by the sea,
nd blew out of a cloud, chilling
  My beautiful Annabel Lee;
at her high-born kinsmen came
  And bore her away from me,
ut her up in a sepulchre,
  In this kingdom by the sea.

The angels, not half so happy in Heaven,
  Went envying her and me —
Yes! — that was the reason (as all men know,
  In this kingdom by the sea)
That the wind came out of the cloud by night,
  Chilling and killing my Annabel Lee.

But our love it was stronger by far than the love
  Of those who were older than we —
  Of many far wiser than we —
And neither the angels in Heaven above,
  Nor the demons down under the sea
Can ever dissever my soul from the soul
  Of the beautiful Annabel Lee : —

For the moon never beams, without bringing me dream
  Of the beautiful Annabel Lee;
And the stars never rise, but I feel the bright eyes
  Of the beautiful Annabel Lee ; —
And so, all the night-tide, I lie down by the side
Of my darling — my darling — my life and my bride
  In her sepulchre there by the sea —
  In her tomb by the sounding sea.

Edgar A. Poe.

11   Manuscript of 'Annabel Lee' in Poe's own handwriting. The signature is taken from a manuscript of 'The Raven'. Courtesy of the Richard Gimbel collection, Free Library of Philadelphia

12 *Above left:* Russell Square, London. The statue of Francis, Duke of Bedford, was erected in 1809 and must have been familiar to Poe when he lived in the district. *Photograph by Gideon Koppel*

13 *Above right:* The house in Amity Street, Baltimore, where Poe lived with Mrs Clemm and Virginia from 1832 to 1835. It is now a museum. *Photograph by Ruth Sinclair*

14 *Below left:* The Church Home and Infirmary in Baltimore. In Poe's time it was the Washington College Hospital, and the room where he died (now a staircase) is marked by the second window from the bottom on the left of the rotunda. *Photograph by Ruth Sinclair*

15 *Below right:* Poe's grave in the little cemetery at the corner of Fayette and Green Streets, Baltimore. *Photograph by Ruth Sinclair*

no strong thought elaborated into weakness. Logic and imagination were combined in rare consistency.

At first the committee thought the premium should go to 'A Descent into the Maelstrom', Latrobe said, but finally it was decided that 'MS Found in a Bottle' had the edge because of 'the originality of its conception and its length' rather than by 'any superior merit in its execution'.

The triumvirate then discovered that Poe had submitted a poem, too — 'The Coliseum':

> Type of the antique Rome! Rich reliquary
> Of lofty contemplation left to Time
> By buried centuries of pomp and power!
> At length — at length — after so many days
> Of weary pilgrimage and burning thirst
> (Thirst for the springs of lore that in thee lie),
> I kneel, an altered and an humble man,
> Amid thy shadows, and so drink within
> My very soul thy grandeur, gloom and glory!
> . . .
>
> Not all our power is gone — not all our fame —
> Not all the magic of our high renown —
> Not all the wonder that encircles us —
> Not all the mysteries that in us lie —
> Not all the memories that hang upon
> And cling around about us as a garment,
> Clothing us in a robe of more than glory.

Latrobe remembered: 'I am not prepared to say that the committee may not have been biased in awarding the prize' to Henry Wilton because the prose honours were already going to Poe. There was, however, a further reason for bias. Henry Wilton was the pen-name of John H. Hewitt, who was then editor of the *Visiter*. Latrobe said, 'we agreed that, under the circumstances, the excellence of Mr Hewitt's poem deserved a reward, and we gave the smaller prize to him with clear consciences'. Latrobe admitted that Poe's poem was better than Hewitt's, but claimed that the committee had not wanted to give two prizes to the same man.

'MS Found in a Bottle' is, like 'Metzengerstein', a patently absurd mixture of the natural and the supernatural that becomes only too credible through the writer's skilful description and controlled exaggeration. It capitalizes on contemporary interest in accounts of fantastic voyages to unknown lands, but takes that 'one step beyond' at which Poe was so brilliant. His ability to take real or reported events and backgrounds and to instil them with an indefinable air of impending doom is one of the chief delights of his stories. He saw powerful and evil forces at work, guiding puny mankind towards some fearful destiny. It is this vision of disintegration, and his capacity for describing it, that makes Edgar Poe unique as a writer.

As its title suggests, 'MS Found in a Bottle' takes the form of a message from the dead, cast adrift at the last moment by a luckless mariner who, after an unnaturally violent storm, finds himself in a huge ghostly ship named *Discovery*, which is dragged to destruction by a strange, irresistible current:

> In the meantime the wind is still in our poop, and, as we carry a crowd of canvas, the ship is at times lifted bodily from out the sea! Oh, horror upon horror! — the ice opens suddenly to the right, and to the left, and we are whirling dizzily, in immense concentric circles, round and round the borders of a gigantic amphitheatre, the summit of whose walls is lost in the darkness and the distance. But little time will be left me to ponder upon my destiny! The circles rapidly grow small — we are plunging madly within the grasp of the whirlpool — and amid a roaring, and bellowing, and thundering of ocean and tempest, the ship is quivering — oh God! and — going down!

Like 'Metzengerstein', the story begins calmly, almost discursively, but again the menace grows ever stronger as the narrative proceeds. The crew of the great black ship 'glide to and fro like the ghosts of buried centuries'; the captain — 'His forehead, although a little wrinkled, seems to bear upon it the stamp of a myriad of years. His grey hairs are records of the past, and his greyer eyes are sybils of the future' — is found in a cabin whose floor 'was thickly strewn with strange, iron-clasped folios, and mouldering instruments of science, and obsolete long forgotten charts' and 'he pored with a fiery, unquiet eye, over a paper which I took to be the commission, and which, at all events, bore the signature of a monarch'. In a few short brush-strokes the artist has imbued his picture with the shadow of the shroud. No wonder it gave Miller and Kennedy something to think about as Latrobe read it out in the judges' comfortable room through the reek of cigar smoke and fine wine.

It is worth noting that the other story mentioned by Latrobe, 'A Descent into the Maelstrom', has a similar theme, though the story-teller actually survives his terrifying plunge. This tale was not published until 1841 and it is possible that Latrobe confused it with 'MS Found in a Bottle' when, more than thirty years after the event, he recalled the details of the competition.

At any rate, for once in his life Edgar Allan Poe was a success, and he could hardly contain his delight. The family were by this time crammed into a small house on Amity Street, Baltimore, but now they had money, a whole fifty dollars, and all thanks to 'Eddy's' continual writing in an attic room with a ceiling so low that a man of average height could barely stand upright in it. Poe's Southern courtesy demanded that thanks should be given for this piece of good fortune, and accordingly he called on each of the three judges on the Monday after his prizewinning story had been published in the *Visiter*. Latrobe remembered his meeting well:

He was if anything below the middle size, and yet could not be described as a small man. His figure was remarkably good, and he carried himself erect and well, as one who had been trained to it. He was dressed in black, and his frock coat was buttoned to the throat, where it met the black stock, then almost universally worn. Not a particle of white was visible. Coat, hat, boots, and gloves had evidently seen their best days, but so far as mending and brushing go, everything had been done apparently, to make them presentable. On most men his clothes would have looked shabby and seedy, but there was something about this man that prevented one from criticizing his garments, and the details I have mentioned were only recalled afterwards. The impression made, however, was that the award in Mr Poe's favour was not inopportune. Gentleman was written all over him. His manner was easy and quiet, and although he came to return thanks for what he regarded as deserving them, there was nothing obsequious in what he said or did.

His features I am unable to describe in detail. His forehead was high, and remarkable for the great development at the temple. This was the characteristic of his head, which you noticed at once, and which I have never forgotten. The expression of his face was grave, almost sad, except when he became engaged in conversation, when it became animated and changeable. His voice I remember was very pleasing in its tone and well modulated, almost rhythmical, and his words were well chosen and unhesitating . . .

That was Edgar at the top of his form — confident, correct, a little aristocratic, a trifle distant, charming and impressive. It was no ordinary man with whom Latrobe had that one meeting which remained so fresh in his mind thirty years later. Poe had found his way as a writer, not of poetry but of prose, and the dark imaginings which had produced 'MS Found in a Bottle' were to become his stock-in-trade. The path ahead would not be easy, to put it mildly, and paradoxically it would be a poem, not his stories, that brought him the small amount of recognition he received in his lifetime. But, whether he knew it or not as he took his prize from the *Visiter*, he had developed a writing technique that has never been matched in originality or effect. The price he was to pay for immortality, though, would be exorbitant.

Chapter 8

Back to Old Virginia

John Allan was dying. His health had begun to fail towards the end of 1832, but with the best medical attention that money could buy he had fought off illness until in January 1834, when Louisa bore him a third son, he had become seriously disabled with dropsy. Unable to lie down, he spent his days and nights propped up in an armchair, except when he was helped to walk across his room for exercise. In December 1832, realizing that his illness was likely to be terminal, he had drawn up his will, adding a codicil in 1833. He did not consult a lawyer, presumably because there were aspects of the document that he knew would cause trouble and he did not want to become involved with legal objections to clauses which were specifically designed to protect his reputation after his death and which, as it turned out, could have no real status in law.

Obviously, Allan's estate was of great interest to Edgar Poe. In spite of the breach between the two, Poe would have entertained some hopes of a legacy: after all, he had called Allan 'Father' for twenty years and now he was on the verge of recognition as a writer; surely past sins would be forgotten and there would be something for him; surely Allan would not be so implacable as to mock him from beyond the grave. It is more than likely that Edgar heard of the deterioration in Allan's health at the beginning of 1834, and the story goes that he visited Richmond around February of that year in a last vain attempt at reconciliation. According to Tom Ellis, son of Allan's business partner, Mrs Allan was passing through the hall of her home one day when the doorbell rang and she answered it herself. 'A man of remarkable appearance stood there' and asked to see Mr Allan. He did not give his name. Mrs Allan said her husband was in no condition to receive visitors, but the man pushed past her and went straight upstairs to Allan's room. As soon as Allan set eyes on the intruder, he reached for a cane beside his chair and, raising it threateningly, ordered him out of the house, whereupon the visitor withdrew. 'That man,' says Tom Ellis, 'was Edgar A. Poe.'

There is no evidence to corroborate this story, and Ellis admits

that his account of the meeting is second hand, as well as making no
secret of the fact that when he published it in 1881 he did so to
defend the reputation of Louisa Allan, 'one of the most admirable
ladies that I have ever known'. Mrs Allan herself stated that she had
seen Poe only twice, to which Ellis added that he believed the second
time was after Allan's death. But Louisa's recollection is both
prejudiced and confusing, for on the one hand she says that she and
Allan never spoke of Poe, while on the other she talks of her husband
having 'banished Poe from his affections' after the insulting letter
Edgar had sent to Sergeant Graves. It may be that she was trying too
hard to protect herself from charges that she had influenced Allan
against Poe — alternatively she communicated with her husband in
some strange, non-verbal way.

At any rate, the story must be given some credence, if only
because it is impossible to disprove it. No more is known about Poe's
activities in 1834 than in 1832. It is probable that he had heard of
Allan's impending death: the Scotsman was a prominent citizen of
Richmond, and news of him would have been likely to circulate
among Poe's Baltimore acquaintances who had contacts in Virginia.
Flushed with the success of his story in the *Visiter* competition — as
well as being in a position to pay the fare from his fifty-dollar prize
— Edgar might well have gone to Richmond to pay his last respects
and to try to discover how he stood with regard to the Allan fortune.
If he did so, he was disappointed.

Allan died on 27 March 1834, and though his will caused quite a
stir it had nothing to do with Edgar Poe, who was not mentioned.
'Pa' had suffered an attack of conscience over Mrs Wills and her
children, but the ice had not melted as far as his adopted son was
concerned:

> I desire that my executors shall out of my estate provided
> give to − − a good English education for two boy sons of
> Mrs Elizabeth Wills, which she says are mine. I do not
> know their names, but the remaining fifth, four parts of
> which I have disposed of must go in equal shares to them
> or the survivor of them but should they be dead before
> they attain the age of 21 years then their share to go to my
> sister's Fowlds children in equal proportions with the
> exception of three thousand dollars, which must go to Mrs
> Wills and her daughter in perpetuity.
>
> John Allan, Dec. 31st, 1832
>
> This memo, in my own handwriting is to be taken as a
> codicil and can easily be proven by any of my friends . . .

The twins were born sometime about the 1st of July,

1830. I was married on the 5th October in New York, my fault therefore happened before I ever saw my present wife and I did not hide it from her. In case therefore these twins should reach the age of 21 & from reasons they cannot get their share of the fifth reserved for them, they are to have $4000 each out of my whole estate to enable them to prosecute some honest pursuit, profession or calling.

March 15th, 1833, I understand one of Mrs Wills' twin sons died some weeks ago, there is therefore only one to provide for.

My wife is to have all my furniture, books, bedding, linen, plate, wines, spirits &c &c, Glass and China ware . . .

Louisa, who had been left 'one third of the net annual income of my whole estate during her natural life, or until our eldest child becomes of age', was furious (suggesting that she had not been fully aware of Allan's obligations, despite his statement in the codicil to his will), and the whole scandal of Allan's amours became public knowledge when she challenged the will in the Henrico County Court, renouncing her position as executor and leaving it to the court to disentangle the strange document by seeking her rights under the intestacy rules. It was several years before matters were settled, and a lot of lawyers made a lot of money, but the result was the same for Poe: nothing. The man who had taken him in, seen that he was educated, and brought him up to be a gentleman, had finally banished him from his family as completely as if he had never existed. The actors' orphan was no better off than if he had not been 'adopted' in the first place — indeed, he was in a sense worse off, for he had been led into expectations that were not to be fulfilled. Allan had been strong-minded, stubborn, even domineering, but the boy he had once called his son had refused to be dominated and thereby had placed himself beyond the pale of his guardian's goodwill. When Allan had sent Edgar a few dollars, it had been to protect his own reputation in the eyes of the world, to demonstrate that he had done what he could to save an ungrateful reprobate whose only reply had been to brand him a drunkard. When it came to drawing up his will, there was no need to consider Edgar because Louisa, as she later proved, had been well enough primed to defend her husband against any charges in that direction; it was far more important, from the point of view of posthumous reputation, to ward off any possible charges of shabby treatment from Mrs Wills and her offspring (and the fact that the lady's daughter was mentioned in the will seems to confirm that Allan was her father as well).

Thus it has been left to history to spot the villain in the relationship between Poe and his guardian, and even now it is not easy to point an unwavering finger at John Allan, so unpredictable do his actions appear from a distance of almost one hundred and fifty years, and so cleverly did he provoke Edgar into one act of folly after another, exposing the young man's own weakness of character and stubborn pride. All that can be said now is that if Allan had behaved differently, had he been more generous and more tolerant, he would have made life less miserable, and perhaps less tragic, for Edgar Poe — though one might ask whether, by so doing, he would have helped to rob the world of some fine writing, for it is questionable that Poe would have written as he did without the misery, deprivation and pain that he suffered. 'His Talents,' as Allan himself put it, 'are of an order that can never prove a comfort to their possessor.'

Poe's talents, however, seemed to be doing him some good in the spring of 1834. His success in the *Visiter* had led to friendship with one of the competition judges, John Pendleton Kennedy, a man of note and influence in Baltimore — lawyer, author and later on member of Congress. Aged thirty-eight when Poe met him, Kennedy had established a literary reputation with a novel entitled *Swallow Barn* (he later wrote the classic novel of the Revolution, *Horse-Shoe Robinson*), and he encouraged Edgar to send his 'Folio Club' stories to his own publishers, Carey and Lea, to whom Poe had vainly tried to sell his poetry in 1829. Kennedy also advised his young friend which periodicals would be most likely to look with favour upon his fiction, though the only immediate result of this seems to have been the publication of 'The Visionary' (now better known as 'The Assignation' and as a crib from the famous tale of Hoffman, 'Doge und Dogaressa'). The prize money had not lasted long, and by the end of the year the inhabitants of the little house in Amity Street were in desperate straits again. In November, Poe wrote to Kennedy:

> Dr. Sir, — I have a favor to beg of you which I thought it better to ask in writing, because, sincerely, I had not the courage to ask it in person. I am indeed well aware that I have no claim whatever to your attention, and that even the manner of my introduction to your notice was, at best equivocal. Since the day you first saw me my situation in life has altered materially. At that time I looked forward to the inheritance of a large fortune, and in the meantime was in receipt of an annuity sufficient for my support. This was allowed to me by a gentleman of Virginia (Mr Jno. Allan) who adopted me at the age of two years (both my parents being dead) and who, until lately always

treated me with affection of a father. But a second marriage on his part, and I dare say many follies of my own at length ended in a quarrel between us. He is now dead and has left me nothing. I am thrown entirely upon my own resources with no profession, and very few friends. Worse than all this, I am at length penniless. Indeed no circumstances less urgent would have induced me to risk your friendship by troubling you with my distresses. But I could not help thinking that if my situation was stated — as you could state it — to Carey and Lea, they might be led to aid me with a small sum in consideration of my Ms now in their hands. This would relieve my immediate wants, and I could then look forward more confidently to better days. At all events receive the assurance of my gratitude for what you have already done.

Most respy, yr. obt. st.,
Edgar Allan Poe

The little romance about Poe's relationship with John Allan was designed, of course, to give the impression of gentility fallen upon hard times, and the innuendo about the second marriage helps to explain why Tom Ellis felt obliged to leap to the defence of Louisa Allan so many years later. At any rate, the kindly Mr Kennedy was touched by the appeal and contacted his publishers to see what could be done. He wrote to Edgar on 22 December with the news that Mr Carey doubted that there would be any profit in publishing the 'Folio Club' collection — 'not from want of merit,' Kennedy hastily added, 'but because small books of detached tales, however well written, seldom yield a sum sufficient to enable the bookseller to purchase a copyright'. But there was still hope: Carey sought permission to sell some of the tales to the flourishing literary annuals of the day and, said the thoughtful Kennedy, 'I thought you would not object to this if the right to publish the same tale was reserved for the volume [that Poe hoped to publish]'. Accordingly, the letter went on, Carey had sent fifteen dollars from the sale of a story to the *Atlantic Souvenir.* 'If other tales can be sold in the same way, you will get more for the work than by an exclusive publication.' The title of the successful tale was not mentioned, and nothing by Poe appeared in the *Souvenir*, so the conclusion must be drawn that Kennedy had found a tactful way to distribute a little charity. It is also worth noting that Carey and Lea never did publish the tales in spite of Kennedy's assurance that they would do so, their doubts notwithstanding.

Kennedy's kindness went considerably farther than the fifteen-dollar 'payment'. Indeed Poe later wrote that, 'Mr Kennedy has been, at all times, a true friend to me — he was the first true friend I ever had — I am indebted to him for *life itself*'. In his diary, Kennedy noted that he had given Poe 'clothing, free access to my table and the use of a horse for exercise whenever he chose; in fact brought him up from the very edge of despair'. But material help was only part of it: Kennedy actually changed the whole course of Poe's life when he encouraged him to submit some stories to a new magazine, *The Southern Literary Messenger*, founded in Richmond in 1834 by Thomas Willis White with the hope of improving the quality of Southern letters and increasing local interest in literature. White was a printer, not an editor, so he entrusted the day-to-day running of the magazine to literary journalists. From the spring of 1835 Poe began to have his tales printed in the *Messenger* and also contributed book reviews. Kennedy, however, had other ideas. On 13 April 1835 he wrote to White pointing out that Poe was *'very* poor' and suggesting that the publisher might give him a permanent job on the magazine: 'He is very clever with his pen — classical and scholar-like . . . highly imaginative, and a little given to the *terrific* . . . I have turned him to drudging upon whatever will make money, and I have no doubt you and he will find your account in each other.'

Poe was pathetically grateful, writing to thank White for the trifling sums he received for his work and saying, 'My poor services are not worth what you give me for them.' But reward, of a kind, was on its way. In June White asked Edgar if he would be willing to move to Richmond and help out on the *Messenger*, the editing of which he had at that time taken upon himself. Poe was hardly likely to turn down the offer. 'Nothing would give me greater pleasure,' he told White, who had apparently mentioned some deficiency in the proof-reading of his magazine. On 7 July an event occurred that made the need for a permanent job all the more pressing — Grandmother Poe died, aged 78, and with her expired the hard-won pension of two hundred and forty dollars a year from the government in respect of her husband's war service. It meant that the household at Number 3 Amity Street was robbed of the only firm basis for its finances. Accordingly, Poe moved to Richmond at the beginning of August and started work at the *Messenger* offices as White's assistant, on trial at ten dollars a week. It was not much — board and lodging cost him four dollars a week — but it was regular and he could send Mrs Clemm a little money from time to time because his actual contributions to the magazine were paid for at the same rate as before. He began to dream of a better life, of a little house with a garden in a secluded corner of Richmond — with Virginia Clemm as his wife.

The relationship between Edgar and his delicate, beautiful cousin is one of the great mysteries of his life, but at least the beginnings of it are not too difficult to trace. Virginia was six when Edgar first appeared at the house in Mechanics Row, a mysterious and magnetic stranger who suddenly became a member of the family. On his part, Poe found a rather plump but pretty little girl with brown curls, dark eyes and a spring of natural affection that was impossible to resist. At first Virginia reminded him of his sister, Rosalie, and on his return to Baltimore after the disaster of West Point, he seems to have taken it upon himself to educate her — his friend Lambert Wilmer remembered 'finding him engaged, on a certain Sunday, in giving Virginia lessons in Algebra'. But as the little girl began to grow into a woman, perhaps another image appeared in Edgar's mind, the memory of his lost love Elmira Royster. The feelings he had experienced for Elmira may have been transferred to Virginia, his new ideal.

There was a problem, though: Virginia was Edgar's first cousin and he seems to have been worried about a liaison between what he regarded as such close relatives, almost as if it would have been incestuous. His feelings are made plain in 'Berenice', one of the stories he wrote while he was living with Mrs Clemm:

> Berenice and I were cousins, and we grew up together in my paternal halls. Yet differently we grew — I of ill health, and buried in gloom — she agile, graceful and overflowing with energy; hers the ramble on the hill-side — mine the studies of the cloister — I living within my own heart, and addicted body and soul to the most intense and painful meditation — she roaming carelessly through life with no thought of the shadows in her path, or the silent flight of the raven-winged hours. Berenice! — I call upon her name — Berenice! — and from the grey ruins of memory a thousand tumultuous recollections are startled at the sound! Ah! vividly is her image before me now, as in the early days of her light-heartedness and joy! Oh! gorgeous yet fantastic beauty! . . .

The parallel is obvious. The narrator is Poe, weighed down by cares from which he cannot escape; Berenice is Virginia, the happy, careless child who sees only the novelty and excitement of the world. Presently, however, a strange, distorted relationship grows up between the two. Berenice 'had loved me long' but 'I had seen her — not as the living and breathing Berenice, but as the Berenice of a dream — not as a being of the earth, earthy, but as the abstraction of

such a being . . .' Then Berenice is afflicted by a fatal disease the
spread of which has the effect of increasing the narrator's intensity
of feeling for her until it becomes a form of monomania fixed upon
her teeth — 'they were here, and there, and everywhere, and visibly
and palpably before me; long, narrow, and excessively white, with
the pale lips writhing about them, as in the very moment of their
first terrible development'. So what we have, in the crudest terms, is
a madman passionately and unnaturally attached to an invalid. 'How
is it,' the narrator asks, 'that from beauty I have derived a type of
unloveliness? — from the covenant of peace a simile of sorrow? But,
as in ethics, evil is a consequence of good, so, in fact, out of joy is
sorrow born . . .' The result of the liaison is pure horror. Berenice,
having fallen into a trance, is given up for dead and is buried; the
narrator is still haunted by the sight of her teeth and falls into an
auto-suggested trance himself:

> There came a light tap at the library door, and pale as the
> tenant of a tomb, a menial entered upon tiptoe. His looks
> were wild with terror, and . . . He told of a wild cry
> disturbing the silence of the night . . . of a search in the
> direction of the sound . . . of a violated grave — of a
> disfigured body enshrouded, yet still breathing, still
> palpitating, still *alive*!
>
> He pointed to my garments; — they were muddy and
> clotted with gore. I spoke not and he took me gently by
> the hand; — it was indented with the impress of human
> nails. He directed my attention to some object against a
> wall . . . it was a spade. With a shriek I bounded to the
> table, and grasped the box that lay upon it. But I could
> not force it open; and in my tremor it slipped from my
> hands, and fell heavily, and burst into pieces; and from
> it . . . there rolled out some instruments of dental surgery,
> intermingled with thirty-two small, white and ivory-
> looking substances that were scattered to and fro about
> the floor.

Of course, it is unwise to relate a writer's work too closely to the
circumstances of his life, and Poe himself described 'Berenice' as 'the
ludicrous heightened to the grotesque'. So it is not to be taken too
seriously. And yet that sentence 'Berenice and I were cousins, and we
grew up together in my paternal halls' was written at a time when
Edgar and Virginia were 'growing up together' under the same roof
and when Poe was thinking of her at one and the same time as a
sister and as a wife: in a letter to Mrs Clemm from Richmond in

August 1835 he spoke of Virginia as both 'my sweetest Sissy' and 'my darling little wifey'. Furthermore, the subject of 'unnatural' male-female relationships recurs in Poe's work, most notably with the brother and sister in 'The Fall of the House of Usher', and the conclusion that he was worried by his sexual feelings is difficult to escape when one considers that death invariably results from the associations he describes.

Nowhere, perhaps, is the 'incest' theme more clearly and more sensitively treated than in the tale of 'Eleonora', first published in 1842. The domestic background is highly significant:

> She whom I loved in youth . . . was the sole daughter of the only sister of my mother long departed. Eleonora was the name of my cousin. We had always dwelled together, beneath a tropical sun, in the Valley of the Many-Coloured Grass. No unguided footstep ever came upon that vale; for it lay far away up among a range of giant hills that hung beetling around about it, shutting out the sunlight from its sweetest recesses. No path was trodden in its vicinity; and, to reach our happy home, there was need of putting back, with force, the foliage of many thousands of forest trees, and of crushing to death the glories of many millions of fragrant flowers. Thus it was that we lived all alone, knowing nothing of the world without the valley, — I, and my cousin, and her mother.

Thus Edgar lived with Virginia and Mrs Clemm, except that they were cut off from the outside world only by poverty.

The narrator of 'Eleonora' is twenty and his cousin fifteen when 'Love entered within our hearts . . . and now we felt that we had enkindled within us the fiery souls of our forefathers. The passions which had for centuries distinguished our race, came thronging with the fancies for which they had been equally noted, and together breathed a delicious bliss over the Valley . . .' The couple are shut up 'as if for ever, within a magic prison-house of grandeur and of glory'. Of course, it cannot last, and before long Eleonora 'had seen that the finger of Death was upon her bosom —that, like the ephemeron, she had been made perfect in loveliness only to die . . . I threw myself hurriedly at the feet of Eleonora, and offered up a vow, to herself and to Heaven, that I would never bind myself in marriage to any daughter of the Earth — that I would in no manner prove recreant to her dear memory . . . And she said to me, not many days afterwards, tranquilly dying, that, because of what I had done for the comfort of her spirit, she would watch over me in that spirit when departed, and, if so it were permitted to her, return to me visibly in the watches of the night ... And, with these words upon her lips, she yielded up her innocent life, putting an end to the first epoch of my own.' The lover's vow is broken — but not before he has quit the valley of innocence in favour of the 'terrible temptations' and 'turbulent triumphs' of the outside world and by so doing is 'absolved, for reasons which shall be made known to thee in Heaven', of his vows to Eleonora.

So it seems that love between cousins, if we are to relate 'Berenice' and 'Eleonora' to the true circumstances of Poe's life, can flower only in Paradise nurtured by innocence and purity; released into the physical world, it becomes horribly distorted and leads to disaster. And either way, death is its vehicle. Perhaps these were the thoughts that haunted Edgar as passion stirred for twelve-year-old Virginia: there was joy in the purity of his feelings towards the 'sister', but at the same time there was a terrible gnawing guilt over the desire for the 'wife'.

None of this, however, would have been apparent to the Poe relatives as Edgar, preparing to move to a regular job in Richmond, confessed to Mrs Clemm his hope of marrying Virginia. They would simply have considered marriage unthinkable for a twelve-year-old girl. Neilson Poe, Edgar's cousin, certainly had his doubts. He had married Virginia's half-sister, Josephine Clemm, and presumably kept in pretty close touch with the family in Amity Street, probably helping out financially from time to time. When news of Edgar's plans reached him, he realized that Mrs Clemm's maternal affection for her nephew would almost certainly lead her into acquiescence and he acted quickly to prevent such an unsuitable marriage. Edgar was already looking for a house to rent in Richmond when he received a letter from Mrs Clemm telling him that Neilson, who was about his own age, had offered to take Virginia into his home outside Baltimore, to educate her and generally to prepare her for entry into Maryland society. To Edgar, cut off in Richmond from both his own family and the family to which he had almost belonged, the news was a body-blow. His mother gone, Jane Stanard gone, Elmira Royster gone — was he now to lose Virginia, too? On 29 August 1835, Poe wrote to Mrs Clemm one of the most revealing of all his letters:

> My dearest Aunty,
> I am blinded by tears while writing this letter — I have no wish to live another hour. Amid sorrow, and the deepest anxiety your letter reached me — and you well know how little I am able to bear up under the pressure of grief — My

bitterest enemy would pity me now could he read my heart — My last my last my only hold on life is cruelly torn away — I have no desire to live and *will not.* But let my duty be done. I love, *you know* I love Virginia passionately devotedly. I cannot express in words the fervent devotion I feel towards my dear little cousin — my own darling. But what can I say. Oh think for me for I am incapable of thinking. All thoughts are occupied with the supposition that both you & she will prefer to go with N. Poe; I do sincerely believe that your *comforts* will for the present be secured — I cannot speak as regards your peace — your happiness. You have both tender hearts — and you will always have the reflection that my agony is more than I can bear — that you have driven me to the grave — for love like mine can never be gotten over. It is useless to disguise the truth that when Virginia goes with N.P. that I shall never behold her again — that is absolutely sure. Pity me, my dear Aunty, pity me. I have no one now to fly to — I am among strangers, and my wretchedness is more than I can bear. It is useless to expect advice from me — what can I say? Can I, in honour & truth say — Virginia! do not go! — do not go where you can be comfortable and perhaps happy — and on the other hand can I calmly resign my — life itself. If she had truly loved me would she not have rejected the offer with scorn? Oh God have mercy on me! If she goes with N.P. what are you to do, my own Aunty?

I had procured a sweet little house in a retired situation on Church hill — newly done up and with a large garden and every convenience — at only $5 per month. I have been dreaming every day & night since of the rapture I should feel in seeing my only friends — all I love on Earth with me there; the pride I would take in making you both comfortable & in calling her my wife. But the dream is over God have mercy on me. What have I *to live for?* Among strangers and with *not one soul to love me.*

He went on to say that any hopes he had entertained of becoming editor of the *Messenger* had been dashed by the appointment to that post of a man named Branch T. Saunders. White had not promised Edgar anything, but Poe's customary wishful thinking had no doubt been at work. On the other hand, White had

engaged to make my salary $60 a month, and we could live in comparative comfort & happiness — even the $4 a week

I am now paying for board would support us all — but I shall have $15 a week & what need would we have of more? I had thought to send you on a little money every week . . . and then we could get a little furniture for a start . . . After that all would go well . . . There is little danger of the house being taken immediately . . .

And the letter ends:

The tone of your letter wounds me to the soul — Oh Aunty, Aunty you loved me once — how can you be so cruel now? You speak of Virginia acquiring accomplishments, and entering into society — you speak in so *worldly* a tone. Are you sure she would be more happy — Do you think any one could love her more dearly than I? She will have far — very far better opportunity of entering into society here than with N.P. Every one here receives me with open arms.

Adieu my dear Aunty. I *cannot advise you.* Ask Virginia. Leave it to her. Let me have, under her own hand, a letter, bidding me *good bye* — forever — and I may die — my heart will break — but I will say no more.

                                                        E.A.P.

Kiss her for me — a million times
For Virginia,

My love, my own sweetest Sissy, my darling little wifey, think well before you break the heart of your cousin Eddy.

That letter came straight from the heart, exposing Poe in all his weakness, his inability to deal with emotional crises, his urge towards self-sacrifice, and his pathetic dependence upon other people. And yet in a postscript to it he was composed enough to ask Mrs Clemm to get him a copy of the *Republican* magazine in which there was a notice about the *Messenger.* What a strange mind, what an unbalanced personality Edgar had. One minute he was ready to die of a broken heart, and the next his thoughts had turned to mundane considerations of his work. It shows the curious inner strength, among all the weaknesses, that enabled him to continue writing even though his world was collapsing about his ears. Had he not possessed that peculiar detachment, the chances are that we should never have heard of Edgar Allan Poe.

Yet despair was always just under the surface in Poe's mind. On 11 September he wrote to John P. Kennedy in Baltimore:

Dr. Sir, — I received a letter yesterday from Dr Miller in which he tells me you are in town. I hasten therefore, to write to you, — and express by letter what I have always found impossible to express orally — my deep sense of gratitude for your frequent and effectual assistance and kindness. Through your influence Mr White has been induced to employ me in assisting him with the Editorial duties of his Magazine — at a salary of $520 per annum. The situation is agreeable to me for many reasons — but alas! it appears to me that nothing can now give me pleasure — or the slightest gratification. Excuse me, my Dear Sir, if in this letter you find much incoherency. My feelings at this moment are pitiable indeed. I am suffering under a depression of spirits such as I have never felt before. I have struggled in vain against the influence of this melancholy — *you will believe me* when I say that I am still miserable in spite of the great improvement in my circumstances. I say you will believe me, and for this simple reason, that a man who is writing for effect does not write thus. My heart is open before you — if it be worth reading, read it. I am wretched, and know not why. Console me — for you can. But let it be quickly — or it will be too late. Write me immediately. Convince me that it is worth one's while, that it is necessary to live, and you will prove yourself my friend. Persuade me to do what is right. I do not mean this — I do not mean that you should consider what I now write you a jest — oh pity me! for I feel that my words are incoherent — but I will recover myself. You will not fail to see that I am suffering under a depression of spirits which will ruin me should it be long continued. Write me then, and quickly. Urge me to do what is right. Your words will have more weight with me than the words of others — for you were my friend when no one else was. Fail not — as you value your peace of mind hereafter.

And even to that terrible letter was added a postscript discussing Poe's professional concerns and accusing another writer of plagiarism.

However, in the summer of 1835 there was an external reason for Poe's sudden swings from manic depression and incoherence to calm lucidity: he had started drinking again. The letters to Mrs Clemm and Kennedy show only too plainly that Poe could not overcome the normal setbacks and difficulties of life by himself — he sought help anywhere he was likely to find it, preferably direct, personal aid. During this stay in Richmond he had to rely on letters to see him through, but they gave only temporary comfort when he really needed someone at his side constantly to reassure and encourage him. In desperation, he reached for the anaesthetic of alcohol, which in view of his weak constitution was the worst thing he could have done. The dramatic effect on him of even a small amount of alcohol has already been discussed, and it was not long before he was labelled a drunkard — and sacked from the *Messenger*. In a letter written on 29 September, Thomas White indulged in some straight talking:

> Dear Edgar, — Would that it were in my power to unbosom myself to you in language such as I could on the present occasion, wish myself master of. I cannot do it — and therefore must be content to speak to you in my plain way.
>
> That you are sincere in all your promises, I firmly believe. But Edgar, when you once again tread these streets, I have my fears that your resolves would fall through, — and that you would sip the juice, even till it stole away your senses. Rely on your own strength and you are gone! Look to your Maker for help, and you are safe.
>
> How much I regretted parting with you, is unknown to anyone on this earth, except myself. I was attached to you — and am still, and willingly would I say return, if I did not dread the hour of separation very shortly again.
>
> If you could make yourself contented to take up your quarters in my family, or in any other private family, where liquor is not used, I should think that there were hopes of you. — But, if you go to a tavern, or to any other place where it is used at table, you are not safe. I speak from experience.
>
> You have fine talents, Edgar, — and you ought to have them respected as well as yourself. Learn to respect yourself, and you will very soon find that you are respected. Separate yourself from the bottle, and bottle companions, forever!
>
> Tell me if you can and will do so — and let me hear that it is your fixed purpose never to yield to temptation.
>
> If you should come to Richmond again, and again be an assistant in my office, it must be expressly understood by us that all engagements on my part would be dissolved, the moment you get drunk.

No man is safe who drinks before breakfast! No man can do so, and attend to business properly . . .

I am your true Friend
T. W. White

Once more Poe had been defeated by his own weakness. Just at the moment when he seemed to be rising out of the slough of poverty and despair, he had encountered a setback he could not cope with, and that difficulty had pushed him into another which ultimately destroyed all his hopes. The fear of one loss had led to the loss of everything.

Chapter 9

The Demon Drink?

Edgar Poe's sacking from the *Messenger*, as explained in Thomas White's letter, provides the first concrete evidence for his legendary drunkenness. The letter is firm but kind, clearly written out of concern and a desire to save a soul from the demon drink, and not from any malicious motive. At first sight, it appears irrefutable, yet there are two factors that militate against the conclusion that Poe was a drunkard. For a start, America in the 1830s was in the grip of a religious revival which took several paths not strictly associated with Christianity: there were campaigns against meat-eating, against restrictive clothing, against male supremacy, and against alcohol. In 1826, the American Temperance Union was founded and set about recruiting a so-called 'Cold Water Army' of thousands of fervent abstainers who sought not to restrain the drinking of alcohol but to stamp it out altogether. Hundreds of thousands of people were persuaded to 'sign the pledge', and in some states movements arose dedicated to having the sale of liquor banned by law. At that particular time, the temperance movement did not have a great deal of success in the South, with its aristocratic tradition of over-indulgence, but Thomas White's letter to Poe makes it clear that the abstainers had found at least one supporter there.

The second factor that puts into a new light the charges of drunkenness so consistently levelled against Poe is the product of hindsight, so it involves circumstances White could not possibly have known about, namely Poe's personality and general health. I have already suggested, in Chapter 4, that Edgar did not actually like strong drink, and that he began to indulge in it at university partly because it was expected of him by the fast set in which he moved, and partly because it increased his confidence and obscured the fact that he was not really a member of the set. Anyone who drinks alcohol, whether he likes it or not, is bound to notice what are commonly and erroneously regarded as its short-term 'restorative' or 'stimulative' effects, and there is no doubt that Poe, with his basic weakness of character, turned to drink for support from time to time

— indeed he frankly admitted that, at a later period in his life, he depended on drink so much that he could not tell whether he was saner when drunk or when sober. His case was that he resorted to alcohol only very infrequently and at moments of what was to him unbearable stress; that he was not even an habitual drinker, let alone a drunkard. All unbiased evidence seems to support this claim. For instance, there is no mention of drinking in recollections which have survived from the period of Poe's life between his leaving West Point and his employment on the *Messenger*, until White's letter, that is. The drinking that prompted White's action was undoubtedly the result of stress: Edgar had enjoyed the support of Mrs Clemm and at least some measure of security for four years, but with his removal to Richmond in the summer of 1835, that security and support disappeared. Furthermore, he had the problem of Virginia to deal with — alone, it seemed to him, since he could communicate with Mrs Clemm only by letter and even then could not absolutely count on her, tempted as she must have been by Neilson Poe's offer.

Now we must consider the effect of alcohol on Edgar, and how much that was conditioned by his general health. Those who recalled his drinking at university were at pains to point out that small amounts of alcohol wreaked havoc with him, that he was 'used up' after only one glass of peach and honey. It is well known that individual tolerance of alcohol varies widely, but the fact that Poe was so rapidly and seriously affected by it seems to suggest some underlying cause, physical or mental. Modern medical science is aware of a condition known as alcoholic mania, in which a small amount of strong drink produces a violent reaction in young neurotic people predisposed to madness through heredity. It may well be argued that Poe was neurotic, but we do not know whether there was any insanity in his family. His father drank heavily and could apparently be roused to violent rage, but this is hardly enough to go on. In any case, alcoholic mania generally produces a state of high excitement and fury leading to violence, attempted murder, or suicide, and as far as is known Poe was not prey to any abnormally violent emotions when he had been drinking (and though he did attempt suicide at one point, there is evidence to suggest that it was more of a cry for attention than a wholehearted attempt to kill himself).

A more likely explanation for Edgar's inability to tolerate alcohol is some form of metabolic disorder which, either of itself or as a consequence of his intake of alcohol, produced mental disturbance as he grew older. It is well established that in his youth Poe was strong and healthy, good at swimming and fond of sports, but his letters show that in later life he became increasingly concerned about his health and was often ill. The onset of sickness seems to have come during his last days at West Point. In January 1831 he told John Allan that 'my future life (which thank God will not endure long) must be passed in indigence and sickness. I have no energy left, nor health.' A month later he was bemoaning the fact that 'my only crime was being *sick*', and by the end of the year he was 'in bad health and unable to undergo as much hardships as formerly'. So between his leaving the army at Fort Monroe and his dismissal from West Point, something had interfered with his metabolism — and the chances are that his life with the Clemms, uncertain where the next meal was coming from and at best on a very poor diet, did nothing to improve his health. Shortly before moving to Richmond he wrote to Thomas White apologizing for his failure to do justice to John P. Kennedy's novel *Horse-shoe Robinson* in a review for the *Messenger*: he said he was ashamed of what he had written, and went on, 'I fully intended to give the work a thorough review, and examine it in detail. Ill health alone prevented me from doing so. At the time I made the hasty sketch I sent you, I was so ill as to be hardly able to see the paper on which I wrote, and I finished it in a state of complete exhaustion.'

George Woodberry, one of the early Poe biographers, wrote in 1885 that after the letter to White in May 1835 Poe 'frequently complains of nervous exhaustion, which can be ascribed only to the reaction of drugs and stimulants on a weakened system'. All the evidence now available points to the fact that Poe was not addicted to drugs, and as far as the 'stimulants' are concerned, I believe Woodberry got things the wrong way round. It was not alcohol that weakened Poe's system and produced nervous exhaustion: it was his previously weakened system which permitted small amounts of alcohol to have such a devastating effect on him. In other words, he was ill to start with, suffering from some metabolic disorder, and drinking merely caused a reaction which made his illness worse.

It remains to ask what that metabolic disorder could have been. Obviously it was a disease that began in a mild form and grew worse with age; it would probably also have had to be related in some degree to the quality of diet, and it would certainly have had to be something aggravated by alcohol; finally, it would have had to be an illness which, if untreated, would have been fatal. After careful research and consultation with medical experts, I have reached the conclusion that Edgar Poe suffered from diabetes — or, to be absolutely precise, diabetes mellitus (there is another, rarer, form of the disease known as diabetes insipidus).

Diabetes would explain a great deal about Poe's life and character. It often manifests itself in early adult life, is debilitating over a fairly long period, and results in death if no treatment is available. The disease is a result of a deficiency of insulin, a hormone secreted by the pancreas to regulate the body's use of sugar: either the victim's pancreas does not produce enough insulin or the patient's body does not use the hormone properly and therefore needs more than the pancreas can secrete. The form that begins in childhood or early maturity is known as juvenile diabetes and, apart from the fact that it has a tendency to run in families, no cause is known. The disease was first noted in the second century AD, but it was not until the late nineteenth century that doctors isolated its main characteristic and it remained incurable until 1921, when fairly pure insulin was isolated and could be injected into the patient.

The most obvious symptoms of diabetes are severe thirst and increased volume of urine, which contains unusually high amounts of sugar. Secondary effects include loss of weight and weakening of the muscles, poisoning of the system producing acidosis and ultimately coma, and increased susceptibility to bacterial infections. In an advanced stage, diabetes can cause defective vision or even blindness and peripheral neuritis, which is a tingling sensation or pains in the limbs. A carefully controlled diet is vital to the sufferer's health, and if the untreated diabetic drinks alcohol he may suffer personality changes and an effect known as the Korsakow syndrome (caused by a deficiency of B vitamins) which involves loss of memory for recent events and often the patient's invention of elaborate lies to disguise this lack.

Now, it is possible to strain credulity almost to breaking point in order to prove some pet theory, and I must confess that I have long believed that Poe suffered from some chronic illness which affected not only his physical health but also his mental balance and which can explain the mystery of his tragic death. But, with as much objectivity as I can muster, I submit that there is enough circumstantial evidence among what we know and can discover about Poe to suggest very strongly that he was a diabetic, that even if he did not know what he was suffering from he realized that he was doomed to an early death, and that the realization had a profound effect upon his work.

The progress of Poe's illness will be revealed as it becomes appropriate during the course of his life, but it is worth summarizing here the clues that lead to the diagnosis of diabetes. We do not know about the state of Poe's urine, or whether he was continually thirsty, but there is plenty of evidence that he lost weight over the years, becoming quite haggard in later life. It is also clear that he suffered from headaches, possibly associated with his eyes, and from muscular spasms, bouts of fever, stomach trouble and periods of unconsciousness — all of which can be connected with diabetes. His mental depression is well known, as is his uncertain memory, and his invention of complicated lies is notorious: these may be seen as manifestations of a Korsakow syndrome, together with personality changes that became apparent as he grew older.

As far as the hereditary aspect of diabetes is concerned, there is little evidence to hand because the time and circumstances of David Poe's death are not known. In early biographies it was suggested that Edgar had inherited from his father a tendency towards alcoholism, what was termed 'a fatal weakness'. That weakness could, of course, have been diabetes. If that sounds like a mere assertion, there is further circumstantial evidence that may tie in with it. Edgar's brother, William Henry, also had a drink problem, and while it seems that he drank a great deal more than Edgar and could have been described as an alcoholic, it is possible that the rapid deterioration in his health and his early death resulted from the action of an excessive amount of alcohol on some inherited weakness like diabetes. This may be supported by the fact that Henry died of consumption: in the nineteenth century, when the first steps towards understanding diabetes were taken, it was noted that diabetics often fell victim to consumption and died early. It is surely arguable that both Edgar and Henry suffered from genetically transmitted diabetes and that Henry's death from consumption at the age of twenty-four was the result of a weakened metabolism further disrupted by heavy drinking, while Edgar's survival for eighteen years more was made possible by his long periods of abstinence from alcohol, though his health was deteriorating all the time and the likelihood of early death was increased by his disordered way of life and poor diet.

All this was for the future, however. In the summer of 1835 Poe's health did not seem to be seriously in doubt — he even mocked a Dr Buckley of Baltimore who had 'assured me that nothing but a long sea voyage would save me' — and his erratic behaviour was firmly attributed to over-indulgence in strong drink. It was a dejected young man who made his way back to Baltimore that September to salvage what he could from his wrecked hopes. He was kindly received by Mrs Clemm, who by that time had apparently made up her mind that Virginia should not join Neilson Poe's family, and who had realized that Edgar was not safe on his own. She told him that if he made his peace with White and promised to behave himself in return for his reinstatement on the *Messenger*, they would all go to live in Richmond. Edgar did patch things up with White, and by 20 October he, Virginia and Mrs Clemm were settled in a boarding house at the corner of Bank and Twelfth Streets, on the south-east border of Capitol Square and a mere block away from Poe's one-time home in Tobacco Alley.

What Poe's exact position was on the *Messenger* is in some doubt. Thomas White told a friend that Edgar had been engaged to contribute to the magazine, but he was not to be called its editor. Edgar had other ideas, and there is no doubt that at some point he did take over complete editorial supervision from White, but when this actually happened, and whether it was official, is not certain. In the issue of September 1835, Poe contributed all the reviews and two stories, 'Loss of Breath' and 'King Pest the First', as well as a poem entitled 'Lines Written in an Album'. Clearly White needed him, but the proprietor was not inclined to let him have total control, as Edgar would have liked, and this was to lead to friction later.

There were no issues of the *Messenger* in October and November, but in December the editorial announced that the proprietor was now being 'assisted by a gentleman of distinguished literary talents', and singled out Poe among the magazine's contributors as having a 'uniquely original vein of imagination, and of humorous, delicate satire'. That number also contained Poe's first and last dramatic work, now known as *Politian* but then called simply 'Scenes from an Unpublished Drama'. It was based on a famous murder case in Kentucky ten years before, but Poe, writing in blank verse, turned it into high historical tragedy, which did the story no good at all.

White seemed happy with his talented and industrious assistant, Poe appeared keen to settle in Richmond, but the *Messenger* salary, though more than Edgar was used to, was not much to support Mrs Clemm and Virginia as well. One can imagine Edgar and his aunt discussing money-making schemes and looking forward to a better life than they had known for several years past. Finally it occurred to them that instead of living in a boarding house they should run one, or rather Mrs Clemm should while Edgar built up his literary reputation. Of course, capital would be needed for the project, and on 12 January 1836 Edgar wrote to his second cousin, George Poe Jr (son of the George Poe to whom Edgar's father had appealed for money shortly after the birth of his second child), who was a bank cashier in Mobile, Alabama:

> Dear Sir, — I take the liberty of addressing you in behalf of a mutual relation, Mrs William Clemm, late of Baltimore — and at her earnest solicitation.
>
> You are aware that for many years she has been suffering privations and difficulties of no ordinary kind. I know that you have assisted her at a former period, and she has occasionally received aid from her cousins, William and Robert Poe, of Augusta. What little has been heretofore in my own power I have also done.

Having lately established myself in Richmond, and undertaken the editorship of the Southern Literary Messenger, and my circumstances having thus become better than formerly, I have ventured to offer my aunt a home. She is now therefore in Richmond, with her daughter Virginia, and is, for the present boarding at the house of a Mrs Yarrington. My salary is at present only about $800 per ann., and the charge per week for our board, (Mrs Clemm's, her daughter's and my own) is $9. I am thus particular in stating my precise situation that you may be the better enabled to judge in regard to the propriety of granting the request which I am now about to make for Mrs Clemm.

It is ascertained that if Mrs C. could obtain the means of opening, herself, a boarding-house in this city, she could support herself and daughter comfortably with something to spare. But a small capital would be necessary for an undertaking of this nature, and many of the widows of our first people are engaged in it, and find it profitable. I am willing to advance, for my own part, $100, and I believe that Wm. & R. Poe will advance $100. If then you would so far aid her in her design as to loan her yourself $100 she will have sufficient to commence with. I will be responsible for the repayment of the sum, in a year from this date, if you can make it convenient to comply with her request.

I beg you, my dear Sir, to take this subject into consideration. I feel deeply for the distresses of Mrs Clemm, and I am sure *you* will feel interested in relieving them.

P.S. I am the son of David Poe, Jr. Mrs C's brother.

George felt interested enough to send a cheque for a hundred dollars, and William and Robert chipped in, too. Things were certainly looking up. On 22 January Edgar wrote to John P. Kennedy to say that having 'fought the enemy manfully' he was 'in every respect, comfortable and happy'. His health was better than for years past, his mind was occupied, his pecuniary difficulties had vanished, and he had 'a fair prospect for success'. Whether he and Mrs Clemm were really serious about the boarding house idea is open to question: certainly, nothing ever came of it, and the money Edgar had begged was squandered.

Professionally speaking, Poe's horizons were expanding rapidly, largely through the literary criticism he was contributing to the

Messenger, which brought him to the notice of such men of letters as James Kirke Paulding and Nathaniel Beverley Tucker. Paulding, friend and collaborator of Washington Irving, was a bastion of the New York literary establishment who had achieved fame with his humorous essays, *The Salamagundi Papers*, a number of anti-British political works and, in 1835, a fine biography of George Washington, as well as many other books and collections of graceful though commonplace poetry. His dislike of the British, which he had inherited from his revolutionary father, extended into the field of literature and he was keen to encourage native American talent to smash the mother country's domination: he regarded Poe as a writer worthy of encouragement and, impressed by the 'Folio Club' tales which had been rejected and finally returned by Carey and Lea, Paulding submitted them to the New York publishers Harper and Brothers. But Harpers were not interested either — they said a novel had more chance of success than a collection of 'detached tales', and anyway most of the stories had already been published in magazines; apart from that, the tales were 'too learned and mystical'. Paulding agreed that Poe would do better to 'undertake a Tale in a couple of volumes, for that is the magical number'. He pointed out, too, that the 'Folio Club' satire would be lost on the average American reader.

If Harpers had lacked confidence in the tales, they did have some nice things to say about Poe the critic: they liked his 'bold, decided, energetic tone' and promised to send him any of their books they thought worthy of his notice. It was also as a literary critic that Edgar attracted the attention of Beverley Tucker, though he did not speak from Paulding's Olympian peak. Tucker was a Virginian, from Williamsburg, with a substantial reputation in Southern circles, and he was impressed by Poe's original style. He pointed out, however, in a letter to White, that such originality needed 'the black rod of that master of ceremonies, Criticism', to keep it in order. Poe was flattered by the older man's interest and the two exchanged letters on the rights and wrongs of versification which, to be frank, Poe did not entirely grasp.

Poe's technique of criticism was to assume in himself a superiority of taste, perhaps of intellect, not enjoyed by ordinary mortals and because of this further to assume a mandate for attacking without quarter any piece of writing that did not rise to meet his principles — and those principles were no more than attempts to justify prejudices that he started out with. In other words, he began with a conclusion, and then proceeded to work backwards until he came across something which would support that conclusion as the result of intellectual activity rather than exposing it for what it actually was: some prejudice (often well founded, it is true) or pet theory based on emotion, intuition, instinct or whatever. It was all part of the half-educated Poe's pretence of scholarship. He was never content to rely on his natural, highly-developed literary instincts, and he spent a great deal of time attempting, vainly as it turned out, to explain to himself and the world why he wrote what he wrote. As far as the technique of working backwards is concerned, Edgar explained it well in *The Philosophy of Composition*, published in 1842, though in this case the process is applied to fiction:

> Charles Dickens, in a note now lying before me, alluding to an examination I once made of the mechanism of *Barnaby Rudge*, says — 'By the way, are you aware that Godwin wrote his *Caleb Williams* backwards? He first involved his hero in a web of difficulties, forming the second volume, and then, for the first, cast about him for some mode of accounting for what had been done.'
>
> I cannot think this the *precise* mode of procedure on the part of Godwin — and indeed what he himself acknowledges, is not altogether in accordance with Mr Dickens' idea — but the author of *Caleb Williams* was too good an artist not to perceive the advantage derivable from at least a somewhat similar process. Nothing is more clear than that every plot, worth the name, must be elaborated to its *denouement* before anything be attempted with the pen. It is only with the *denouement* constantly in view that we can give a plot its indispensable air of consequence, or causation, by making the incidents, and especially the tone at all points, tend to the development of the intention.

Well, it is a point of view, though one that not all of us would agree with today when it comes to writing fiction. Where we do find it, however, is in criticism, in which the denouement is obviously the conclusion reached by the critic and the tone and development of the review, equally clearly, reflects that conclusion. It seems obvious, yet it must be remembered that in the America of the 1830s such a technique of criticism was unknown outside the pages of the great British magazines like *Blackwood's*, the *Quarterly Review* and the *Edinburgh Review*, thus Edgar was breaking new ground in American literary journalism. The difference between the hatchet men of those fearsome British publications and Poe was that they were working to carefully thought-out and scholarly ground rules, while Edgar had only his own vague, instinctive theories to go on. Nevertheless, the effect of both was the same, because if Edgar lacked the intellectual background, he was a first-class writer and his skill more than made up for his lack of academic knowledge. Indeed, so effective were his reviews that the *Messenger*, started by White as a self-congratulatory outlet for Southern talent, soon attracted the attention of the big Northern literary magazines. That was to lead to trouble.

Puffery was the stock-in-trade of American literary journalists in those days, with a number of powerful clans of writers indulging in a mutual protection racket — praising each other in tight circles and fighting off unacceptable outsiders. Reviews tended to be superficial and often misleading, their tone dependent on whether the work in question came from a member of the clique or not. The most powerful and inward-looking coteries were in Boston and New York, and it was with the latter that Poe tangled, to the detriment of his entire career.

It came about in the December 1835 issue of the *Messenger*, when Poe expended four thousand words on a review of a novel entitled *Norman Leslie*, published anonymously but in fact written by Theodore Sedgwick Fay, an associate editor of the *New York Mirror*, at that time the country's best-known literary weekly. There was nothing anonymous about *Norman Leslie* as far as the *Mirror* was concerned: four months before the novel's publication, a two-column foretaste appeared in the weekly under the heading, 'Mr Fay's Novel — Norman Leslie'. The *Mirror's* introduction to the extract spoke of Mr Fay's 'powers of descriptive pathos, and his facility of touching the feelings'. A month later, the clan was at it again, this time with a full-page extract and an even more fulsome curtain-raiser: 'The last extract we gave from Mr Fay's forthcoming novel having been extensively copied, and spoken of in high terms by our bretheren of the press, we are induced to present them with another selection from these beautiful volumes, which we shall continue from time to time until their publication.' That was how it was done. The magazine which supported a particular member of the clan puffed his work and thus allowed other magazines to pick it up and introduce it to their own readers; then it was the custom of the first magazine to reprint the flattering comments of its followers (those having assumed that because the first magazine had given space to the work in question, it must be an important one). By the time the book came out, it had been so widely publicized, quoted from and praised, that it was bound to be a success. The *Mirror* printed a third *Norman Leslie* excerpt at the end of August 1835, quoted from it in September, and gave yet another section in October. When Harper and Brothers finally published the book in November, another organ of the New York clique, *The Knickerbocker Magazine*, reviewed it as follows:

With some faults, incident to a first attempt, this work of
Mr Fay is said by those critics who have perused it, — (a
pleasure in which, owing to absence from town, we have
been unable to participate,) to possess scenes of great
power, and to be often characterized by that quiet ease of
style and purity of diction for which the author is distinguished, and of which we have heretofore spoken in this
Magazine. It may be taken as a conclusive evidence of the
power of the novel to awaken interest, that in two weeks
after the publication of the first large edition, not a copy
remained in the hands of the publishers.

Puffery at its worst — and the 'reviewer' had not even read the work!
Poe the crusader had some corrupt fortresses to besiege. Taking his
cue from the literary generals in London and Edinburgh, he sent in
the battering ram first:

Well! — here we have it! This is *the* book — *the* book *par
excellence* — the book bepuffed, beplastered, and
be-*Mirrored*: the book 'attributed to' Mr Blank, and 'said
to be from the pen' of Mr Asterisk: the book which has
been 'about to appear' — 'in press' — 'in progress' — 'in
preparation' — and 'forthcoming': the book 'graphic' in
anticipation — 'talented' *a priori* — and God knows what *in
prospectu.* For the sake of every thing puffed, puffing and
puffable, let us take a peep at its contents!
  Norman Leslie, gentle reader, a Tale of the Present
Times, is, after all, written by nobody in the world but
Theodore S. Fay, and Theodore S. Fay is nobody in the
world but 'one of the Editors of the New York Mirror'.

Having smashed his way in, Poe proceeded to lay about him in all
directions. He summarized the plot of *Norman Leslie* in great detail,
calling it 'a monstrous piece of absurdity and incongruity'; the
characters, he said, 'have no character'; the writing style was 'unworthy of a school-boy'; in sum, the novel was 'the most inestimable
piece of balderdash with which the common sense of the good
people of America was ever so openly or so villainously insulted'.
  The *Mirror* and the *Knickerbocker* were stunned into silence, but
Poe's Southern colleagues went wild with delight, and complimentary notices of his review appeared in several magazines, among
them the *Lynchburg Virginian* and the *Petersburg Constellation.*
Even some of the Northern journals praised Poe, with the *New
Yorker* crying, 'May he live a thousand years!' Others accused him of

personal hostility towards Fay or 'undue severity'. Glorying in fame, Poe persuaded White to include in the January 1836 issue of the *Messenger* a special supplement quoting the comments about his review made by other editors. Perhaps it was on the principle that any publicity is good publicity that, a couple of months later, Harpers expressed their approval of Poe's reviewing style. Certainly he had done *Norman Leslie* no real harm, for a second edition was soon under way and it was also turned into a successful stage play. But perhaps, too, it was Poe's attack on the New York clan that helped to make up Harpers' mind to reject his tales. In April, the *New York Mirror* commented:

> Those who have read the notices of American books in a certain 'southern' monthly which is striving to gain notoriety by the loudness of its abuse, may find amusement in the sketch, in another page, entitled 'The Successful Novel'. The Southern Literary Messenger knows *by experience* what it is to write a successless novel.

That was a clear reference to Harpers' rejection, though it was, of course, a collection of short stories rather than a novel that Poe had submitted. Then the clique closed ranks, with the *New York Commercial Advertiser* accusing Poe of 'gross blunders' and sanctimoniously intoning that, 'The duty of the critic is to act as judge, not as enemy, of the writer whom he reviews.' The *Philadelphia Gazette* also joined in: it was edited by Willis Gaylord Clark, brother of the *Knickerbocker* editor, who described Poe's reviewing style as 'decidedly *quacky*'. In the April number of the *Messenger*, Poe was moved to justify his stand:

> There was a time, it is true, when we cringed to foreign opinion — let us even say when we paid a most servile deference to British critical dicta. That an American book could, by any possibility, be worthy of perusal, was an idea by no means extensively prevalent in the land; and if we were induced to read at all the productions of our native writers, it was only after repeated assurances from England that such productions were not altogether contemptible . . . Not so, however, with our present follies. We are becoming boisterous and arrogant in the pride of a too speedily assumed literary freedom. We throw off with the most presumptuous and unmeaning hauteur, *all* deference whatever to foreign opinion — we forget, in the puerile inflation of vanity, that *the world* is the true

theatre of the biblical histrio — we get up a hue and cry about the necessity of encouraging native writers of merit — we blindly fancy that we can accomplish this by indiscriminate puffing of good, bad and indifferent, without taking the trouble to consider that what we choose to denominate encouragement is thus, by its general application, precisely the reverse. In a word, so far from being ashamed of the many disgraceful failures to which our own inordinate vanities and misapplied patriotism have lately given birth, and so far from deeply lamenting that these daily puerilities are of home manufacture, we adhere pertinaciously to our original blindly conceived idea, and thus often find ourselves involved in the gross paradox of liking a stupid book the better, because, sure enough, its stupidity is American.

This passage is taken from what is now Poe's best-known piece of criticism written for the *Messenger*, the so-called 'Drake-Halleck Review', which further upset the New York literati partly because it dealt with the poetry of two more of its favourite sons, Fitzgreene Halleck and Joseph Rodman Drake, and partly because it attacked the puffing system. It was even too much for some of the Southern journals, and Poe was sniped at from South Carolina, from North Carolina, from Baltimore and even from Richmond itself, for the savagery of his reviewing. Poe defended himself with spirit, and at the same time massacred in the *Messenger* a novel entitled *Ups and Downs in the Life of a Distressed Gentleman*, which just happened to be the work of Colonel William L. Stone, editor of the *New York Commercial Advertiser*.

All this was very good for the sales of the *Messenger* (which between Edgar's arrival and departure rose from five hundred copies a month to three thousand five hundred) and for its reputation, which rapidly spread throughout America. Even magazines that criticized Poe's 'hanged, drawn and *Quarterly*' technique admitted that the *Messenger* was one of the best literary journals in the country and complimented it on, among other things, its typography. But although Thomas White was glad to see his investment paying off, he also recognized that his magazine was going far beyond the limited aims he had envisaged for it. In a word, it was becoming professional, and that was not at all the intention. The bulk of the *Messenger's* contributors were genteel amateurs, writing sloppy, sentimental poetry and turgid, nostalgic prose either anonymously or under pen-names. It was a closed, cosy little world, and the last thing that the inhabitants of that world wanted to feel was the sharp, cold wind of professionalism. Apart from anything else, what chance would their efforts stand of being published if the *Messenger* became a national institution, able to pick its material from among the best-known writers of the day?

To some extent, Poe sympathized with the views of his contributors and was always patient, courteous and gentle with poetesses and gentlemen authors. It is no accident that most of the poetry he chose for publication during his editorship in Richmond dealt with the 'death of beauty', a favourite theme of Southern writers and one which, of course, constantly recurs in Poe's own work. He himself was a Southerner, after all, and his feelings for the planter gentry have already been discussed. On the other hand, he wanted professional success — needed it, in fact, since it seemed that was the only way he was ever going to be comfortable in the material sense — and to achieve that success he had to take on the best in the land and beat them. He would have liked to have been part of the old order, but he recognized the gathering twilight of those particular gods and at the same time realized, John Allan having died and left him nothing, that he was never going to be one of their number. The split this produced in his attitudes is well illustrated by a commentary he wrote on a speech by Lucian Minor, a Virginia lawyer and Jeffersonian politician:

> The most lukewarm friend of the State must perceive — if he perceives anything — that the glory of the Ancient Dominion is in a fainting — is in a dying condition. Her once great name is becoming, in the North, a byeword for imbecility — all over the South, a type for 'the things that *have been*'. And tamely to ponder upon times gone by is not to meet the exigencies of times present or to come. Memory will not help us. The recollection of our former estate will not benefit us . . .

It is worth noting that Minor was a close friend of Thomas White, and had been offered the editorship of the *Messenger* before Poe's time there, but that does not entirely explain these un-Poe-like thoughts. As editor (official or otherwise) of the *Messenger* he had nailed his colours to a new mast, that of the aspiring middle class, seeing in professional success the chance of reconciling his idealism with his material needs. But by taking this course, he was once more contributing to his own professional failure.

Chapter 10

The Child Bride

Know all men by these presents, That we Edgar A. Poe and Thomas W. Cleland are held and firmly bound unto Wyndham Robertson, Lieutenant Governor and acting as governor of the Commonwealth of Virginia, in the just and full sum of one hundred and fifty dollars, to the payment whereof, well and truly to be made to the said acting Governor, or his successors, for the use of the said Commonwealth, we bind ourselves and each of us, our and each of our heirs, executors and administrators, jointly and severally, firmly by these presents. Sealed with our seals, and dated this 16th day of May 1836. The condition of the above obligation is such, That whereas a marriage is shortly intended to be had and solemnized between the above bound Edgar A. Poe and Virginia E. Clemm of the City of Richmond. Now if there is no lawful cause to obstruct said marriage, then the above obligation to be void, else to remain in full force and virtue.

So read the marriage bond Edgar Poe filed at the Court of Hustings in Richmond. Of course, there was 'lawful cause to obstruct said marriage'. Virginia Clemm was not quite fourteen years old. However, Thomas Cleland signed a false affidavit to the effect that the bride-to-be 'is of the full age of twenty-one years', and the marriage was indeed solemnized in the evening of 16 May at Mrs Yarrington's boarding house, the ceremony being conducted by a Presbyterian minister, the Reverend Amasa Converse. Either the clergyman had been persuaded to keep his mouth shut, or Virginia was a very well-developed thirteen-year-old; alternatively, it may have been assumed that she was twenty-one but in some way retarded. Whatever the small party of wedding guests thought, Edgar and his pubescent wife set off for their honeymoon at the home of Hiram W. Haines, proprietor of the *Constellation* magazine in Petersburg, set among rolling hills some twenty miles south of

Richmond. That night was the first that Virginia had ever spent away from her mother: whether it was anything more, whether it was a 'wedding night' in the true sense of the phrase, is a matter for conjecture.

Nothing is known about the sex life of Edgar and Virginia, though as usual with Poe's life there are plenty of rumours, some of them hinting darkly at perversion — drawing all sorts of Freudian conclusions from the fact that Edgar frequently referred to his child bride as 'Sissy' — while others suggest an unnatural distaste for matters physical leading to celibacy, reinforced by the knowledge that Virginia never produced a child. It is true that there is something strange about a twenty-seven-year-old man taking as his wife a thirteen-year-old girl, but Edgar was probably still worried about the possibility of Virginia being sent to live with Neilson Poe and, fearing that another female in his life was to be snatched from him, badgered Mrs Clemm into consenting to the marriage, which was the only way of securing the relationship. And, in the words of the song, 'little girls get bigger every day': the child Virginia soon became a woman, and with that process her relationship with Edgar would also develop. For the first few years of her marriage, life was hardly any different from what it had been before; she was still living with and protected by her mother and the likelihood is that the marriage was in name only — but there is no reason to suppose that was always the case, that as Virginia reached seventeen, or eighteen, or nineteen, physical love did not play the part it does in any 'normal' marriage.

Edgar's published writings give no real clue that would help to clear up the mystery. In the story that most closely resembles his relationship with Virginia, 'Eleonora', the narrator says, 'I am come from a race noted for vigour of fancy and ardour of passion', and later speaks of the god Eros enkindling 'within us the fiery souls of our forefathers' so that 'The passions which had for centuries distinguished our race came thronging . . .' The story goes on:

> A change fell upon all things. Strange brilliant flowers, star-shaped, burst out upon the trees where no flowers had been known before. The tints of the green carpet deepened; and when, one by one, the white daisies shrank away, there sprang up, in place of them, ten by ten of the ruby-red asphodel. And life arose in our paths; for the tall flamingo, hitherto unseen, with all gay glowing birds, flaunted his scarlet plumage before us. The golden and silver fish haunted the river, out of the bosom of which issued, little by little, a murmur that swelled, at length, into a lulling melody more divine than that of the harp of

Aeolus — sweeter than all save the voice of Eleonora. And now, too, a voluminous cloud, which we had long watched in the regions of Hesper, floated out thence, all gorgeous in crimson and gold, and settling in peace above us, sank, day by day, lower and lower, until its edges rested upon the tops of the mountains, turning all their dimness into magnificence, and shutting us up, as if for ever, within a magic prison-house of grandeur and of glory.

To the sophisticated reader of today, when awareness of sexual feeling has reached such a pitch that it intrudes upon everything, that passage might appear to be a masterly piece of erotic writing — it could even be seen as a symbolic description of sexual intercourse, with star-shaped flowers bursting out all over the place, life arising 'in our paths', the murmuring of the river, and finally the crimson and gold cloud (of after-love) settling over the scene. Modern eyes might see Poe, in an age when physical love was hardly ever written about, trying to express his own sexual feelings in poetic terms, and might further assume that because the story seems to be about Virginia it follows that Edgar felt that way about her. But our obsession with seeking out sexual significance, encouraged by Freudian psychologists, may blind us to symbols of a different kind. For example, the asphodel Poe mentions is a kind of lily that the ancient Greeks always associated with death: asphodels (of which the modern 'daffodil' appears to be a corruption) were always placed on graves, and the departed souls lived as ghosts on the Plain of Asphodel. Then there is the cloud from 'the regions of Hesper' — and Hesper is the star associated with the ending of the day. The passage begins to take on new significance, particularly when two paragraphs later Eleonora sees 'that the finger of death was upon her bosom — that, like the ephemeron, she had been made perfect in loveliness only to die'. The changes in the Valley of the Many-Coloured Grass, far from reflecting the joys of physical love, are precursors of death, glimpses of the Paradise to come. This impression is reinforced by Poe's reference in the story to 'the bard of Schiraz', the fourteenth-century Persian poet Hafiz, whose odes dealt with love, beauty, and the temporary nature of all things human.

So the tale that has been called the most 'amorous' story to come out of nineteenth-century America, and which can be directly traced to Poe's love for Virginia Clemm, still leaves a question-mark over his physical relationship with his bride. That he loved her cannot be doubted, but *how* he loved her is a mystery — and perhaps that is just as well. My own feeling, and it can be no more than that, based on the picture of Poe that has been built up, is that the marriage was somewhat abnormal, not only because when it took place Virginia was so young but also because Edgar makes it clear in his tales that he was obsessed by the idea of physical decay, of disease and of death, and this probably aroused some distaste for bodily contact, possibly leading to impotence, which most commonly has a psychological cause. Added to this is the fact that nineteenth-century doctors noted loss of sexual potency as a frequent symptom among untreated diabetics, which might provide another indication of what Poe himself called his 'long and dangerous illness', as well as of the state of his sex life. The balance of probabilities is that although Edgar needed women — Virginia in particular — and constantly sought their company, it was not for the desires of the flesh that he needed them: they were surrogates for the lost mothers and sister of his life and for the lost goddesses of his imagination.

At any rate, in May 1836 Edgar was a married man, and his responsibilities towards Virginia and Mrs Clemm became institutionalized. As usual, however, Poe made a mess of things. Having begged three hundred dollars from relatives to set up a boarding house, he spent two hundred on furniture for a house Thomas White had bought and which he proposed to rent to Mrs Clemm with himself and his family as boarders. This, at least, is what Poe told John P. Kennedy when he wrote to him in June asking for a loan, explaining that in the event the house had proved barely large enough to accommodate one family, let alone two. 'The plan was highly advantageous to us,' Poe wrote, but it is difficult to see how that could have been the case. If White had bought the house and was proposing to rent it to Mrs Clemm, it would hardly be likely that he would have paid her to let his family board there, and if he did not pay her while she had to pay rent, there would have been no difference from boarding at Mrs Yarrington's. It sounds like no more than a complicated excuse to borrow money. Whether it worked is not known.

Poe made another attempt to raise money in that same month by writing to a lawyer whom he asked to press a claim against the United States government for forty thousand dollars spent by his grandfather, 'General' Poe, in fitting out and providing for troops during the War of Independence. The claim came to nothing, because Grandmother Poe had died before the decision to allow such applications had been enacted in July 1836.

Troubles other than financial ones were also gathering. Poe had brought national fame to the *Southern Literary Messenger*, but he had made enemies faster than friends, and White was beginning to worry. The September number of the magazine was late, because, it was stated, 'both Publisher and Editor' (Poe's status must have been official by then) were ill: in letters, White and Poe referred to their illnesses, but White also told his friend Lucian Minor that he had sacked Poe, who — as he later admitted — had been drinking again. Edgar was still at his desk in October, however, and he wrote some reviews for that month's issue and for the following one. In December there was a printers' strike and a serious interruption of the money supply following President Andrew Jackson's anti-inflation Specie Circular, which required land sales to be paid for in gold and silver rather than in banknotes, thus seriously damaging confidence in paper money and tightening credit: again the *Messenger* did not appear. 'We are all without money in Richmond,' said White. But that was not his only complaint. He feared that he was losing control of his magazine, as he told Lucian Minor:

> . . . I am cramped by him [Poe] in the exercise of my own judgment, as to what articles I shall or shall not admit into my work. It is true that I neither have his sagacity, nor his learning — but I do believe I know a handspike from a saw. Be that as it may, however, — and let me even be a jackass, as I dare say I am in his estimation, I will again throw myself on my own resources — and trust my little bark to the care of those friends who stood by me in my earlier, if not darker days . . .

The *Messenger* was White's 'little bark', not the great battleship that Poe was trying to make of it. And so, 'Highly as I think of Mr Poe's talents, I shall be forced to give him notice in a week or so at farthest that I can no longer recognize him as editor of my Messenger.' Although the next edition of the magazine contained reviews, poems and the beginning of a story by Poe, he ceased to be editor on 3 January 1837, his attention having been called in another direction, according to the small 'Valedictory' in the *Messenger*. He was not sorry to leave. White, he said later, was a vulgar and illiterate man, though well meaning, who lacked both the capacity to appreciate his editor's labours and the will to reward them properly. This was a harsh and probably an unfair judgment, and certainly White remained warm in his praise of Poe long afterwards.

Edgar, however, had his sights set on the literary constellation of New York. He had scorched through it like a meteor with his reviews in the *Messenger*; now the time had come to try to establish himself as one of its stars. The time, however, could hardly have been more ill chosen. The Specie Circular and run on the banks of late 1836 had been merely an augury of the economic troubles in store for Jackson's successor as President, Martin Van Buren, and soon the country was wracked by the worst depression it had ever known. In such circumstances, the literary magazines of New York were not about to risk their precarious fortunes on an interloper from the South, and one who had already shaken their foundations to boot. Thus when Poe arrived in the great, turbulent city in February 1837, with Virginia and Mrs Clemm in tow, he was not welcomed with bands and bunting. He haunted the 'magazine quarter' around Broadway, approaching any of his acquaintances who might offer him a job — but when people can barely afford to buy bread, they are unlikely to spend their money on literature, and the magazine editors, whether or not the word about Poe had gone out from the Clarks and their supporters, were more concerned with survival than with encouraging new talent.

Mrs Clemm came to the rescue, as she was so often to do. The little family had settled in Greenwich Village, and it was there that Mrs Clemm at last achieved her ambition to open a boarding house. Her first tenant was, appropriately enough, a bookseller, a man named William Gowans, who was apparently much impressed by Edgar's intelligence and Southern good manners, and also by the beauty of Virginia. It may have been Gowans who introduced Poe to the editor of the *New York Review*, a meeting which led to a commission for Edgar to write a review of a new book by the traveller and archaeologist John Lloyd Stephens, *Incidents of Travel in Egypt, Arabia and the Holy Land.* Unfortunately, before Edgar could do anything the financial panic worsened, the banks stopped issuing paper money, and the *Review* was obliged to close down temporarily. (Poe did complete the review, and it was published when the magazine reappeared in October 1837.) The economic crisis was good for Mrs Clemm, however, for scores of businessmen were being driven into liquidation, forced to sell their homes and seek accommodation. It was not long before the boarding house could move, accompanied by Gowans, to larger premises at 113½ Carmine Street, in the Village, and take in more tenants. It was ironic that while most people were hard up, and many were bankrupt, Edgar should be in comparatively comfortable circumstances, having been used to poverty for virtually all of his adult life. But he made good use of his situation, working hard at his writing and staying well away from alcohol, as Gowans later testified.

Edgar had taken James Kirke Paulding's advice and had embarked upon a novel. Two instalments of it had appeared in the *Southern Literary Messenger* — the second in the January issue that marked Poe's departure — but in the spring of 1837 Harpers agreed to publish it in book form and Edgar set to work either finishing it or polishing it. The story never made the two volumes Paulding had suggested, yet it is by far the longest Poe ever wrote. It is now known as *The Narrative of Arthur Gordon Pym*, but Poe's full title is worth giving because it must establish some sort of record for length. It is:

'The Narrative of Arthur Gordon Pym of Nantucket. Comprising The Details of a Mutiny and Atrocious Butchery on Board of the American Brig Grampus, on Her Way to the South Seas, in the Month of June, 1827, — with an Account of the Recapture of the Vessel by the Survivors; Their Shipwreck, and Subsequent Horrible Sufferings, from Famine; Their Deliverance by Means of the British Schooner Jane Guy; The Brief Cruise of this Latter Vessel in the Antarctic Ocean; Her Capture, and of the Massacre of Her Crew, among a Group of Islands in the 84th Parallel of the Southern Latitude, together with the Incredible Adventures and Discoveries still further South, to which that Distressing Calamity gave Rise.'

Notwithstanding this impressive, indeed awe-inspiring beginning, the book was, in Gowans's words, 'the most unsuccessful of all his writings'. Poe's talent for making the most incredible events seem real, so effective in his short tales, comes unstuck in *Pym* because he tries too hard and gets bogged down in detail. The writing is beautiful, the descriptions masterly, the climax unforgettable — but *Pym* lacks the simple menace, the growing sense of horror that makes 'MS Found in a Bottle' one of the last stories you would want to read alone in bed on a stormy night. Harpers published *Pym* in the summer of 1838, hoping to cash in on the current vogue for stories, real and imagined, of adventure and exploration: Poe had borrowed a good deal of background material from a speech by one Jeremiah N. Reynolds urging Congress to put up the money for an expedition to the South Seas, and also from a book by Benjamin Morell entitled *Narrative of Four Voyages to the South Seas and Pacific*, published in 1832. Some people took *Pym* for a true story — it sold well as such in England, for example, though of course Poe earned nothing out of that owing to the lack of copyright agreements — but most ignored it altogether, and the few press comments it attracted were unfavourable, the Philadelphia *Gentleman's Magazine* describing it as an 'impudent attempt at humbugging the public'. Poe himself later called *Pym* 'a very silly book', but this may have been based less on the fact that he was unhappy with it than on a desire to write it off because it was so unsuccessful. The book did find one notable champion, in France, when Baudelaire called it an 'admirable novel . . . purely realistic . . . purely human'. But by that time Poe was dead.

One thing *Pym* did provide was an opportunity for Lewis Gaylord
Clark, of the *Knickerbocker*, to get his own back on the man who had
so grievously offended him. In August 1838 Clark wrote:

> There are a great many tough stories in this book, told in a
> loose and slip-shod style, seldom chequered by any of the
> more common graces of composition, beyond a Robinson
> Crusoe-ish sort of simplicity of narration. This work is one
> of much interest, with all its defects, not the least of which
> is, that it is too liberally stuffed with 'horrid circumstances
> of blood and battle'. We would not be so uncourteous as
> to insinuate a doubt of Mr Pym's veracity, now that he *lies*
> 'under the sod'; but we should very much question that
> gentleman's word who should affirm, after having
> thoroughly perused the volume before us, that he *believed*
> the various adventures and hairbreadth 'scapes therein
> recorded.

As they say, it is an ill wind that does nobody any good.

By the time that review appeared, though, Poe had tired of the
closed doors of New York and, no doubt further depressed by the
failure of *Pym*, had taken Virginia and Mrs Clemm to try their luck
in the second most important publishing centre of the United States,
Philadelphia. But it was not in fact in Philadelphia that one of his
most popular and enduring tales was published in September 1838.
'Ligeia', the classic study of a love that defies death, graced the first
issue of a magazine started by two of Edgar's Baltimore friends, Dr
Nathan C. Brooks and Dr Joseph E. Snodgrass, and called *The
American Museum of Literature and the Arts*. In the story the
narrator, distracted by the death of his wife Ligeia, the personification of Beauty, takes as his second wife the Lady Rowena
Trevanion of Tremaine and settles with her in a half-ruined abbey
with 'verdant decay hanging about it' in 'one of the wildest and least
frequented portions of fair England'. The story fairly drips with
gloom and despair as the dead Ligeia haunts the narrator's mind and
he grows to hate his second wife. Lady Rowena falls ill and is
ultimately despatched through poison delivered by a ghostly hand —
but, horror upon horror, her body slowly begins to assume an
awesome new character, until the breathtaking climax is reached:

> . . . Rushing to the corpse, I saw — distinctly saw — a
> tremor upon the lips. In a minute afterwards they relaxed,
> disclosing a bright line of the pearly teeth . . . There was
> now a partial glow upon the forehead and upon the cheek
> and throat; a perceptible warmth pervaded the whole

frame; there was even a slight pulsation of the heart. The lady *lived*. . .

The greater part of the fearful night had worn away, and she who had been dead, once again stirred — and now more vigorously than hitherto, although arousing from a dissolution more appalling in its utter hopelessness than any . . . The hues of life flushed up with unwonted energy into the countenance — the limbs relaxed — and, save that the eyelids were yet pressed heavily together, and that the bandages and draperies of the grave still imparted their charnel character to the figure, I might have dreamed that Rowena had shaken off, utterly, the fetters of Death . . .

I trembled not — I stirred not — for a crowd of unutterable fancies connected with the air, the stature, the demeanour of the figure, rushing hurriedly through my brain, had paralysed — had chilled me into stone . . . Could it, indeed, be the *living* Rowena who confronted me? Could it indeed be Rowena *at all* — the fair-haired, the blue-eyed Lady Rowena Trevanion of Tremaine? . . . One bound, and I had reached her feet! Shrinking from my touch, she let fall from her head, unloosened, the ghastly cerements which had confined it, and there streamed forth, into the rushing atmosphere of the chamber, huge masses of long and dishevelled hair; *it was blacker than the raven wings of the midnight!* And now slowly opened *the eyes* of the figure which stood before me. 'Here then, at least,' I shrieked aloud, 'can I never — can I never be mistaken — these are the full, and the black, and the wild eyes — of my lost love — of the lady — of the *Lady Ligeia*'.

If Edgar Poe had written nothing else, that story alone might have endowed his name with immortality. But consideration of the mind that was filled with such terrible visions brings an echo of John Allan's prophecy: 'His Talents are of an order that can never prove a comfort to their possessor.' Poe's talents were evident in 'Ligeia' but it provided little material comfort for the trio in Philadelphia. In September 1838 he wrote to Dr Brooks thanking him for a payment, presumably for 'Ligeia', of ten dollars — and that was the most the few other pieces be contributed to the *Museum* that year brought in. The family were obliged to quit their first Philadelphia home for a smaller house, and Edgar began to look around for anything in the way of writing or editorial work that would provide ready cash. He found it in a piece of shameful hack work to which only desperation could have driven him. Late in 1838 he was approached by a marine biologist,

Thomas Wyatt, who had earlier that year produced a lavish and expensive textbook on conchology and who was annoyed with his publishers, Harpers, because they refused to issue a cheaper edition of his work to bring it within the financial range of the general public. What Wyatt proposed was to bring out a second version of the book, using a Philadelphia publisher, but that version had to be different enough from the first to prevent Harpers from suing for breach of copyright. Would Poe, Wyatt asked, care to take on the preparation of this book, using material from the first edition and anything else he could lay his hands on? Edgar had taken an interest in the pursuits of the naturalist since his excursions with Dr Ravenel on Sullivan's Island, when he was in the army, so he may have felt that he possessed enough knowledge of the subject to undertake the work. More important, however, he needed the money.

The Conchologist's First Book appeared early in 1839 under the imprint of Haswell, Barrington and Haswell and under the name of Edgar A. Poe. It consisted of an introduction paraphrased from a British book, *The Conchologist's Text-Book*, by Captain Thomas Brown, published in Glasgow in 1837; illustrations and an 'explanation of the parts of shells' copied directly from Brown; a classification lifted from Wyatt's first book (and acknowledged as such); descriptions of the shells rewritten from the Harper book; some translation of the work of the eminent French anatomist and zoologist Georges Cuvier; and an original glossary and index contributed by Wyatt. It was a great success, and ran to a second edition, though whether that was any good to Poe is doubtful — he was almost certainly paid a flat fee. He may have been pleased to have his name associated with a successful book, but he probably soon forgot about it . . . until a few years later, when it returned to trouble him with a charge of plagiarism.

In the meantime, Edgar was building up his journalistic contacts in Philadelphia, and among them was an Englishman, William Evans Burton, an actor with literary ambitions, who had launched the *Gentleman's Magazine* in July 1837. In spite of the depression, Burton's gamble came off and by 1839 the magazine was well established, publishing both pirated works of British authors and the effusions of native talents, including Poe's friends Nathan Brooks, co-proprietor of the *Museum*, and Lambert Wilmer, formerly of the *Baltimore Saturday Visiter*. Wilmer was then living in Philadelphia, and it may have been he who introduced Poe to Burton. Edgar had been writing steadily but still lacked an income, and in the spring of 1839 he suggested to Burton that he might share the editorial duties of the *Gentleman's Magazine*, citing the success of the *Messenger* as evidence of his journalistic skill. Burton needed help because he was also planning to become the owner of a theatre, and on 11 May he told Poe he could offer him ten dollars a week until the end of the year for 'two hours a day, except occasionally', with a contract to follow in 1840. He pointed out that competition was hot, printing costs were high, and these and other difficulties prevented him from taking up Poe's proposition immediately. Poe was disappointed by the offer and made another approach in terms which evidently upset Burton, for on 30 May he wrote to Edgar telling him, more or less, to buck up his ideas and to stop feeling sorry for himself. With no other prospect in view, Edgar took the job — not realizing that the ten dollars a week would include payment for any stories or articles he might contribute to the magazine. In June, Burton announced that Poe was to become his assistant and in July the magazine carried Edgar's name on the title-page: he was back on the journalistic tread-mill.

The August issue of the *Gentleman's* carried one of Poe's best 'comic' stories, 'The Man That Was Used Up', a neat burlesque of public adulation for the heroes of the Indian wars provoked by the government's resettlement policy. The hero, Brevet Brigadier-General John A. B. C. Smith, 'six feet in height, and of a presence singularly commanding', turns out to be almost completely man-made, having lost all his limbs and most of his other physical accoutrements fighting 'the Bugaboo and Kickapoo campaign'. Then, in September, the magazine published Edgar's most famous tale, arguably the greatest 'horror story' ever written, 'The Fall of the House of Usher':

> During the whole of a dull, dark and soundless day in the autumn of the year, when the clouds hung oppressively low in the heavens, I had been passing alone, on horseback, through a singularly dreary tract of country, and at length found myself, as the shades of evening drew on, within view of the melancholy House of Usher. I know not how it was — but, with my first glimpse of the building, a sense of insufferable gloom pervaded my spirit. I say insufferable; for the feeling was unrelieved by any of that half-pleasurable, because poetic, sentiment with which the mind usually receives even the sternest natural images of the desolate or terrible. I looked upon the scene before me — upon the mere house, and the simple landscape features of the domain — upon the bleak walls — upon the vacant eye-like windows — upon a few rank sedges — and upon a few white trunks of decayed trees — with an utter depression of soul which I can compare to no earthly sensation more properly than to the after-dream of the

reveller upon opium — the bitter lapse into every-day life — the hideous dropping off of the veil. There was an iciness, a sinking, a sickening of the heart — an unredeemed dreariness of thought which no goading of the imagination could torture into aught of the sublime.

The opening sentences of 'Usher' are a splendid example of Poe's economy of style. Each word is a brick in the construction of a house of horrors, and trapped inside that house is a mind in mortal terror of decaying into madness. Roderick Usher is Poe's nightmare vision of himself, and of what he might become.

A cadaverous complexion; an eye large, liquid, and luminous beyond comparison; lips somewhat thin and very pallid, but of a surprisingly beautiful curve; a nose of a delicate Hebrew model, but with a breadth of nostril unusual in similar formations; a finely moulded chin, speaking, in its want of prominence, of a want of moral energy; hair of a more than web-like softness and tenuity; — these features, with an inordinate expansion of the regions above the temple, made up altogether a countenance not easily to be forgotten.

This is nothing less than a description of Edgar Poe himself. And in Roderick Usher reposes Edgar's fear for himself:

'I *must* perish in this deplorable folly. Thus, thus, and not otherwise shall I be lost. I dread the events of the future, not in themselves, but in their results. I shudder at the thought of any, even the most trivial, incident, which may operate upon this intolerable agitation of soul. I have, indeed, no abhorrence of danger, except in its absolute effect — in terror. In this unnerved, in this pitiable, condition I feel that the period will sooner or later arrive when I must abandon life and reason together, in some struggle with the grim phantasm, FEAR.'

Usher is even credited with the composition of one of Poe's finest poems, 'The Haunted Palace' (published in the *Museum* in April 1839 and then incorporated in 'Usher'):

In the greenest of our valleys
　By good angels tenanted,
Once a fair and stately palace —
　Radiant palace — reared its head.

In the monarch Thought's dominion —
   It stood there!
Never seraph spread a pinion
   Over fabric half so fair!

The palace is the human body, within which lives the soul, 'the ruler of the realm'. But when the palace falls into ruin, what happens to its tenant?

But evil things, in robes of sorrow,
   Assailed the monarch's high estate.
(Ah, let us mourn! — for never morrow
   Shall dawn upon him desolate!)
And round about his home the glory
   That blushed and bloomed,
Is but a dim-remembered story
   Of the old time entombed.

And travellers now within that valley,
   Through the red-litten windows see
Vast forms, that move fantastically
   To a discordant melody,
While, like a ghastly rapid river,
   Through the pale door
A hideous throng rush out forever,
   And laugh — but smile no more.

In the story, Usher gives the narrator the poem to read, and 'in the under or mystic current of its meaning, I fancied that I perceived, and for the first time, a full consciousness on the part of Usher of the tottering of his lofty reason upon her throne'.

Once again there is a woman in the case, this time not a cousin or a bride but Usher's twin sister, the lady Madeline, the only person who can ensure his survival. She is in the grip of a deadly disease, though, and as Usher watches her slow dissolution, he sees his existence slipping away, too. In due course she dies and is entombed — then returns from the grave to claim her brother.

As if in the superhuman energy of his utterance there had been found the potency of a spell, the huge antique panels to which the speaker pointed threw slowly back, upon the instant, their ponderous and ebony jaws. It was the work of the rushing gust — but then without those doors there *did* stand the lofty and enshrouded figure of the lady

Madeline of Usher. There was blood upon her white robes, and the evidence of some bitter struggle upon every portion of her emaciated frame. For a moment she remained trembling and reeling to and fro upon the threshold — then, with a low moaning cry, fell heavily inward upon the person of her brother, and in her violent and now final death-agonies, bore him to the floor a corpse, and a victim of the terrors he had anticipated.

I have already pointed out the danger of associating an artist's work too closely with the details of his life, but there are certain Poe stories, of which 'Usher' is one, in which the association is inescapable, and the only question that remains is whether the parallels were deliberate or unconscious. Poe claimed that he always wrote *for effect*, which is perhaps a way of saying that his tales should not be taken too seriously, but given that he based his 'adventure stories' and later his detective or ratiocination pieces on real events, there is every reason to believe that his despairing cries of the soul in torment came from the dreams, terrors and troubles that beset and upset his delicately balanced mind. It is the quality of inner torture that distinguishes the great stories and poems from the lesser, that is the ones which are merely experiments in creating effects, no matter how skilful. D. H. Lawrence summed it up in an essay he wrote in 1923, when he said that Poe 'is absolutely concerned with the disintegration-processes of his own psyche . . . Doomed to seethe down his soul in a great continuous convulsion of disintegration, and doomed to register the process . . .'

Poe disagreed with this assessment, at least in his public pronouncements. He was writing for money, after all, and he apparently believed that he was able to construct and control his tales and poems in order to achieve precisely the effects that he desired. His essay 'The Philosophy of Composition', which is derived from lectures he gave towards the end of his life, is adamant on this point, and goes into great detail — for example, on the length of a piece:

If any literary work is too long to be read at one sitting, we must be content to dispense with the important effect derivable from unity of impression — for, if two sittings be required, the affairs of the world interfere, and everything like totality is at once destroyed . . . It appears evident, then, that there is a distinct limit, as regards length, to all works of literary art — the limit of a single sitting . . .

He was talking principally about the composition of poetry here, and he did admit that 'in certain classes of prose composition . . . (demanding no unity) this limit may be advantageously over-passed . . .' In his own work, though, he obviously applied the same limits to prose as to poetry, since he never wrote anything longer than a substantial short story, so the points he made in 'The Philosophy of Composition' seem to apply to his tales as well as his verse.

Having dealt with length, he turned his attention to the aim of the work:

> My next thought concerned the choice of an impression, or effect, to be conveyed: and here I may as well observe that, throughout the construction, I kept steadily in view the design of rendering the work *universally* appreciable . . .

And he went on to describe how he composed his most famous poem, 'The Raven', claiming that each move was carefully calculated to achieve 'such combinations of event, or tone, as shall best aid me in the construction of the effect'.

Of course, there is a great deal of truth in all this. As Poe pointed out, writers do not generally 'compose by a species of fine frenzy', and as Thomas Carlyle put it, genius 'means transcendent capacity of taking trouble, first of all'. But what Poe left out of his considerations was the reason for writing in the first place. He was confusing technique with motivation. It was not at all the 'philosophy' of composition that he was talking about but the actual process. He forgot that in every work of art there are aspects of the artist's personality that do not appear as the result of any conscious effort and may not even be visible to the artist himself. He answered the question, in part at least, *how* he wrote what he did, but not the question *why*.

We know that Edgar had a peculiarly sensitive nature; all the evidence from people who knew him supports this. We know, too, that his personality was crippled by weakness; his letters make this only too clear. A person who is both sensitive and weak is likely to be much afflicted by fear, and it is fear that is the common denominator in all Poe's horror stories — fear of madness, fear of death, and perhaps even fear of love, for love is so often linked to death in Poe's tales and poems. I think Lawrence was right: Poe's greatest stories (as opposed to the hack tales he wrote for the market) and poems were, whether their author knew it or not, records of the terrors and troubles that beset him.

In 1839 there were terrors and troubles aplenty to come. That autumn, the Poes and Mrs Clemm had to move to a new home a little way out of Philadelphia, near Fairmount Park. The move was for reasons of health rather than finance. Virginia, the child bride, now seventeen, was growing up into a sick wife.

Chapter 11

Tricks of Fate

As the year 1839 drew towards its close, Edgar Poe began to approach the zenith of his literary fortunes (though his financial position was as weak as it had ever been). By that time he had written, apart from *Arthur Gordon Pym* twenty-five short stories of which all save one — a lightweight effort, called 'Why the Little Frenchman Wears His Hand in a Sling' — had been published in magazines. Now they were to appear in book form, two volumes of two hundred and forty pages each. The Philadelphia publishers Lea and Blanchard had agreed to print 'at our own risque' *Tales of the Grotesque and Arabesque.* Edgar must have been thrilled, though his delight would have been dampened somewhat by the fact that all he was going to get out of the publication was a few complimentary copies for his friends. Lea and Blanchard kept the edition to under two thousand, and, 'This sum if sold — will pay but a small profit which if realized is to be ours.' Edgar had apparently persuaded them to publish by saying that his interest did not lie in any money the book might make. His ten dollars a week from Burton did not go very far, however, and shortly before the *Tales* were due to appear he sought better terms, offering the copyright to the publishers. Lea and Blanchard would have none of that. On 20 November, they wrote:

Edgar A. Poe, — We have your note of to-day. The copyright of the Tales would be of no value to us; when we undertook their publication, it was solely to oblige you and not with any view to profit, and on this ground it was urged by you. We should not therefore be now called upon or expected to purchase the copyright when we have no expectation of realizing the Capital placed in the volumes. If the offer to publish was now before us we should certainly decline it, and would feel obliged if you knew and would urge some one to relieve us from the publication at cost, or even at a small abatement.

In the event Lea and Blanchard's caution was justified. The *Tales* appeared in December, and sales were small, in spite of favourable press comment like the following notice from the *New York Mirror*:

> Had Mr Poe written nothing else but 'Morella', 'William Wilson', 'The House of Usher' and the 'MS Found in a Bottle', he would deserve a high place among imaginative writers, for there is fine poetic feeling, much brightness of fancy, and excellent taste, a ready eye for the picturesque, much quickness of observation, and great truth of sentiment and character in all of these works. But there is scarcely one of the tales published in the two volumes before us, in which we do not find the development of great intellectual capacity, with a power for vivid description, an opulence of imagination, a fecundity of invention, and a command over the elegance of diction which have seldom been displayed, even by writers who have acquired the greatest distinction in the republic of letters.

Of course, praise, no matter how welcome, was not at all what Poe needed from his *Tales*. He had rent to pay and food to buy, and he was finding it more and more difficult to manage on the pittance he was paid by Burton. When he realized that he was not going to receive any extra payment for his contributions to the *Gentleman's*, his anxiety about money turned to resentment of his employer, upon whose honesty and character he began to cast doubts. For example, there was the matter of some prizes Burton announced for contributions. Poe claimed there was no intention of paying them, and in a letter to his friend Dr Snodgrass in December 1839 said:

> Touching the Premiums. The Advertisement respecting them was written by Mr Burton, and is not I think as explicit as it might be. I can give you no information about their designation further than is shown in the advertisement itself. The truth is, I object, in toto, to the whole scheme — but merely followed in Mr B's wake upon such matters of business.

Snodgrass apparently submitted an entry for Burton's competition and became concerned about its fate. In June 1840, Poe was even more explicit:

> Touching your Essay, Burton not only *lies*, but deliberately and wilfully lies; for the last time but one that

I saw him I called his attention to the MS. which was then at the top of a pile of other MSS. sent for premiums, in a drawer of the office desk. The last day I was in the office I saw the Essay in the same position, and am perfectly sure it is there still. You know it is a peculiar looking MS. and I could not mistake it. In saying it was not in his possession his sole design was to vex you, and through you myself. Were I in your place I would take some summary method of dealing with the scoundrel, whose infamous line of conduct in regard to this whole Premium scheme merits, and shall receive exposure. I am firmly convinced that it was never his intention to pay one dollar of the money offered; and indeed his plain intimations to that effect, made to me personally and directly, were the immediate reason of my cutting the connexion so abruptly as I did. If you could, in any way, spare the time to come on to Philadelphia, I think I could put you in the way of detecting this villain in his rascality. I would go down with you to the office, open the drawer in his presence, and take the MS. from beneath his very nose. I think this would be a good deed done, and would act as a caution to such literary swindlers in the future . . .

By the time that letter was written, as it makes plain, Edgar had quit the *Gentleman's*. The story spread by Burton was that Poe had been habitually drinking and that, having abandoned one issue of the magazine, leaving Burton to work through the night in order to make sure it appeared on time, he had been sacked. Poe emphatically denied the charge in a letter to Snodgrass written a year later:

In regard to Burton. I feel indebted to you for the kind interest you express; but scarcely know how to reply. My situation is embarrassing. It is impossible, as you say, to notice a buffoon and a felon, as one gentleman would notice another. The law, then, is my only recourse. Now, if the truth of a scandal could be admitted in justification — I mean what the law terms a *scandal* — I would have matters all my own way. I would institute a suit, forthwith, for his personal defamation of myself. He would be unable to prove the truth of his allegations. I could prove their falsity and their malicious intent by witnesses who, seeing me at all hours of every day, would have the best right to speak — I mean Burton's own clerk, Morrell, and the compositors of the printing office. In fact, I could

prove the scandal almost by acclamation. I should obtain
damages. But, on the other hand, I have never been
scrupulous in regard to what I have said of him. I have
always told *him* to his face, and everybody else, that I
looked upon him as a blackguard and a villain. This is
notorious. He would meet me with a cross action. The
truth of the allegation − which I could as easily prove as
he would find it difficult to prove the truth of his own
respecting me − would not avail me. The law will not
admit, as justification of my calling Billy Burton a
scoundrel, that Billy Burton is really such. What then can I
do? If I sue, he sues: you see how it is . . .

So far for the matter inasmuch as it concerns Burton. I
have now to thank you for your defence of myself, as
stated. You are a physician, and I presume no physician
can have difficulty in detecting a *drunkard* at a glance.
You are, moreover, a literary man, well read in morals.
You will never be brought to believe that I could write
what I daily write, *as* I write it, were I as this villain would
induce those who know me not, to believe. In fine, I
pledge you, before God, the solemn word of a gentleman,
that I am temperate even to rigor. From the hour in which
I first saw this basest of calumniators to the hour in which
I retired from his office in uncontrollable disgust at his
chicanery, arrogance, ignorance and brutality, *nothing
stronger than water ever passed my lips.*

The next paragraph of the letter is important in determining the
truth or falsehood of the Poe legends about drink.

It is, however, due to candor that I inform you upon what
foundation he has erected his slanders. At no period of my
life was I ever what men call intemperate. I never was in
the *habit* of intoxication. I never drunk drams, &c. But,
for a brief period, while I resided in Richmond, and edited
the *Messenger* I certainly did give way, at long intervals, to
the temptation held out on all sides by the spirit of
Southern conviviality. My sensitive temperament could not
stand an excitement which was an every day matter to my
companions. In short, it sometimes happened that I was
completely intoxicated. For some days after each excess I
was invariably confined to bed. But it is now quite four
years since I have abandoned every kind of alcoholic drink
− four years, with the exception of a single deviation,

which occurred shortly *after* my leaving Burton, and when
I was induced to resort to the occasional use of *cider*, with
the hope of relieving a nervous attack.

I can find no reason to doubt the sincerity and veracity of this
statement. Edgar admits his lapses in Richmond, to which White
referred in his letter of September 1835, and it seems to me that the
point he makes about 'what I daily write, *as* I write it' is perfectly
valid. Even the publisher of the *Gentleman's Magazine*, C. W.
Alexander, writing ten years after Poe's time there and accepting that
he was a drunkard, conceded that 'the monthly issue was never
interrupted upon any occasion, either from Mr Poe's deficiency, or
from any other cause, during my publication of it, embracing the
whole time of Mr Poe's connection with it'. Mr Poe's failing, said
Alexander, 'was well known in the literary circles of Philadelphia': of
course it was — hadn't Burton been telling everybody who would
listen that Poe was a drunkard? It seems strange that if Poe's drinking
was so bad, 'he alone was the sufferer, and not those who received
the benefit of his preeminent talents', as Alexander put it. The truth
of the quarrel between Poe and Burton, I think, is also to be found
among Alexander's reminiscences: 'The absence of the principal
editor on professional duties left the matter frequently in the hands
of Mr Poe . . .' The two hours a day suggested by Burton in his
original offer to Poe had become considerably more, and Edgar was
still getting only ten dollars a week, with nothing for the articles,
reviews and stories he wrote. On top of that, the *Gentleman's* was in
financial difficulties and Burton stopped paying altogether for contributions, as Poe told Snodgrass in a letter in November 1839. Burton
was far more interested in a new acquisition, the National Theatre in
Philadelphia, so Poe was left to do all the work on the magazine,
which, as well as denting his pride, also rankled because he was held
responsible for what he saw as his employer's 'chicanery'. The last
straw came at the end of May, when Burton apparently wrote to
Edgar charging him with some debt of a hundred dollars. Poe stood
on his dignity in his reply:

Sir, — I find myself at leisure this Monday morning, June
1, to notice your very singular letter of Saturday. I have
followed the example of Victorine and slept upon the
matter, and you shall now hear what I have to say. In the
first place, your attempts to bully me excite in my mind
scarcely any other sentiment than mirth. When you
address me again, preserve, if you can, the dignity of a
gentleman. If by accident you have taken it into your head

that I am to be insulted with impunity I can only assume
that you are an ass. This one point being distinctly understood I shall feel myself more at liberty to be explicit. As
for the rest, you do me gross injustice; and you know it.
As usual, you have wrought yourself into a passion with
me on account of some imaginary wrong; for no real
injury, or attempt at injury have you ever received at my
hands. As I live, I am utterly unable to say why you are
angry, or what true grounds of complaint you have against
me. You are a man of impulses; have made yourself, in
consequence, some enemies; have been in many respects
ill-treated by those you had looked upon as friends — and
these things have rendered you suspicious. You once wrote
in your magazine a sharp critique upon a book of mine — a
very silly book — Pym. Had I written a similar criticism
upon a book of yours, you feel that you would have been
my enemy for life, and you therefore imagine in my
bosom a latent hostility towards yourself. This has been a
mainspring in your whole conduct towards me since our
first acquaintance. It has acted to prevent all cordiality. In
a general view of human nature your idea is just — but you
will find yourself puzzled in judging me by ordinary
motives. Your criticism was essentially correct, and therefore, although severe, it did not occasion in me one
solitary emotion either of anger or dislike. But even while I
write these words, I am sure you will not believe them. Did
I not still think you, in spite of the exceeding littleness
of some of your hurried actions, a man of many honorable
impulses, I should not now take the trouble to send you
this letter. I cannot permit myself to suppose that you
would say to me in cool blood what you said in your letter
of yesterday. You are, of course, only mistaken, in
asserting that I owe you a hundred dollars, and you will
rectify the mistake at once when you come to look at your
accounts.

Soon after I joined you, you made me an offer of
money, and I accepted $20. Upon another occasion, at my
request, you sent me enclosed in a letter $30. Of this 30, I
repaid 20 within the next fortnight (drawing no salary for
that period). I was thus still in your debt $30, when not
long ago I again asked a loan of $30, which you promptly
handed to me at your own home. Within the last three
weeks, three dollars each week have been retained from
my salary, an indignity which I have felt deeply but did

not resent. You state the sum retained as $8, but this I
believe is through a mistake of Mr Morrell. My postage bill,
at a guess, might be $9 or $10 — and I therefore am
indebted to you, upon the whole, in the amount of about
$60. More than this sum I shall not pay. You state that
you can no longer afford to pay $50 per month for 2 or 3
pp. of MS. Your error here can be shown by reference to
the Magazine. During my year with you I have written —

In July	5pp	
„ August	9pp	
„ Sept.	16pp	
„ Oct.	4pp	
„ Nov.	5pp	
„ Dec.	12pp	
„ Jan.	9	
„ Feb.	12	
„ March	11	
„ April	17	
„ May	14 + 5 copied — Miss McMichael's MS.	
„ June	9 + 3 „	Chandlers
	132 [his arithmetic had gone astray]	

Dividing this sum by 12 we have an average of 11 pp. per
month — not 2 or 3. And this estimate leaves out of
question everything in the way of extract or compilation.
Nothing is counted but *bona fide* composition. 11 pp. at
$3 per p. would be $33, at the usual Magazine prices.
Deduct this from $50, my monthly salary, and we have
left $17 per month, or $4 25/100 per week, for the
services of proof-reading; general superintendence at the
printing office; reading, alteration and preparation of
MSS., with compilation of various articles, such as Plate
articles, Field sports, &c. Neither has anything been said of
my name upon your title page, a small item — you will say
— but still something, as you know. Snowden pays his
editresses $2 per week each for their names *solely*. Upon
the whole, I am not willing to admit that you have greatly
overpaid me. That I did not do four times as much as I did
for the Magazine was your own fault. At first I wrote long
articles, which you deemed inadmissable, and never did I
suggest any to which you had not some immediate and

decided objection. Of course I grew discouraged, and could feel no interest in the journal.

I am at a loss to know why you call me selfish. If you mean that I borrowed money of you — you know that you offered it, and you know that I am poor. In what instance has any one ever found me selfish? Was there selfishness in the affront I offered Benjamin (who I respect, and who spoke well of me) because I deemed it a duty not to receive from any one commendation at your expense? ... Place yourself in my situation and see whether you would not have acted as I have done. You first 'enforced', as you say, a deduction of salary: giving me to understand thereby that you thought of parting company. You next spoke disrespectfully of me behind my back — this as an habitual thing — to those whom you supposed your friends, and who punctually retailed to me, as a matter of course, every ill-natured word which you uttered. Lastly, you advertised your magazine for sale without saying a word to me about it. I felt no anger at what you did — none in the world. Had I not firmly believed it your design to give up your journal, with a view of attending to the Theatre, I should never have dreamed of attempting one of my own. The opportunity of doing something for myself seemed a good one — (and I was about to be thrown out of business) — and I embraced it. Now I ask you, as a man of honor and as a man of sense — what is there wrong in all this? What have I done at which you have any right to take offence? ... The charge of $100 I shall not admit for an instant. If you persist in it our intercourse is at an end, and we can each adopt our own measures.

> In the meantime, I am
> Yr. Obt. St.,
> Edgar A. Poe.

The magazine of his own to which Poe referred in that long and spirited letter was a dream which he would constantly try to realize. The opinions of first White and later Burton which he expressed in his letters show that he had little faith in the kind of people who were behind the journals of the day, indeed he regarded them as ignorant, arrogant and brutal, and it irked him to have to work for them. The obvious course was to raise the money to publish his own magazine, and his departure from the *Gentleman's*, together with its apparent difficulties, seemed to provide the ideal opportunity. On 13 June 1840, just two weeks after the final break with Burton, Poe inserted an announcement in the *Philadelphia Saturday Chronicle*, setting forth his personal vision of what a literary magazine should be:

PROSPECTUS
OF
THE PENN MAGAZINE,

A MONTHLY LITERARY JOURNAL,

To be edited and published in the City of Philadelphia

By EDGAR A. POE

TO THE PUBLIC. — Since resigning the conduct of the Southern Literary Messenger, at the commencement of its third year, I have always had in view the establishment of a Magazine which should retain some of the chief features of that journal, abandoning or greatly modifying the rest. Delay, however, has been occasioned by a variety of causes, and not until now have I found myself at liberty to attempt the execution of the design.

I will be pardoned for speaking more directly of the Messenger. Having in it no proprietary right, my objects too being at variance in many respects with those of its very worthy owner, I found difficulty in stamping upon its pages that *individuality* which I believe essential to the full success of all similar publications. In regard to their permanent influence, it appears to me that a continuous definite character, and a marked certainty of purpose, are requisites of vital importance; and I cannot help believing that these requisites are only attainable when one mind alone has the general direction of the undertaking. Experience has rendered obvious — what might indeed have been demonstrated *a priori* — that in founding a Magazine of my own lies my sole chance of carrying out to completion whatever peculiar intentions I may have entertained.

To those who remember the early days of the Southern periodical in question, it will be scarcely necessary to say that its main feature was a somewhat overdone causticity in its department of Critical Notices of new books. The Penn Magazine will retain this trait of severity insomuch only as the calmest yet sternest sense of justice will permit. Some years since elapsed may have mellowed down the petulance without interfering with the rigor of the critic. Most surely they have not yet taught him to read through the medium of a publisher's will, nor convinced him that the interests of letters are unallied with the interests of truth. It shall be the first and chief purpose of the Magazine now proposed to become known as one where may be found at all times, and upon all subjects, an honest and a fearless opinion. It shall be a leading object to assert in precept, and to maintain in practice, the rights, while in effect it demonstrates the advantages, of an absolutely independent criticism; — a criticism self-sustained; guiding itself only by the purest rules of Art; analyzing and urging these rules as it applies them; holding itself aloof from all personal bias; acknowledging no fear save that of outraging the right; yielding no point either to the vanity of the author, or to the assumptions of antique prejudice, or to the involute and anonymous cant of the Quarterlies, or to the arrogance of those organized *cliques* which, hanging on like nightmares upon American literature, manufacture, at the nod of our principal booksellers, a pseudo-public-opinion by wholesale. These are objects of which no man need be ashamed. They are purposes, moreover, whose novelty at least will give them interest. For assurance that I will fulfill them in the best spirit and to the very letter, I appeal with confidence to those friends, and especially to those Southern friends, who sustained me in the Messenger, where I had but a very partial opportunity of completing my own plans.

In respect to the other characteristics of the Penn Magazine a few words here will suffice.

It will endeavor to support the general interests of the republic of letters, without reference to particular regions — regarding the world at large as the true audience of the author. Beyond the precincts of literature, properly so called, it will leave in better hands the task of instruction upon all matters of *very* grave moment. Its aim chiefly shall be *to please* — and this through means of versatility, originality and pungency. It may be as well here to observe that nothing said in this Prospectus should be construed into a design of sullying the Magazine with any tincture of buffoonery, scurrility, or profanity, which are the blemish of some of the most vigorous of the European prints. In all branches of the literary department, the best aid, from the highest and purest sources, is secured.

To the mechanical execution of the work the greatest attention will be given which such a matter can require. In this respect it is proposed to surpass, by very much, the ordinary Magazine style. The form will somewhat resemble that of The Knickerbocker; the paper will be equal to that of The North American Review . . .

Of course, Poe was right in what he was trying to do, but at the same time he was reaching for the moon. Many are the editors and publishers who have failed to realize that in setting standards of perfection for themselves they are doing so for their readers, too, and rarely do such standards appear in enough people to make a publication viable. It is more comfortable, and may even be more sensible, to accept imperfections than to strive all the time for perfection, and it is the refusal to admit this that makes the idealist's task so hard. Standards there have to be, but if they are pitched too high, the normal, wayward human being will not only fail to reach them but will even stop trying to do so. One of the tragedies of Edgar Allan Poe was that he would never compromise his art.

The first issue of the 'Penn Magazine' was promised for January 1841, but Edgar was taken ill that winter and had to delay the launching until March. He was in high spirits when he wrote to Snodgrass on 17 January saying that the prospects for the magazine 'are *glorious*', but just as he was overcoming his internal difficulties external ones were massing. The fruits of the 1837 depression were still in evidence, and there was a new economic slump after the Whig Party defeated Van Buren's Democrats in the 1840 election for the Presidency. Poe had no chance of raising the capital he needed to start his magazine, even though he had built up a reasonable list of subscribers: 'It would have appeared under glorious auspices, and with capital at command, in March, as advertised, but for the unexpected bank suspensions,' he told Snodgrass. It seemed the fates were against him.

But the abandonment of the 'Penn' did not leave Edgar destitute. He had met a young Philadelphian, George Rex Graham, who had been a cabinet-maker, a lawyer, and had at length secured the position of an assistant editor on the *Saturday Evening Post*. Finding journalism to his liking, he bought a lowbrow monthly called the *Casket* and, when Burton put the *Gentleman's* up for sale in 1840, he decided to merge the two in a new magazine that would appeal to readers of all types — *Graham's Lady's and Gentleman's Magazine*, 'embracing every department of literature, embellished with engravings, fashions, and music arranged for a piano-forte, harp and guitar'. *Graham's* started with a circulation of five thousand and sought to improve on this by paying handsome fees to writers like Longfellow and Fenimore Cooper, but it needed above all the services of a skilful editor. Poe was certainly well thought of in Philadelphia journalistic circles at the time, and the ideals of the prospectus for the 'Penn Magazine' may well have appealed to George Graham, who was a shrewd judge of men. At any rate, he offered Edgar eight hundred dollars a year to edit his magazine, plus a page rate for his own writing. The salary was far from princely — Longfellow got fifty dollars for a single poem — but it was almost double what Burton had been paying, and at least Poe had the opportunity to increase his earnings with his pen. Although disappointed at the failure of his 'Penn' scheme, he set to work with a will, and as *Graham's* prospered under his care — the circulation rising to twenty-five thousand a month by the end of 1841 — he became one of the literary personalities of Philadelphia.

In April 1841 there appeared in *Graham's* the first of the detective stories — Poe called them tales of ratiocination — that so influenced the creator of Sherlock Holmes, Sir Arthur Conan Doyle. It was 'The Murders in the Rue Morgue', in which Poe, through the character of the amateur detective C. Auguste Dupin, solves a horrible and baffling murder through a staggering process of analysis. 'Poe transported the detective story from the group of tales of adventure into the group of portrayals of character,' a twentieth-century critic wrote. 'By bestowing upon it a human interest, he raised it in the literary scale.' It is not the mystery that captures the attention of the reader, but the process of solving it and the extraordinary analytical talents of the detective. Conan Doyle built a legend on this foundation, but it was Poe who gave him the idea. C. Auguste Dupin is the prototype of Sherlock Holmes.

Yet even as he settled in at *Graham's,* Edgar was reviving his plan for a magazine of his own, and hoping that George Graham would help him. In June 1841 he mentioned the idea in a letter to John P. Kennedy, citing the prospectus of the 'Penn' as an example of what the new publication would be like, and he also put a proposal to Longfellow, who was a regular contributor to *Graham's,* but nothing came of these approaches. At the same time, there was the prospect of a government job in Washington. The Whig President, General William Henry Harrison, had died in March after only a month in office, and had been succeeded by his Vice-President, John Tyler. The fact that Tyler was a Virginian prompted one of Poe's old Baltimore friends, Frederick Thomas, to suggest to Edgar that he might obtain one of the 'jobs for the boys' that followed the inauguration of the new President. Thomas, a lawyer, had himself found a place as a clerk in the Treasury Department. He asked Edgar:

> How would you like to be an office holder here at $1500 per year payable monthly by Uncle Sam, who, however slack he may be to his general creditors, pays his officials with due punctuality. How would you like it? You stroll to your office a little after nine in the morning leisurely, and you stroll from it a little after two in the afternoon homeward to dinner, and return no more that day. If, during office hours, you have anything to do, it is an agreeable relaxation from the monotonous laziness of the day. You have on your desk everything in the writing line in apple-pie order, and if you choose to lucubrate in a literary way, why you can lucubrate . . .

Edgar liked the idea very much. How different that sort of life was from the alarums and excursions of a magazine office. He told Thomas that in spite of Graham's 'unceasing civility and real kindness, I feel more and more dissatisfied with my situation'. He went on:

> Would to God I could do as you have done. Do you seriously think that an application on my part to Tyler would have a good result? My claims, to be sure, are few. I am a Virginian — at least I call myself one, for I have resided all my life, until within the last few years, in Richmond. My political principles have always been, as nearly as may be, with the existing administration, and I battled with right good will for Harrison, when opportunity offered. With Mr Tyler I have some slight personal acquaintance, although it is a matter which he has possibly forgotten. For the rest I am a literary man, and I see a disposition in Government to cherish letters. Have I any chance? I would be greatly indebted to you if you would reply to this as soon as you can, and tell if it would, in your opinion, be worth my while to make an effort; and, if so, put me on the right track. This could not be better done than by detailing to me your own mode of proceeding.

Thomas evidently did reply as soon as possible, suggesting that Edgar might employ the good offices of John P. Kennedy. Poe received the advice gratefully, and asked Thomas to approach

Kennedy on his behalf. He added: 'I wish to God I could visit Washington, but — the old story, you know — I have no money; not enough to take me there, saying nothing of getting back. It is a hard thing to be poor; but as I am kept so by an honest motive, I dare not complain.'

It is true that Poe had a natural sympathy with the Whigs, for they were the defenders of wealth and privilege which he so admired and to which he had once aspired. But.the Whigs had won the election by turning the tables on the Democrats and presenting themselves as representatives of the people. They had depended upon the personal appeal of Harrison, the military hero, but he had let them down by dying at the wrong moment, and the infuriated Democrats, not to mention a disaffected Whig faction led by a disappointed presidential candidate, Henry Clay, were giving Tyler a rough ride. The President had no time to worry about the future of an obscure literary man who had been adopted into his home state. Once again, Poe was out of luck.

So Edgar remained at *Graham's*, on the one hand nursing dreams of having his own magazine, and on the other producing splendid tales like 'A Descent into the Maelstrom', 'Eleonora', 'The Masque of the Red Death', and masterly criticism of such giants as Dickens and Macaulay (in the *Saturday Evening Post* of 1 May 1841, to which he contributed through Graham, he solved the murder in *Barnaby Rudge* having read only eleven chapters in a magazine serialization). His financial circumstances did not improve much, and neither did Virginia's health. George Graham later wrote: 'I have seen him hovering around her when she was ill, with all the fond fear and tender anxiety of a mother for her first-born — her slightest cough causing in him a shudder, a breast chill that was visible . . .' Graham also recalled that Poe handed his monthly salary straight to Mrs Clemm — 'twice only I remember his purchasing some rather expensive luxuries for his house', one of which was a piano for Virginia, who loved singing. 'His love for his wife was a sort of rapturous worship of the spirit of beauty which he felt was fading before his eyes,' Graham said. It must have been obvious by then, if it had not been before, that Virginia was suffering from consumption.

Yet in spite of the setbacks, and the fears about Virginia, Poe's artistic spirit remained unbowed. He worked steadily and was praised on all sides. In August 1841 he decided to attempt a new collection of his tales and wrote, rather optimistically, to Lea and Blanchard:

> Gentlemen: I wish to publish a new collection of my prose
> Tales with some such title as this: —

'The Prose Tales of Edgar A. Poe, including "The Murders in the Rue Morgue", the "Descent into the Maelstrom", and all his later pieces, with a second edition of the "Tales of the Grotesque and Arabesque".'

The later pieces will be eight in number, making the entire collection thirty-three, which would occupy two *thick* novel volumes.

He was not worried about receiving any money, only about getting his work into book form:

> I am anxious that your firm should continue to be my publishers, and, if you would be willing to bring out the book, I should be glad to accept the terms which you allowed me before, that is, you receive all profits, and allow me twenty copies for distribution to friends.

He had broken off relations with Lea and Blanchard after their curt letter concerning *Tales of the Grotesque and Arabesque*, but he was under the impression, as he told Snodgrass, that the book had sold out. The publishers were quick to enlighten him:

> Edgar A. Poe
> We have yrs of the 15th inst. in which you are kind enough to offer us a 'new collection of prose Tales'.
> In answer we very much regret to say that the state of affairs is such as to give little encouragement to new undertakings. As yet we have not got through the edition of the other work and up to this time it has not returned to us the expense of its publication. We assure you that we regret this on your account as well as on our own — as it would give us great pleasure to promote your views in relation to publication.

Another disappointment in a year of unfulfilled promises. But at least the little family had a roof over its head and food on its table at what one visitor described as 'a pretty little rose-covered cottage on the outskirts of Philadelphia'. As things turned out, they were days that could be looked back on with envy. The first intimation of decline came some time in January 1842. There was a small party at the Poe house, and Virginia was entertaining with a song. Suddenly she coughed, and blood trickled from her mouth. There was no doubt now that consumption was far advanced. It seemed she would die within hours, but once she had been seen by a doctor she recovered slightly, though she needed constant nursing. 'She could not bear the slightest exposure,' wrote one of the family's friends, A. B. Harris. 'All those conveniences as to apartment and surroundings which are so important in the case of an invalid were almost matters of life and death to her . . ..she lay for weeks, hardly able to breathe, except as she was fanned . . .' To Edgar it seemed that the horrible prophecy of 'Eleonora', lately published in *The Gift*, was coming true. Harris wrote that 'no one dared to speak, Mr Poe was so sensitive and irritable . . . And he would not allow a word about the danger of her dying; the mention of it drove him wild.'

Out of his mind with worry, and clinging to Virginia's life to save his own, as Roderick Usher had clung to his sister Madèline, Edgar, as might be expected, turned to drink, and the drink had its usual effect. Years later he wrote: 'I became insane, with long intervals of horrible sanity. During these fits of absolute unconsciousness I drank, God only knows how often or how much.' The course of Virginia's illness at the time, however, was not all downward. Sometimes it seemed that she would recover completely, and at those times Edgar was his old self. In March 1842, for instance, he was composed enough to write to Charles Dickens, then on his first visit to the United States, asking for an interview. Poe greatly admired Dickens's work, and in *Barnaby Rudge* had found the inspiration for what was to be his greatest poem, 'The Raven'. Dickens, who was staying at the United States Hotel in Philadelphia, replied considerately:

> My Dear Sir, — I shall be very glad to see you whenever you will do me the favour to call. I think I am more likely to be in the way between half past eleven and twelve than at any other time. I have glanced over the books you have been so kind as to send me, and more particularly at the papers to which you called my attention. I have the greater pleasure in expressing my desire to see you on this account . . .

Poe must have made a very favourable impression on the great English novelist, for when he returned home Dickens tried vainly to persuade a London publisher to handle Poe's work. In November 1842 he wrote to Edgar: 'Do not for a moment suppose that I have ever thought of you but with a pleasant recollection; and that I am not at all times prepared to forward your views in this country.' On his second visit to America, many years after Poe's death, Dickens visited old Mrs Clemm and gave her some money.

Sometimes what Poe's contemporaries were pleased to call his 'irregular' behaviour — which I have indicated was probably not drunkenness but the effect of drinking on a weakened constitution — caused difficulties in the *Graham's* office. George Graham began to find Edgar eccentric and querulous and partly because of that, also because the magazine was expanding rapidly, he took on an associate editor to complement the editorial staff of four he had hired the previous winter. Poe had never been entirely committed to his job, as witness his attempts not only to revive plans for his own magazine but also to get a post in Washington, and his anxiety over Virginia made him even less interested. Graham understood the problem, and sympathized, but he was running what had become the country's best monthly journal and, reluctant as he was to part with Edgar, the magazine had to come first. Edgar left in May 1842, telling Frederick Thomas:

> My reason for resigning was disgust with the namby-pamby characteristics of the Magazine — a character which it was impossible to eradicate. I allude to the contemptible pictures, fashion-plates, music and love-tales. The salary, moreover, did not pay me for the labour which I was forced to bestow. With Graham, who is really a very gentlemanly, although an exceedingly weak man, I had no misunderstanding.

He was succeeded by the recently acquired associate editor, the Reverend Rufus W. Griswold, a Baptist minister and literary publicist who had worked on several newspapers in Boston and New York and who had just published a popular anthology entitled *Poets and Poetry of America*, which included some verses and a biographical sketch of Poe. If there was one man whom Poe's ghost should have haunted it was Griswold, for it was he who, almost single-handed, blackened Poe's character after his death and consigned him to the obscurity that allowed his work to be ignored for so many years. But Griswold's lies and distortions were for the future, and in 1842 Edgar had nothing against him — indeed the two were quite friendly; 'I have no quarrel with either Mr Graham or Mr Griswold'.

But, quarrel or not, Edgar was out of a job. In the letter to Thomas quoted above he asked again if there was any chance of his obtaining a government post, but it is almost certain that the hopes held out by Thomas were entirely without foundation. There remained the prospect of the 'Penn Magazine' and he began to try to raise interest in it again. At the same time he was attempting to have his cherished second edition of the Tales published, and he prepared an elaborate two-volume selection which he called 'Phantasy Pieces'. It never appeared in print.

Meanwhile, the family had put the 'rose-covered cottage' behind them and moved back into the centre of Philadelphia, to Spring Garden, near the journalists' quarter. This time it was not a question of health, but of money. The 'good days', such as they were, had come to an end.

Chapter 12

Down and Out

It was like the early days in Baltimore all over again. Thomas Mayne Reid, the Irish-born author of such adventure stories as *Rifle Rangers* and *The Headless Horseman*, visited the Poes frequently at Spring Garden and later described their way of life:

> Mrs Clemm was the ever-vigilant guardian of the home, watching it against the silent but continuous sap of necessity, that appeared every day to be approaching closer and nearer. She was the sole servant, keeping everything clean; the sole messenger, doing the errands, making pilgrimages between the poet and his publishers, frequently bringing back such chilling responses as 'The article not accepted', or 'The check not to be given until such and such a day', — often too late for his necessities. And she was also the messenger to the market; from it bringing back not 'the delicacies of the season', but only such commodities as were called for by the dire exigencies of hunger.

Throughout the summer and early autumn of 1842 there was still some hope of that government post for Edgar. Thomas wrote to say that he had enlisted the aid of the President's son, Rob Tyler, and that appointments were about to be made to the Custom House in Philadelphia. In June, after a short visit to New York in an unsuccessful attempt to sell his 'Phantasy Pieces', Edgar wrote to another Washington friend thanking him for his efforts in regard to the Custom House appointment, 'which has become so vitally necessary to me', and thanking him also for the gift of twenty dollars. In September, Thomas visited Philadelphia to deliver a political address, but Edgar could not attend because he was 'too ill to venture out'. Thomas, apparently unaware that the Poes had moved, looked for them at their former home near Fairmount Park. In November, the Custom House appointments were published. Edgar wrote to Thomas:

My Dear Friend, — Your letter of the 14th gave me new
hope — only to be dashed to the ground. On the day of its
receipt, some of the papers announced four removals and
appointments. Among the latter I observed the name —
Pogue. Upon inquiry among those behind the curtain, I
soon found that no such person as — Pogue had any expectation of an appointment, and that the name was a mis-
print or rather a misunderstanding of the reporters, who
had heard *my own* name spoken of at the Custom
House . . .'

But he was wrong. After waiting in an agony of suspense for two
days, he called at the Custom House and inquired of a Mr Smith, 'a
Whig of the worst stamp', if there was a job for him, mentioning Rob
Tyler's name. Mr Smith took the use of the name as a slight upon the
President, and replied pompously, according to Poe: 'Hem! I have
received orders from *President* Tyler to make no more appointments,
and shall make none.' Edgar ended his letter: 'I would write more,
my dear Thomas, but my heart is too heavy. You have felt the
misery of hope deferred, and will feel for me.'

Desperation had driven him to sell two stories, 'The Mystery of
Marie Roget' — again featuring the detective Dupin, and based on a
real murder in New York — and 'The Landscape Garden', to the
rather unedifying *Snowden's Lady's Companion*, then he noticed the
announcement of a new magazine to be published in Boston by
James Russell Lowell, whose poetry he had praised in *Graham's*.
Edgar lost no time in writing to Lowell:

Dr Sir, — Learning your design of commencing a Magazine,
in Boston, upon the first of January next, I take the
liberty of asking whether some arrangement might not be
made, by which I should become a regular contributor.

I should be glad to furnish a short article each month —
of such character as might be suggested by yourself — and
upon such terms as you could afford 'in the beginning'.

That your success will be marked and permanent I will
not doubt. At all events, I most sincerely wish you well;
for no man in America has excited in me so much admiration — and, therefore, none so much of respect and
esteem . . .

Lowell, who admired Poe's talent but later came to despise his
weakness of character, accepted his offer, and Edgar took his place in
the new magazine, *The Pioneer*, alongside Nathaniel Hawthorne and

Washington Irving. His first piece, published in the inaugural issue, was 'The Tell-Tale Heart', which he had passed on to Lowell after it had been rejected by the editor of the Boston *Miscellany*, whom Edgar had once referred to as 'insufferably tedious and dull'. Like 'William Wilson', it is a story of conscience: a murderer is driven to confess his crime by the ghostly thumping of his victim's heart. It is also one of a number of stories in which the narrator vehemently denies that he is mad — Edgar's fear of insanity, like Roderick Usher's, was growing under the strain of his soul-mate's precarious health. Yet Poe retained a keen interest in professional matters. Shortly after the first issue of *The Pioneer* appeared in January 1843 he wrote to Lowell:

> For some weeks I have been daily proposing to write and congratulate you upon the triumphant debut of the 'Pioneer', but have been prevented by a crowd of more worldly concerns.
>
> Thank you for the compliment of the foot-note. Thank you, also, for your attention in forwarding the Magazine.
>
> As far as a $3 Magazine can please me at all, I am delighted with yours. I am especially gratified with what seems to me a certain coincidence of opinion and of taste, between yourself and your humble servant, in the minor arrangements, as well as in the more important details of the journal, for example — the poetry in the same type as the prose — the designs from Flaxman — &c. As regards the contributors our thoughts are one. Do you know that when, some time since, I dreamed of establishing a Magazine of my own, I said to myself — 'If I can but succeed in engaging, as permanent contributors, Mr Hawthorne, Mr Neal, and two others, with a certain young poet of Boston, who shall be nameless, I will engage to produce the best journal in America.' At the same time, while I thought, and still think highly of Mr Bryant, Mr Cooper, and others, I said nothing of *them*.
>
> You have many warm friends in this city — but the reforms you propose require time in their development, and it may be even a year before 'The Pioneer' will make due impression among the Quakers. In the meantime, persevere . . .
>
> I duly received from Mr Graham, $10 on your account, for which I am obliged. I would prefer, however, that you would remit directly to myself through the P. Office . . .

Encouraged by Lowell's example, Edgar issued a few weeks later yet another prospectus for his own magazine. He had found a partner in Thomas C. Clarke, owner of the Philadelphia weekly the *Saturday Museum*, which towards the end of February published a long biographical article about Poe, together with a portrait and a number of his poems. Another interested party was Felix Darley, who was contracted to provide illustrations for the new magazine. He recalled Poe as 'a refined and very gentlemanly man; exceedingly neat in his person; interesting always, from the intellectual character of his mind, which appeared to me to be tinged with sadness. His manner was quiet and reserved; he rarely smiled.' The prospectus was published in the *Saturday Museum* on 4 March 1843: the new magazine was to be called 'The Stylus', and its objects were to be the same as those of the abortive 'Penn'. Poe wanted what would now be described as an up-market publication, hence his rather scathing comment about the three-dollar *Pioneer* in the letter to Lowell. 'The Stylus' would appeal to 'the *true* intellect of the land' rather than currying popular favour.

Early in March, Edgar travelled to Washington, ostensibly to collect subscriptions for 'The Stylus' but also to try once more for a government job. Unfortunately he was entertained too well, and on 12 March his friend J. E. Dow had a sorry tale to tell Thomas Clarke:

Dear Sir, — I deem it to be my bounded duty to write you this hurried letter in relation to our mutual friend E.A.P.

He arrived here a few days since. On the first evening he seemed somewhat excited, having been over-persuaded to take some Port wine.

On the second day he kept pretty steady, but since then he has been, at intervals, quite unreliable.

He exposes himself here to those who may injure him very much with the President, and thus prevents us from doing for him what we wish to do and what we can do if he is himself again in Philadelphia. He does not understand the ways of politicians, nor the manner of dealing with them to advantage. How should he?

Mr Thomas is not well and cannot go home with Mr P. My business and the health of my family will prevent me from so doing.

Under all the circumstances of the case, I think it advisable for you to come on and see him safely back to his home. Mrs Poe is in a bad state of health, and I charge you, as you have a soul to be saved, to say not one word to her about him until he arrives with you. I shall expect you or an answer to this letter by return of mail.

Should you not come, we will see him on board the cars bound to Phila., but we fear he might be detained in Baltimore and not be out of harm's way.

I do this under a solemn responsibility. Mr Poe has the highest order of intellect, and I cannot bear that he should be the sport of senseless creatures who, like oysters, keep sober, and gape and swallow everything.

I think your good judgment will tell you what course you ought to pursue in this matter, and I cannot think it will be necessary to let him know that I have written you this letter; but I cannot suffer him to injure himself here without giving you this warning.

Poe apparently recovered himself during the next few days, and on 15 March arrived alone and, as he put it, 'in perfect safety, and *sober*' in Philadelphia, where Mrs Clemm was waiting for him. Next day he wrote to Dow and Thomas asking them to pass on apologies for his behaviour in Washington and promising to repay some money he had borrowed from them. He said he was ill, had taken some medicine, and was staying indoors for the day. To this letter Thomas added a note to the effect that accounts of Poe's drinking bouts were greatly exaggerated and that he suffered gravely for them, becoming very ill, which accords with the idea that he was a diabetic.

The Washington debacle, however, did not seriously damage Poe in the eyes of his partner, and plans for 'The Stylus' went ahead. The example of *The Pioneer* was soon removed: the magazine folded after the March issue, leaving Lowell sick with ophthalmia and heavily in debt. Edgar wrote to him on 27 March:

My Dear Friend, — I have just received yours of the 24th and am deeply grieved, first that you should have been so unfortunate, and, secondly, that you should have thought it necessary to offer me any apology for your misfortunes. As for the few dollars you owe me — give yourself not one moment's concern about *them*. I am poor, but must be very much poorer, indeed, when I even think of demanding them.

But I sincerely hope all is not so bad as you suppose it, and that, when you come to look about you, you will be able to continue 'The Pioneer'. Its decease, just now, would be a most severe blow to the good cause — the cause of a Pure Taste. I have looked upon your Magazine, from

its outset, as the best in America, and have lost no opportunity of expressing the opinion . . .

. . . On the first of July next I hope to issue the first
number of 'The Stylus', a new monthly, with some novel
features. I send you, also, a paper containing the Prospectus. In a few weeks I hope to forward you a specimen
sheet. I am anxious to get a poem from yourself for the
opening number, but, until you recover your health, I fear
that I should be wrong in making the request . . .

It was not to be. In June 'The Stylus' project was abandoned.
Presumably Clarke got cold feet — Poe called him an idiot in a letter
to Lowell announcing that the magazine was stillborn. But the news
was not all bad. That same month, Edgar earned a hundred dollars
with his story 'The Gold Bug', which won a competition run by *The
Dollar Newspaper*, where it was published in two parts on 21 and 28
June. Two months later the *United States Saturday Post* (the
temporarily renamed *Saturday Evening Post*) printed 'The Black Cat', a
drunkard's nightmare.

. . . my general temperament and character — through the
instrumentality of the fiend Intemperance — had (I blush
to confess it) experienced a radical alteration for the
worse. I grew, day by day, more moody, more irritable,
more regardless of the feelings of others. I suffered myself
to use intemperate language to my wife. At length, I even
offered her personal violence . . .

Poe obviously realized the risks he was running when he took a drink.

One night, returning home, much intoxicated, from one of
my haunts about town, I fancied that the cat avoided my
presence. I seized him; when, in his fright at my violence,
he inflicted a slight wound upon my hand with his teeth.
The fury of a demon instantly possessed me. I knew myself no longer. My original soul seemed, at once, to take its
flight from my body; and a more than fiendish malevolence,
gin-nurtured, thrilled every fibre of my frame. I took from
my waistcoat pocket a pen-knife, opened it, grasped the
poor beast by the throat, and deliberately cut one of its eyes
from the socket!

It is Poe's ability to lay bare his own inner torment that gives his
tales their special quality, that places them far above what are
generally called 'horror stories'. On the one hand Edgar was the

victim of these terrible uncertainties, fears and urges, and yet on the
other there was a part of his mind that could rise above them, look
down upon them with dispassionate interest, and describe them with
a sort of mystical reverence. The strange thing is that the setting
down of the awful visions does not seem to have been therapeutic in
Poe's case. No sooner had his artistic self finished its work than he
was back in his nightmare world again, a weak, slight, rather pathetic
figure wounded by 'the slings and arrows of outrageous fortune' and
completely unable to come to grips with the life he had chosen and
in which he was trapped. It is astonishing that the 'artistic self'
remained apparently undamaged as Poe's tortures worsened and his
decline accelerated. In the midst of all his troubles of 1843 —
'domestic and pecuniary', he told Lowell — among all his broken
dreams, and in spite of his periodic drinking, he continued to write
steadily, not only tales but also criticism, which was published in
Graham's. He even tried to circulate his 'Prose Romances' in a new
form, persuading a Philadelphia publisher to bring out a serial
edition, 'each number complete in itself', at twelve and a half cents a
volume. The first number, containing 'The Murders in the Rue
Morgue' and 'The Man That Was Used Up', sold so few copies that no
more were issued.

That he was desperately hard up during this period is not in doubt.
Any scruples he had entertained about asking the downcast Lowell
for the money *The Pioneer* owed him were quickly forgotten; he
could not afford to ignore even ten dollars. Rufus Griswold claimed,
too, that Edgar approached him for money, in the following terms:

> Dear Griswold: — Can you not send me $5? I am sick, and
> Virginia is almost gone. Come and see me. Peterson [who
> worked in the *Graham's* office] says you suspect me of a
> curious anonymous letter. I did not write it, but bring it
> along with you when you make the visit you promised to
> Mrs Clemm. I will try to fix that matter soon. Could you
> do anything with my *note*?
>
> > Yours truly,
> > E.A.P.

The letter, which was published in Griswold's memoir of Poe in
1850, was said by that worthy to have been written on 11 June
1843. There is no trace of the original, which might seem suspicious
in view of the fact that Griswold forged several 'Poe letters'. Certainly Edgar had no very high opinion of his successor at *Graham's*
(he told Lowell that Griswold 'lacks independence, or judgment, or
both'), but that would not necessarily have prevented him from

seeking a loan. Proud Poe was, but not too proud to seek help from any quarter whence it might be offered.

At the turn of the year, Edgar found a new outlet: the lecture circuit. He had a good speaking voice, and much has been said about his pleasing appearance. People were happy to pay twenty-five cents apiece to listen to him. His debut was in Baltimore at the end of January 1844, when he spoke on American poetry, reading examples in his fine clear voice with its musical Southern intonation. He gave the same talk in several other places and, perhaps in order to add distinction to his presence, began to sport the moustache shown in the portraits of him most frequently reproduced tóday. Part of the lecture was a fierce attack on *Poets and Poetry of America*, which had then just gone into a third edition and which was edited, of course, by Rufus W. Griswold, who based his selections not on merit but on the favours he received or might expect from the versifiers he chose. The *Saturday Museum* had carried a notice of the third edition which had ridiculed Griswold in bitter terms and contrasted him unfavourably with none other than Edgar Allan Poe. If Griswold had his suspicions regarding the authorship of that review, they were no doubt confirmed by Edgar's lectures. Several years later Griswold was to find that revenge was sweet.

Still Edgar clung to the dream of a literary magazine of real quality. On 30 March 1844 he wrote to Lowell, by then fully recovered from his eye trouble and celebrating the success of his second published volume of poetry:

> How dreadful is the present condition of our Literature! To what are things tending? We want two things, certainly:— an International Copy-Right Law, and a well-founded Monthly Journal, of sufficient ability, circulation, and character, to control and so give tone to, our Letters. It should be, externally, a specimen of high but not too refined Taste:— I mean, it should be boldly printed, on excellent paper, in single column, and be illustrated, not merely embellished, by spirited wood designs . . . Its chief aims should be Independence, Truth, Originality. It should be a journal of some 120 pp., and furnished at $5. It should have nothing to do with Agents or Agencies. Such a Magazine might be made to exercise a prodigious influence, and would be a source of vast wealth to its proprietors. There *can* be no reason why 100,000 copies might not, in one or two years, be circulated; but the means of bringing it into circulation should be radically different from those usually employed.

Such a journal might, perhaps, be set on foot by a coalition, and, thus set on foot, with proper understanding, would be irresistible. Suppose, for example, that the elite of our men of letters should combine secretly. Many of them control papers &c. Let each subscribe, say $200, for the commencement of the undertaking; furnishing other means, as required from time to time, until the work be established. The articles to be supplied by the members solely, and upon a concerted plan of action. A nominal editor to be elected from among the number. How could such a journal fail? I would like very much to hear your opinion upon this matter. Could not the 'ball be set in motion'? If we do *not* defend ourselves by some such coalition, we shall be devoured, without mercy, by the Godeys, the Snowdens [proprietors of popular magazines] , *et id genus omne.*

Nowadays such artists' cooperatives as Poe described are commonplace, but in 1844 the idea was ahead of its time by a long way, and Edgar was forced to rely on the Godeys, the Snowdens and their like. He had tried to raise them up by his own vision; he had offered them some of the most acute literary criticism America had ever seen; he had given them some of the finest 'tales of the grotesque and arabesque' the world has ever known; and they had failed him. It is not difficult to imagine the depression, the despair that inspired during his time in Philadelphia the first poem he had written in three years. It was first published by *Graham's* in January 1843, and its title is 'The Conqueror Worm':

Lo! 'tis a gala night
   Within the lonesome latter years!
An angel throng, bewinged, bedight
   In veils, and drowned in tears,
Sit in a theatre, to see
   A play of hopes and fears,
While the orchestra breathes fitfully
   The music of the spheres.

Mimes, in the form of God on high,
   Mutter and mumble low,
And hither and thither fly —
   Mere puppets they, who come and go
At bidding of vast formless things
   That shift the scenery to and fro,

Flapping from out their Condor wings
   Invisible Woe!

That motley drama — oh, be sure
   It shall not be forgot!
With its Phantom chased for evermore
   By a crowd that seize it not,
Through a circle that ever returneth in
   To the self-same spot,
And much of Madness, and more of Sin,
   And Horror the soul of the plot.

But see, amid the mimic rout
   A crawling shape intrude!
A blood-red thing that writhes from out
   The scenic solitude!
It writhes! — it writhes! — with mortal pangs
   The mimes become its food,
And the seraphs sob at vermin fangs
   In human gore imbued.

Out — out are the lights — out all!
   And, over each quivering form,
The curtain, a funeral pall,
   Comes down with the rush of a storm,
And the angels, all pallid and wan,
   Uprising, unveiling, affirm
That the play is the tragedy 'Man,'
   And its hero the Conqueror Worm.

There was little in the rest of that long, miserable, poverty-stricken year to dispel such gloomy thoughts. Any relief was purely temporary, and was more than compensated for by the ever-present fears for Virginia's life. Philadelphia, the Cradle of Liberty, had done its best and its worst for Edgar Allan Poe. By the spring of 1844 there was nothing left in either direction. Taking advantage of an improvement in Virginia's health, Edgar instructed Mrs Clemm to sell what she could of their belongings that remained in the Spring Garden home and, with no more than about ten dollars in his pocket, booked himself and his wife on a train for New York. Twice before he had tried to establish himself in the metropolis and twice he had failed. Perhaps it would be third time lucky.

Chapter 13

War of Words

The letter Edgar wrote to Mrs Clemm the day after the Poes' arrival in New York is not only the most intimate piece of his correspondence to have survived, but it also shows clearly how close he was to his mother-in-law, upon whom he was coming to depend more and more. If proof is needed of how much store Edgar set by his family, this letter provides it:

> New York, Sunday Morning,
> April 7, just after breakfast.

My Dear Muddy,

We have just this minute done breakfast, and I now sit down to write you about everything. I can't pay for the letter, because the P.O. won't be open to-day. In the first place we arrived safe at Walnut St wharf. The driver wanted me to pay a dollar, but I wouldn't. Then I had to pay a boy a levy to put the trunks in the baggage car. In the meantime I took Sis in the Depot Hotel. It was only a quarter past six, and we had to wait till seven. We saw the Ledger and Times — nothing in either — a few words of no account in the Chronicle. We started in good spirits but did not get here until nearly three o'clock. We went in the cars to Amboy, about forty miles from N. York, and then took the steamboat the rest of the way. Sissy coughed none at all. When we got to the wharf it was raining hard. I left her on board the boat, after putting the trunks in the Ladies' cabin, and set off to buy an umbrella and look for a boarding house. I met a man selling umbrellas, and bought one for twenty-five cents. Then I went up Greenwich St and soon found a boarding house. It is just before you get to Cedar St, on the west side going up — the left-hand side. It has brown stone steps, with a porch with brown pillars. 'Morrison' is the name on the door. I made a bargain in a few minutes and then got a hack and went for Sis. I was not gone more than half an hour, and she was quite astonished to see me back so soon. She didn't expect me for an hour. There were two other ladies waiting on board — so she wasn't very lonely. When we got to the house we had to wait about half an hour before the room was ready. the house is old and looks buggy . . . the cheapest board I ever knew, taking into consideration the central situation and the *living*. I wish Kate [Catterina, the family cat] could see it — she would faint. Last night, for supper, we had the nicest tea you ever drank, strong and hot — wheat bread and rye bread — cheese — tea-cakes (elegant), a great dish (two dishes) of elegant ham, and two of cold veal, piled up like a mountain and large slices — three dishes of the cakes and everything in the greatest profusion. No fear of starving here. The landlady seemed as if she couldn't press us enough, and we were at home directly. Her husband is living with her — a fat, good-natured old soul. There are eight or ten boarders — two or three of them ladies — two servants. For breakfast we had excellent-flavored coffee, hot and strong — not very clear and no great deal of cream — veal cutlets, elegant ham and eggs and nice bread and butter. I never sat down to a more plentiful or a nicer breakfast. I wish you could have seen the eggs — and the great dishes of meat. I ate the first hearty breakfast I have ever eaten since I left our little home. Sis is delighted, and we are both in excellent spirits. She has coughed hardly any and had no night sweat. She is now busy mending my pants which I tore against a nail. I went out last night and bought a skein of silk, a skein of thread, two buttons, a pair of slippers, and a tin pan for the stove. The fire kept in all night. We have now got four dollars and a half left. To-morrow I am going to try and borrow three dollars, so that I may have a fortnight to go upon. I feel in excellent spirits and haven't drank a drop — so that I hope soon to get out of trouble. The very instant I scrape together enough money I will send it on. You can't imagine how we both do miss you. Sissy had a hearty cry last night, because you and Catterina weren't here. We are resolved to get two rooms the first moment we can. In the mean time it is impossible we could be more comfortable or more at home than we are. It looks as if it were going to clear up now. Be sure and go to the P.O. and have my letters forwarded. As soon as I write Lowell's article, I will send it to you, and get you to get the money from Graham. Give our best love to C[atterina].

No sign there of the dark, brooding Poe, of Edgar the sick, helpless drunk, or of Edgar A. Poe the literary idealist and seeker after beauty. In that New York boarding house he is, for the moment, homely 'Eddy', appreciating a comfortable room and a good meal, his little wife beside him mending his trousers. Yet it is pointless to pretend that the letter gives a glimpse of the Poe who might have been had life been kinder to him. His nature did have its darker side , his mental balance was unstable, he was possessed at times by what he called 'The Imp of the Perverse', and for him life could not have been otherwise. Even if he had grown up in the comfort and wealth of John Allan's home it would have made no difference. Edgar Allan Poe was a doomed man.

Thoughts of doom, however, were far from Edgar's mind as he set out to conquer New York. One of his first calls was at the offices of the *New York Sun*, where he presented the editor with an elaborately constructed piece of journalistic fiction which pretended that the Atlantic had been crossed by balloon. Such tricks were popular at the time, and the *Sun* knew a winner when it saw one. On 13 April its headlines read: 'Astounding News by Express, via Norfolk! The Atlantic Crossed in Three Days, Signal Triumph of Mr Monck Mason's Flying Machine! Arrival at Sullivan's Island, near Charleston, S.C.' At least Edgar could describe the landing site convincingly: he had seen enough of it during his time at Fort Moultrie. 'The Balloon Hoax' was a huge success. Crowds besieged the *Sun* offices for hours waiting for a promised 'Extra' giving the full story, and when it appeared they paid up to fifty cents a copy for the penny paper. It was a promising start, though not a trick to be repeated too often and, as a mere nine-day wonder, it was not going to pay for bed and board. More substantial work was needed.

Fortunately Edgar had not been completely dazzled by the beacon of New York and had fixed himself up with a correspondent's job for the *Spy* in Columbia, Pennsylvania, to which he regularly contributed his views of Gotham (a name frequently applied to New York after about 1800, presumably coming from the English village of the same name which became synonymous with stupidity). Present day New Yorkers might wish their city were still as Poe described it in May 1844: 'When you visit Gotham, you should ride out the Fifth Avenue, as far as the distributing reservoir, near Forty-third Street, I believe. The prospect of the walk around the reservoir is particularly beautiful. You can see . . . a large portion of the harbour, and long reaches of the Hudson and East rivers.' He was prophetic about the picturesque Manhattan coastline: 'In twenty years, or thirty at farthest, we shall see here nothing more romantic than shipping, warehouses, and wharves.' What would he have said a century later?

In May Mrs Clemm completed the sale of the family's effects in Philadelphia and joined her daughter and son-in-law. As luck would have it, she had sold something that was not theirs to sell — a volume of the *Southern Literary Messenger* which Edgar had borrowed from his friend Henry B. Hirst, who had in turn borrowed it from William J. Duane, a former United States Treasury Secretary and thus a man of some importance. Edgar had reminded Mrs Clemm, in his first letter from New York, to return the book to Hirst, but by then she had already sold it to a Philadelphia bookseller and could not, or would not, reclaim it. Nothing more was said about the matter until October 1844, when Edgar received a letter from Duane seeking the return of the book. Poe questioned Mrs Clemm, who said she had done as he asked and returned the volume to Hirst. Edgar then wrote a rather haughty letter to Duane accusing Hirst of having deposited the book on a shelf and forgotten about it. 'A damned lie,' cried Hirst when Duane put this to him. The book finally turned up in Richmond and Duane was forced to buy it back, even though his name was on the title-page. Poe was furious when he found out but he still defended his mother-in-law, telling Duane to take up the argument with Hirst. Naturally the story got about in Philadelphia, seriously damaging Edgar's reputation. Duane asked him to send the five dollars it had cost to repurchase the book, but, as he himself commented, Poe 'died without doing so, I suppose from inability'. It was a silly and unnecessary little scandal arising in the first place from Mrs Clemm's fear of upsetting her 'son' by telling him the truth and later from her determination that he should not be forced to apologize for something she had done — she preferred that he should brazen it out.

Mrs Clemm presumably boarded with Edgar and Virginia in Greenwich Street for a few weeks, until they all moved into the home of Mr and Mrs Patrick Brennan about five miles out of the city overlooking the Hudson. Edgar had discovered the Brennans' farm during one of the rambles on which he collected material for his *Spy* column, and thinking the country air would be good for Virginia, he asked the kindly family to take them in as boarders. In the peace of the countryside, he settled down to write. He had been experiencing difficulty in selling his tales — half a dozen were in the hands of various editors — but he worked unremittingly, and in July had the satisfaction of seeing 'The Premature Burial' published in the *Dollar Newspaper*. The following month, 'Mesmeric Revelation', an exploration of the afterlife through the then fashionable and exciting medium of hypnosis, appeared in the *Columbian Magazine*, and in

September *Godey's Lady's Book* printed 'The Oblong Box', the story of a husband's attempts to transport his wife's body in secret. Death and its terrors were still very much on Edgar's mind, though at this time the reasons were probably more commercial than psychological. For instance, 'The Premature Burial' played on a common nineteenth-century fear that an attack of catalepsy might be mistaken for death and that the sufferer would be consigned to the grave too soon. (Even men like Hans Christian Andersen and Wilkie Collins carried notes detailing elaborate instructions to be carried out before it was assumed that they were dead.) He was in mischievous mood, too, as witness 'The Literary Life of Thingum Bob', published in the good old *Messenger*, which took a swipe at literary magazines in general and in particular at Lewis Gaylord Clark, whose paragraphs 'were so vigorous and altogether stout, that they seemed not particularly disconcerted by any extreme of position, but looked equally happy and satisfactory, whether on their heads, or on their heels'. That was reopening old wounds Poe had inflicted on the editor of the *Knickerbocker*.

The tenor of Poe's life during this period is reflected in a letter he wrote to Frederick Thomas on 8 September:

> I have been playing the hermit in earnest, nor have I seen a living soul out of my family — who are well and desire to be kindly remembered. When I say 'well', I only mean (as regards Virginia) as well as usual. Her health remains excessively precarious ... I am working at a variety of things (all of which you shall behold in the end) — and with an ardor of which I did not believe myself capable ...

Life on the Brennans' farm was cheap but not free, and the few dollars Edgar was earning here and there from his writing barely provided the necessities of life. The storming of New York was taking longer than he had perhaps expected and the contacts he had maintained elsewhere were proving none too fruitful. Ever the optimist, he had another attempt at getting 'The Stylus' off the ground, again in vain, and he tried to interest Harpers in publishing a new volume of his works — but Harpers had not forgotten the affair of *The Conchologist's First Book*. Things were beginning to look pretty desperate once more, when Mrs Clemm intervened. She was acting as Edgar's copy-runner while he remained at home working, and one of her calls was at the offices of the New York *Evening Mirror*, where she met the editor, Nathaniel Parker Willis, and won his sympathy with a countenance made 'beautiful and saintly by an evident complete giving up of her life to privation and sorrowful tenderness'. The hard days of her early widowhood in Baltimore had aroused in Mrs Clemm a talent for evoking sympathy, and the life she subsequently shared with Poe gave her plenty of further practice. Before she left Willis's office, he had agreed to hire Edgar as a critic and sub-editor (or 'mechanical paragraphist' as he put it). Mrs Clemm must have been delighted with herself: now there would be a salary coming in.

Willis found Poe a courteous and conscientious worker. He had not touched alcohol since leaving Philadelphia, and he was 'at his desk in the office from nine in the morning till the evening paper went to press'. In a tribute published shortly after Edgar's death Willis added:

> With the highest admiration for his genius, and a willing-
> ness to let it atone for more than ordinary irregularity, we
> were led by common report to expect a very capricious
> attention to his duties, and occasionally a scene of violence
> and difficulty. Time went on, however, and he was invari-
> ably punctual and industrious. With his pale, beautiful, and
> intellectual face, as a reminder of what genius was in him,
> it was impossible, of course, not to treat him always with
> deferential courtesy, and to our occasional request that he
> would not probe too deep in a criticism, or that he would
> erase a passage colored too highly with his resentments
> against society and mankind, he readily and courteously
> assented . . .

Back on the treadmill Edgar might have been, but he could rest secure in the knowledge that his 'playing the hermit' had produced something wonderful — his best known poem, 'The Raven'. The poem is chiefly noted for its rhythmic power and hypnotic sonority — indeed it has been called an elocutionist's delight. When one delves behind its verbal virtues, however, it can be seen almost as an auto-biography of Edgar Poe.

> Once upon a midnight dreary, while I pondered, weak and weary,
> Over many a quaint and curious volume of forgotten lore —
> While I nodded, nearly napping, suddenly there came a tapping,
> As of some one gently rapping — rapping at my chamber door.
> ''Tis some visitor,' I muttered, 'tapping at my chamber door —
>   Only this and nothing more.'
>
> Ah, distinctly I remember, it was in the bleak December,
> And each separate dying ember wrought its ghost upon the floor.
> Eagerly I wished the morrow; — vainly I had sought to borrow

From my books surcease of sorrow — sorrow for the lost Lenore —
For the rare and radiant maiden whom the angels name Lenore —
    Nameless here for evermore.

And the silken sad uncertain rustling of each purple curtain
Thrilled me — filled me with fantastic terrors never felt before;
So that now, to still the beating of my heart, I stood repeating
''Tis some visitor entreating entrance at my chamber door —
Some late visitor entreating entrance at my chamber door; —
    This it is and nothing more.'

After the speaker has long stood there 'wondering, fearing/
Doubting, dreaming dreams no mortal ever dared to dream
before'. . .

Open here I flung the shutter, when, with many a flirt and flutter,
In there stepped a stately Raven of the saintly days of yore;
Not the least obeisance made he; not an instant stopped or stayed he;
But, with mien of lord or lady, perched above my chamber door —
Perched upon a bust of Pallas just above my chamber door —
    Perched, and sat, and nothing more.

Then this ebony bird beguiling my sad fancy into smiling,
By the grave and stern decorum of the countenance it wore,
'Though thy crest be shorn and shaven, thou,' I said, 'art sure no craven,
Ghastly grim and ancient Raven wandering from the Nightly shore —
Tell me what thy lordly name is on the Night's Plutonian shore!'
    Quoth the Raven, 'Nevermore'.

And finally . . .

'Be that word our sign of parting, bird or fiend!' I shrieked, upstarting —
'Get thee back into the tempest and the Night's Plutonian shore!
Leave no black plume as a token of that lie thy soul hath spoken!
Leave my loneliness unbroken! — quite the bust above my door!
Take thy beak from out my heart, and take thy form from off my door!
    Quoth the Raven, 'Nevermore'.

And the Raven, never flitting, still is sitting, still is sitting
On the pallid bust of Pallas just above my chamber door;
And his eyes have all the seeming of a demon's that is dreaming,
And the lamp-light o'er him streaming throws his shadow on the floor;
And my soul from out that shadow that lies floating on the floor
    Shall be lifted — nevermore!

Reading that poem today, it is difficult to resist a superior smile at the use of what seem to be incongruous words — 'nearly napping', for example — in order to get the sound right. Yet if you read the whole poem straight off without trying to analyse it you are left with a strange haunted feeling, a sensation of having looked directly into the poet's tortured soul. There is an old English saying about having 'a black dog on your back', which means something like being possessed by the Devil. Poe felt he had a raven on his back, and although the idea for the poem was undoubtedly suggested by 'Grip', the sinister companion of Barnaby Rudge, there is much more to it. The raven has been a bird of ill-omen since Roman times, a harbinger of bad luck, disease and death — as the eighteenth-century pastoralist John Gay put it,

> The boding raven on her cottage sat,
> And with hoarse croakings warned us of our fate.

In his blacker moments, Poe felt that his whole life was a warning of some terrible fate to come. Hence his obsession with death, when it happens, how it happens, why it happens, and what follows it. Hence also the shadow of the Raven out of which his soul 'Shall be lifted — nevermore'.

Out of the sombre came forth success, however. 'The Raven' was a sensation when it was published in 1845, first in the *Mirror* on 29 January and then in the February number of the *American Review*, carrying in the latter case the pseudonym 'Quarles' and in the former Poe's own name. N. P. Willis wrote that it was 'unsurpassed in English poetry for subtle conception, masterly ingenuity of versification, and consistent sustaining of imaginative lift'. Even the *Knickerbocker* was moved to comment that 'The Raven' was 'unique, singularly imaginative, and most musical', though a month later it gleefully printed one of the many parodies that the poem inspired. Edgar became a celebrity. A short biography of him, written by James Russell Lowell, appeared in the February issue of *Graham's*: it was, to say the least, somewhat inaccurate, Poe having given the date of his birth as 1813, suggested that he left West Point because of the birth of an heir to John Allan, and supplied the fiction of his romantic journey to St Petersburg. It all added to the glamour. In the same article, Lowell said Poe 'has that indescribable something which men have agreed to call genius' and although in his literary criticism 'he seems sometimes to mistake his phial of prussic acid for his inkstand', he was 'a man who thinks for himself, and says what he thinks, and knows well what he is talking about'. Later, disillusioned by what he called Poe's pet prejudices, Lowell would write:

> Here comes Poe with his Raven, like Barnaby Rudge,
> Three fifths of him genius, and two fifths sheer fudge.

That pithy summing-up has never been bettered.

For the moment, however, Edgar was enjoying the fruits of literary hero-worship. Everyone was raven-mad. On 28 February he lectured at the New York Historical Society on American poetry, giving three hundred people what appears to have been a selection from his old book reviews. By that time he had thrown off what he saw as the shackles of his lowly position at the *Mirror* and, through the good offices of Lowell, had become joint editor of the *Broadway Journal*, a weekly founded the year before. The *Journal* was owned by two New Englanders, John Bisco, a former publisher of the *Knickerbocker*, and Charles F. Briggs, whose novel *The Adventures of Harry Franco* had been a best-seller. Briggs was a friend of Lowell, who introduced him to Poe, as a result of which Edgar had become a regular contributor to the new magazine. In February 1845, following the success of 'The Raven', Bisco offered Poe the co-editorship in return for a third of the profits; he was also to supply one page of original matter every week. Edgar was thrilled. Never had he enjoyed a literary base over which he exercised so much control. It was the next best thing to having a magazine of his own.

Briggs was rather less enthusiastic. He told Lowell: 'Poe is only an assistant to me, and will in no manner interfere with my own way of doing things. It was requisite that I should have his or some other person's assistance, on account of my liability to be taken off from the business of the paper, and as his name is of some authority I thought it advisable to announce him as an editor.' Still, he liked Edgar well enough and everything seemed set fair for a fruitful relationship. Poe had the chance of becoming an established literary figure instead of the fugitive he had always been. There was a chilling inevitability about the manner in which he proceeded to throw away that chance.

The seeds of downfall had been sown at the *Mirror* when Poe reviewed Longfellow's selection of favourite poems, entitled *Waif*:

> We conclude our notes on the 'Waif' with the observation that, although full of beauties, it is infected with a *moral taint* — or is this a mere freak of our own fancy? We shall be pleased if it be so; — but there *does* appear, in this little volume, a very careful avoidance of all American poets who may be supposed especially to interfere with the claims of Mr Longfellow. These men Mr Longfellow can continuously *imitate* (*is* that the word?) and yet never incidentally commend.

Longfellow's friends protested bitterly at this insinuation of dis-
honesty, and Willis first published what amounted to an apology and
then printed a defence of Longfellow by a correspondent known
only as 'Outis', who slyly accused Poe of plagiarism in the composition of 'The Raven'. Edgar, furious and at the same time anxious to
gain publicity for the *Journal*, embarked upon a reply to 'Outis'
which ran through five consecutive issues. He charged Longfellow
with plagiarism in 'The Midnight Mass for the Dying Year', with
trying to pass off the Scottish ballad 'Bonnie George Campbell' as a
German translation of his own, and with drawing upon Poe's
'Politian' for his 'Spanish Student'. This was all very silly; Edgar
was merely playing with words. Before long he found himself having
to fight with words.

That Poe's views on Longfellow's verse were sincere is beyond
doubt: the tendency towards moral instruction, the weak hexa-
meters, and the air of cultivation rather than inspiration would have
all offended Edgar's taste. What was wrong with his criticisms, however, was the malicious way in which they were delivered − to say
nothing of the ridiculous accusations of plagiarism. Briggs commented: 'Poe is a monomaniac on the subject of plagiarism . . . a very
ticklish hobby . . . which he is bent on riding to death.' But his
co-editor was not about to stop Edgar's mad ride. It was such good
publicity: 'The "Journal" gains strength every day . . .' But it was
gaining more than strength. Poe's old enemies were massing, with
Lewis Gaylord Clark at their head. The *Knickerbocker* fired a
warning shot in July 1845, referring to Poe as a 'nil-admirari critic
. . . one of a numerous class who are "nothing if not critical," and
even less than nothing at that'. Poe snapped back:

> . . . He talks about a *nil admirari* critic; some person, we
> presume, having quizzed him with the information that the
> meaning of *nil admirari* is 'to admire nothing'. We certainly
> do not admire Mr Clarke [sic] − nor his wig − but the true
> English of the Latin phrase is 'to wonder at nothing', and
> we plead guilty to having wondered at nothing since we
> have found the *Knickerbocker* sinking day by day in the
> public opinion in despite of the brilliant abilities and
> thoroughly liberal education of Mr Lewis Gaylord Clarke.

Poe had already dismayed James Russell Lowell with his attacks
on Longfellow, and Lowell's only meeting with Edgar − in the early
summer of 1845 − ended their friendship. Lowell thought Poe had
been drinking and Mrs Clemm, who was present at the meeting,
admitted that he was 'not himself'. For his part, Edgar reported

himself disappointed in Lowell's appearance as an intellectual man — 'He was not half the noble looking person that I expected to see.' Thus the friendship became the first casualty of the so-called Longfellow War.

There was almost a casualty of a different kind that July, if Thomas Holly Chivers, a Georgia-born poet and friend of Poe from the Philadelphia days, is to be believed. Chivers claimed that he met Edgar, 'drunk as an Indian', one day and shortly afterwards they happened upon Lewis Clark talking to another man. Poe became very excited and threatened to assault Clark, while Chivers struggled to restrain him. There was an angry exchange between Poe and Clark, which ended with the latter beating a hasty but dignified retreat and Edgar calling him 'a damned coward'. Chivers's account is probably apocryphal, but some such meeting must have occurred, for Clark was to find ammunition in it later.

For the time being, though, there was a lull in the war of words, and Poe settled down to the business of reprinting some of his stories in the *Broadway Journal* and selling new ones to other publications. Among the fresh material was 'The Facts in the Case of M. Valdemar', which has been described, with some justification, as the most tasteless and disgusting tale Edgar ever wrote. Again mesmerism is the theme, with a dying man being hypnotized, only this time the purpose is to keep his brain alive. In spite of the feelings of revulsion the story may arouse, as an exercise in pure horror and also as a warning against interference in the natural process of death, it is without equal. The ending is gruesome in the extreme:

There was an instant return of hectic circles on the cheeks: the tongue quivered, or rather rolled violently in the mouth (although the jaws and lips remained rigid as before), and at length the same hideous voice which I have described, broke forth:

'For God's sake! — quick! — quick! — put me to sleep — or, quick! — waken me! — quick! — *I say to you that I am dead!*'. . .

As I rapidly made the mesmeric passes, amid ejaculations of 'dead! dead!' absolutely *bursting* from the tongue and not from the lips of the sufferer, his whole frame at once — within the space of a single minute, or less, shrunk — crumbled — absolutely *rotted* away beneath my hands. Upon the bed, before that whole company, there lay a nearly liquid mass of loathsome — of detestable putrescence.

Further success was at hand with the publication of *Tales* by Wiley and Putnam of New York. This was not the impressive volume Edgar would have liked — it contained only a dozen stories out of the seventy-two he had submitted — but for once, possibly for the first time, he was getting royalties, eight cents a copy. The book did well, being hailed in the United States as 'one of the most original' ever published there, and in England, where it was pirated, as a work of genius. Poe had by this time obtained an agent, of sorts, in England, the poet Richard Henry Horne, with whom he had entered into correspondence after his flattering review of Horne's epic poem 'Orion' in 1844. What exactly Horne did in his capacity as agent is unclear, but he never made it possible for Edgar to earn any money from his works that were published in London. Among all the praise for *Tales*, there was also a warning note sounded by an American reviewer who pointed out that the enmity aroused by Poe's critical writings might rebound on his fiction. That proved to be a very shrewd judgment.

As well as danger signals from outside, there were signs of trouble brewing inside Edgar. The statements by Chivers and Lowell that he had once more turned to drink are supported by evidence from Alexander T. Crane, office boy at the *Broadway Journal*, who in an interview published in 1902 recalled:

> Poe had given a lecture in Society library in New York on 'The Poets and Poetry of America'. The lecture had proved a success and he was finally induced to consent to repeat it. The night set for the second lecture was a very bad one. It stormed incessantly, with mingled rain and hail and sleet. In consequence there were scarcely a dozen persons present when Poe came upon the platform and announced that, under the circumstances, the lecture could not be given, and those in the audience would receive their money back at the door. I was one of those present, as Poe had given me a complimentary ticket to the lecture, and badly as I was disappointed, I could see upon his face that my master was much more so. It was a little thing, it is true, but he was a man easily upset by little things. The next morning he came to the office, leaning on the arm of a friend, intoxicated with wine.

If Crane was biased, it was in Poe's favour, for he worshipped 'the gentlest, truest, tenderest and knightliest man I ever knew'. He attributed Poe's drinking to the fact that Edgar was 'very delicate and sensitive, with nerves that throbbed with pain at the slightest contact', and also suggested that he used opium, though there is

absolutely no evidence to support that claim — indeed, what
evidence there is leads to the opposite conclusion. The drink did
enough damage, in any case. Probably it was pressure of work that
sent him back to the bottle: in May 1845 he told Frederick Thomas
that he was working fourteen or fifteen hours a day. Apart from
that, Virginia's health was in one of its periodic declines. The family
had moved from the Brennans' to a boarding house on East Broadway so that Edgar was spared a ten-mile round trip every day, and
this probably did nothing to improve his wife's condition.

Edgar made another enemy in July when Briggs was obliged to
leave the *Journal*. In letters to Lowell, Briggs had been saying that he
was sick of Poe and Bisco, and that he had found a new financial
backer for the magazine. At first, according to Briggs, Bisco agreed to
give up his interest, but later he asked a higher price for it than the
prospective new publisher was prepared to pay and the deal fell
through, causing one issue of the magazine to be cancelled. Then,
said Briggs, Edgar 'got into a drunken spree and conceived an idea
that I had not treated him well . . . and persuaded Bisco to carry on
the "Journal" himself . . .' Briggs was out, and Edgar became sole
editor. Briggs told James Russell Lowell: 'You have formed a correct
estimate of Poe's characterless character. I have never met a person
so utterly deficient of high motive . . .' Here was someone else who
would be waiting for Poe to get his comeuppance.

Edgar, meanwhile was convinced that nothing could stop him.
When things went well, he tended to be carried away by enthusiasm,
like a child, and when the bubble burst, as it invariably did (often at
least partly as a result of his own actions), it seemed to him like the
end of the world. Having taken charge of the *Journal* he continued to
ridicule and insult literary figures with whom he did not agree. He
even turned to dramatic criticism and ended up by being struck off a
theatre free list. And he made himself unpopular in Boston when he
read 'Al Aaraaf' during a lecture there, saying afterwards that he
would not bother to compose a new work — as he had been asked to
do — for the inhabitants of the 'frog-pond'.

Yet he had become accepted on the fringes of New York literary
society and was much sought-after by amateur poetesses at soirées in
the home of Miss Anne Charlotte Lynch, not far from Washington
Square. He moved into the district in the winter of 1845, to number
85 Amity Street: not only was it near the literati, but its airiness and
open aspect were good for Virginia. Poe thrived on admiration, and
he received plenty of it from the middle-aged writers of sentimental
ladies' verses who gathered in various homes in the area to deliver
their effusions amid gasps of delight. Edgar was their hero. He was,
after all, the famous author of 'The Raven' (not to mention the

editor of a magazine in which these ladies might some day see their verses published). There was even more to admire in November when Wiley and Putnam, encouraged by the success of the *Tales*, brought out *The Raven and Other Poems* — and by that time Edgar had become sole proprietor of the *Broadway Journal*.

The magazine was in financial trouble: advertising was increasing and the circulation was rising, but not enough to cover costs. Bisco got into debt and finally became so desperate that he sold his rights in the *Journal* to Poe for a fifty-dollar promissory note. Poe was not exactly creditworthy, so he had the note endorsed by Horace Greeley, politician and owner of the New York *Tribune*. He had sixty days in which to honour the promissory note, and he also needed cash to keep the magazine afloat. From Rufus Griswold, with whom he had resumed cordial relations, he begged a fifty-dollar loan. (Griswold and Poe needed each other at this time, the former having produced *Prose Writers of America*, in which it was necessary to include Poe, in view of his growing reputation, and in which Edgar was very keen to be included. Griswold later forged cringing letters in which 'Poe' sought his favour, but the likelihood is that the reverend gentleman himself made the first approach — he was still awaiting his chance for revenge.) Edgar also approached his cousin George in Alabama for money. While all this was going on he continued to print his stories in the *Journal*, sometimes using the pen-name Little-ton Barry, and kept up his attack against the Clark set, saying: 'The *Knickerbocker* magazine, for November, is really beneath notice and beneath contempt. And yet this work was, at one time, *respectable*. We should regret, for the sake of New York literature, that a journal of this kind should perish, and through sheer imbecility on the part of its conductors . . . Its friends should come to its rescue . . .'

On 26 December the credit note to Bisco became due, and Edgar could not pay — George Poe had refused to help, and although Edgar had raised two or three loans, they were not enough. Accordingly on 3 January 1846 the *Journal* carried the following notice:

> Unexpected engagements demanding my whole attention, and the objects being fulfilled, so far as regards myself personally, for which 'The Broadway Journal' was established, I now, as its Editor, bid farewell — as cordially to foes as to friends.
>
> Mr Thomas H. Lane is authorized to collect all money due to the Journal.

Edgar had achieved the ambition of having his own magazine, and it had died. It had cost him money, it had cost him friends — and its demise left him at the mercy of the *Knickerbocker* clique.

On 14 February 1846 Virginia Poe gave a Valentine to her husband, the first letters of each line adding up to his name:

Ever with thee I wish to roam —
Dearest my life is thine.
Give me a cottage for my home
And a rich old cypress vine,
Removed from the world with its sin and care
And the tattling of many tongues.
Love alone shall guide us when we are there —
Love shall heal my weakened lungs;
And Oh, the tranquil hours we'll spend,
Never wishing that others may see!
Perfect ease we'll enjoy, without thinking to lend
Ourselves to the world and its glee —
Ever peaceful and blissful we'll be.

She was soon to have her wish concerning her home, for in the spring Edgar rented a cottage surrounded by farmland at Fordham, about thirteen miles out of the city (now in the Bronx, and preserved as a museum). But she never did enjoy tranquil hours, or feel love healing her weakened lungs, or see tattling tongues silenced. Rumours were rife about Edgar's relationships with the literary ladies who were so captivated by his Southern charm and accent — while men tended to make fun of the Virginian drawl — and particularly about his intentions towards Mrs Frances Sargent Osgood, a fairly successful poetess in her early thirties who was married to a well-known artist. Poe had written favourable reviews of her verse, and when 'The Raven' was published she sought an introduction to him through Nathaniel Willis, editor of the *Mirror*. She later wrote:

I shall never forget the morning when I was summoned to the drawing-room by Mr Willis to receive him [Poe]. With his proud and beautiful head erect, his dark eyes flashing with the electric light of feeling and of thought, a peculiar, an inimitable blending of sweetness and hauteur in his expression and manner, he greeted me, calmly, gravely, almost coldly, yet with so marked an earnestness that I could not help being deeply impressed by it. From that moment until his death we were friends . . .

Mrs Osgood was described by a friend as 'ardent, sensitive, impulsive . . . a worshipper of the beautiful'. Poe was to her a mysterious, romantic figure, and she courted him in verse through the

Broadway Journal. He revised a poem he had originally written for
Eliza White, daughter of the proprietor of the *Southern Literary
Messenger*, and re-dedicated it 'To Mrs F-----s S-----t O----d'. The
friendship thus established, Mrs Osgood became a regular visitor at
85 Amity Street:

> It was in his own simple yet poetical home that to me the
> character of Edgar Poe appeared in its most beautiful light.
> Playful, affectionate, witty, alternately docile and way-
> ward as a petted child, for his young, gentle, and idolized
> wife, and for all who came, he had, even in the midst of his
> most harassing literary duties, a kind word, a pleasant
> smile, a graceful and courteous attention. At his desk
> beneath the romantic picture of his loved and lost Lenore,
> he would sit, hour after hour, patient, assiduous and
> uncomplaining, tracing, in an exquisitely clear chiro-
> graphy and with almost superhuman swiftness, the
> lightning thoughts − the 'rare and radiant fancies' − as
> they flashed through his wonderful and ever-wakeful
> brain . . .

Obviously the last flowering of a girlish crush, and Virginia recognized it for what it was. She also realized that the friendship was
good for Edgar, who at the insistence of Mrs Osgood had forsworn
alcohol (at least when she was present), so she encouraged the smit-
ten lady to call on and write to Poe. Other members of the literary
sisterhood, however, whether from prudishness or jealousy, saw
rather more in the relationship, and one of them, Mrs Elizabeth
Frieze Ellet, whom Poe had cultivated at the literary soirées, began
writing anonymous letters to Virginia suggesting that Edgar and Mrs
Osgood were motivated by feelings less pure than poetic sympathy.
Virginia was greatly upset by these letters, but they were not the
worst of the matter. On a visit to the cottage at Fordham, Mrs Ellet
picked up a letter from Mrs Osgood to Poe and was shocked at its
romantic excesses. She consulted her friends, prevailed upon Mrs
Osgood to demand the return of such 'compromising' material, and
with this purpose in mind, two tight-lipped literary ladies visited Poe
at Fordham. Edgar was at first amazed and then furious, yelling 'Mrs
Ellet had better come and look after her own letters.' He handed
over Mrs Osgood's outpourings and the two messengers went on their
way, no doubt to warn Mrs Ellet that she, too, could be in danger. A
few days later, Edgar received a threatening communication from Mrs
Ellet's brother-in-law, but by that time he had already returned her
letters. After this episode, Mrs Osgood kept out of the way, and the

whisperers branded Edgar as a womanizer. Later he said that Virginia, on her death-bed, 'declared that Mrs E. had been her murderer'.

While wagging tongues blackened Edgar's personal reputation, the pen of Lewis Gaylord Clark was getting to work on his literary merits. In January 1846, the *Knickerbocker* turned its attention to *The Raven and Other Poems*:

> If we were disposed to retort upon Mr Poe for the exceedingly gross and false statements which, upon an imaginary slight, he made in his paper respecting this Magazine, we could ask for no greater favor than to be allowed to criticize this volume of poems . . .

Those poems, Clark said, could have been written by any boy, 'but very rarely do they publish such verses when they become men'. Poe might be the darling of the ladies' magazines, but 'among men of letters his sword is a broken lath'. To rub in the salt, Clark printed a eulogy of Longfellow, with a sideswipe at 'self-elected poets' who could not reach his standard of excellence.

Deprived of the *Journal*, Edgar had no real base from which to mount a counter-attack, but he had been working on a series of sketches called 'The Literati of New York City — Some Honest Opinions at Random Respecting their Authorial Merits, with Occasional Words of Personality', and in May the first of the series appeared in *Godey's Lady's Book*. There was some sniping at Longfellow and his 'quacks' and an attack on Charles F. Briggs, whom Poe called 'grossly uneducated'. The sketches were so popular that when Clark heard he was to figure in them, he instantly lashed out, describing Poe as 'a wandering specimen of "The Literary Snob" . . . today in the gutter, tomorrow in some milliner's magazine . . .' Worse was to come. One of the articles involved Thomas Dunn English, a twenty-seven-year-old doctor, lawyer, editor, novelist, playwright and balladeer from Georgia (now forgotten except for his ballad 'Ben Bolt', which became a popular song during the Civil War). Edgar had known him in Philadelphia and had quarrelled with him in New York at the time when the *Journal* was going under. His portrait of 'Thomas Dunn Brown' was merciless, and English replied with a scandalous article in the *Mirror* (which was no longer edited by Willis and which had Briggs on its staff) accusing Poe of drunkenness, forgery, and obtaining money by false pretences, as well as hinting at his 'womanizing' and suggesting there was much more mud that could be thrown. The *Mirror* gleefully headlined the piece 'War of the Literati'. Poe filed suit for libel.

Edgar was in a weak position physically as well as professionally. He had been ill throughout the spring of 1846, probably as a result of a drinking bout during a visit to Baltimore, the purpose of which is not clear. The more often he drank, the sicker he became, and it appears that as he grew older the duration of each drink-induced illness became longer. It is interesting to recall the comment of Alexander Crane, the *Journal* office boy, that Poe had 'nerves that throbbed with pain at the slightest contact': if this is to be taken literally, it could indicate the neuropathy commonly associated with diabetes.

Virginia was ailing, too, and life was gloomy in the small, sparsely furnished wooden cottage at Fordham. Mrs Clemm managed as best she could, helped by Mrs Marie Louise Shew, a friend from the Amity Street days who had some practical medical knowledge. Another visitor commented: 'One felt that [Virginia] was almost a disrobed spirit, and when she coughed it was made certain that she was rapidly passing away.'

Weighed down by illness and worry, Edgar wrote little that summer, but his sketch of Lewis Gaylord Clark appeared in *Godey's* in September. 'Mr C, as a literary man,' he said, 'has about him no determinateness, no distinctiveness . . . He is as smooth as oil . . . he is noticeable for nothing in the world except for the markedness by which he is noticeable for nothing . . .'

Clark went mad. Poe, he wrote in the October *Knickerbocker*, was a 'wretched inebriate', a jaded hack for common hire, a 'poor wretch whose want of moral rectitude has reduced his mind and person to a condition where indignation for his vices and revenge for his insults are changed into a compassion for the poor victim of himself'. Strong stuff, and there was more of it. Claiming to quote from 'one of our most respectable journals', Clark retold Chivers's story of his meeting with Poe, who he said was in a condition of 'sad imbecility' and accompanied by 'an aged female relative'. In that one article were all the accusations which were to reverberate around Poe for the rest of his life, and long after his death. Rufus Griswold would complete the character assassination Lewis Clark had begun.

But a blow far worse than any Clark could deliver was about to fall. In the winter of 1846, Virginia was fading fast, and there was not even enough money in the household to make her end dignified and comfortable. She lay on a straw mattress, wrapped in Edgar's greatcoat and with Catterina beside her for extra warmth. On 15 December the *New York Express* carried an advertisement appealing to the Poes' friends to come to their aid, and the plea was taken up by Willis in the *Home Journal*. Within a few days, similar calls for help were appearing in the Philadelphia papers. The death scene now being played out was reminiscent of the long-ago days in Richmond when Edgar's mother had died, and the curtain fell just as inexorably. Virginia died on 30 January 1847.

Edgar had now lost his mother, Jane Stanard, Frances Allan and, most important of all, Virginia. He still had Mrs Clemm, but while he depended upon her maternal care she was not the soul-mate he so desperately needed. It remained to be seen whether there was another woman among those he had met who could save him, or whether the terrible prophecies contained in 'Ligeia' and 'The Fall of the House of Usher' would come to pass.

Chapter 14

Affairs of the Heart

Edgar was in a state of collapse. Virginia had been buried, suitably covered with fine linen sheets provided by Mrs Shew, in the family vault of the Valentines, who owned the Fordham cottage, and her distraught husband would sometimes be found at the tomb on the verge of hysteria. At other times he was too ill to get out of bed, and every night Mrs Clemm or Mrs Shew had to sit with him until he fell asleep – he could not bear to be alone in the dark. Mrs Shew put on her medical hat and came to a conclusion, as John H. Ingram reported in his 1891 biography of Poe:

> I made my diagnosis, and went to the great Dr Mott of the New York University Medical School with it; I told him that at best, when Mr Poe was well, his pulse beat only ten regular beats, after which it suspended, or intermitted (as doctors say). I decided that in his best health he had lesion of one side of the brain, and as he could not bear stimulants or tonics, without producing insanity, I did not feel much hope that he could be raised up from brain fever brought on by extreme suffering of mind and body – actual want and hunger, and cold having been borne by this heroic husband in order to supply food, medicine and comforts to his dying wife – until exhaustion and lifelessness were so near at every reaction of the fever, that even sedatives had to be administered with extreme caution. . . From the time the fever came on until I could reduce his pulse to eighty beats, he talked to me incessantly of the past, which was all new to me, and often begged me to write his fancies for him, for he said he had promised to many greedy publishers his next efforts, that they would not only say that he did not keep his word, but would also revenge themselves by saying all sorts of evil of him if he should die . . .

Of course, Mrs Shew was not a doctor, and her obvious pleasure in her own cleverness makes me mistrust her diagnosis even more than I otherwise would. It is most likely that Edgar was suffering from shock and complete nervous exhaustion, from which, under Mrs Shew's nursing — probably more expert than her diagnosis — he soon began to recover. By February he was corresponding with friends again, and on the seventeenth of the month he received two hundred and twenty-five dollars, plus costs, for the libels in the *Mirror*. He even felt strong enough to consider suing Greeley's *Tribune* for a comment it made on the case (Greeley had not forgotten the promissory note on which he had been obliged to pay fifty dollars) but he was persuaded out of a second court action. He also decided not to take proceedings against the Philadelphia *Saturday Evening Post* over allegations of plagiarism concerning the unfortunate book on conchology. And he had apparently been doing some writing, for a poem in honour of Mrs Shew was published by Willis in March, while later in the year the *American Review* printed my personal favourite among his poems — *Ulalume,* a hymn to the dead Virginia, and a kind of portrait of Roderick Usher in verse:

> The skies they were ashen and sober;
>> The leaves they were crispéd and sere—
>> The leaves they were withering and sere;
> It was night in the lonesome October
>> Of my most immemorial year;
> It was hard by the dim lake of Auber;
>> In the misty mid region of Weir—
> It was down by the dank tarn of Auber;
>> In the ghoul-haunted woodland of Weir.
>
> Here once, through an alley Titanic,
>> Of cypress, I roamed with my Soul—
>> Of cypress, with Psyche, my Soul.
> These were days when my heart was volcanic
>> As the scoriac rivers that roll—
>> As the lavas that restlessly roll
> Their sulphurous currents down Yaanek
>> In the ultimate climes of the pole—
> That groan as they roll down Mount Yaanek
>> In the realms of the boreal pole.
>
> Our talk had been serious and sober,
>> But our thoughts they were palsied and sere—
>> Our memories were treacherous and sere—

For we knew not the month was October,
  And we marked not the night of the year—
  (Ah, night of all nights in the year!)
We noted not the dim lake of Auber—
  (Though once we had journeyed down here)—
Remembered not the dank tarn of Auber,
  Nor the ghoul-haunted woodland of Weir.

For there lay 'the vault of thy lost Ulalume' . . .

Then my heart it grew ashen and sober
  As the leaves that were crispéd and sere—
  As the leaves that were withering and sere;
And I cried— 'It was surely October
  On *this* very night of last year
  That I journeyed—I journeyed down here—
  That I brought a dread burden down here—
  On this night of all nights in the year,
  Ah! what demon has tempted me here?
Well I know, now, this dim lake of Auber—
  This misty mid region of Weir—
Well I know, now, this dank tarn of Auber,
  This ghoul-haunted woodland of Weir.'

Like 'The Raven', this poem may sound slightly comic today, with its use of words like 'sere' and 'boreal pole' and 'scoriac' — it somehow reminds one of Lewis Carroll's great nonsense-poem *Jabberwocky*. Yet its grim message remains as clear as ever: the poet's soul is forever shackled to the corpse of the lost Ulalume; death has only strengthened the ties that bound the lovers in life, and one day the spirit of Ulalume will claim her own. To Edgar it must have seemed sometimes that his own life had ended with Virginia's, that the days left to him were no more than a period of waiting before a journey through the grave to rejoin his wife.

  But while Poe was waiting for death, there was one last great effort that he had to make, one masterpiece that he had to produce, a work that would never die. He had always been interested in science, and now he was going to relate scientific thought to poetic intuition. He called the work *Eureka: A Prose Poem*, and he prefaced it:

To those who love me and whom I love — to those who feel rather than to those who think — to the dreamers and those who put faith in dreams as the only realities — I offer this Book of Truths, not in its character of Truth-

Teller, but for the Beauty that abounds in its Truth; constituting it true. To these I present the composition as an Art-Product alone: — let us say as a Romance; or, if I be not urging too lofty a claim, as a Poem. What I here propound is true: — therefore it cannot die: — or if by any means it be now trodden down so that it die, it will 'rise again to the Life Everlasting.' Nevertheless, it is as a Poem only that I wish this work to be judged after I am dead.

Eureka was a poet's scientific view of the universe, based on the proposition, as Poe expressed it, that because nothing was, therefore all things are. Nothingness, he said, is unity, from which matter was created and to which it returns; the universe of space is infinite, but the universe of stars is limited and contains two forces, attraction (or gravitation) and repulsion (or electricity), which could also be seen as the body and the soul respectively. He formulated a crude theory of relativity, and to support his views quoted Kepler, Newton and the French astronomer and mathematician Laplace. The work is impressive, but not as a scientific treatise. At times it is vague and some threads of argument diverge; parts could be dismissed as mere sophistry. Yet *Eureka* shows that Poe was keenly aware of the scientific thinking of his day and also that he had the intellectual capacity to analyse and develop it in an intuitive and for the most part logical way. If in its forty thousand words one does not find a work of science, there is certainly a work of art.

Edgar delivered part of *Eureka* as a lecture in New York on 3 February 1848, and the publisher George Putnam gave him a fourteen-dollar advance on the volume, which appeared in the early summer, the last book of his Poe ever saw published. Time was passing, and the dead hand of Virginia had still not fallen upon him. The pain of her death had abated, and the completion and publication of *Eureka* brought new hope for the future. He revived the idea of the 'Stylus', even to the extent of designing a cover for it, and planned to expand his sketches of the literati into a book, 'Literary America'. He still had the friendship of Mrs Shew and he continued to attract the attention of society poetesses. It seems to have been Mrs Shew who gave him the idea for the melodic poem 'The Bells' (which was so to impress Rachmaninov that he based a choral symphony upon it):

> Hear the sledges with the bells—
> Silver bells!
> What a world of merriment their melody foretells!
> How they tinkle, tinkle, tinkle,

> In the icy air of night!
> While the stars, that oversprinkle
> All the heavens, seem to twinkle
> With a crystalline delight:
> Keeping time, time, time,
> In a sort of Runic rhyme,
> To the tintinnabulation that so musically wells
> From the bells, bells, bells, bells,
> Bells, bells, bells—
> From the jingling and the tinkling of the bells.

Mrs Shew claimed that she put the idea into Poe's head while he was staying at her home in New York. He had become irritated by the sound of nearby church bells, and to put his annoyance to constructive use she took a piece of paper and wrote on it, 'The Bells, by E. A. Poe. The little silver bells.'

Other women had less worthy tasks for Edgar to perform, and they were aided and abetted by Mrs Clemm, who kept in mind the practical problems of running a home on virtually no income. When poetesses like the repulsive-sounding Sarah Anna Lewis — described by Mrs Shew as fat and gaudily dressed — offered money and aid in return for Edgar's criticism of their poems (favourable criticism, naturally), the businesslike mother-in-law saw no reason why it should not be earned. Edgar tried his best to escape, even to the extent of absenting himself from the cottage when Mrs Lewis arrived, but he also recognized the need for money, though he wanted it to help him launch the 'Stylus' rather than for any mundane domestic purposes, and he stooped to writing the puffs he so despised.

The names of two other ladies of letters, however, were to be writ larger than was Mrs Lewis's in the narrative of Edgar Allan Poe. To the soirée set he was still 'The Raven', and his wife's death enhanced his appeal as far as they were concerned, not only because it added to his air of tragedy but also because he was free to pay them the kind of attention that excited their fantasies. On his side, Edgar needed the company of women, and particularly of women who admired him. He still had his mother-figure in Mrs Clemm, but with Virginia he had lost his wife, sister, and ideal of love and beauty, so he was ripe to fall for one of these sensitive and romantic women. On a visit to the town of Lowell, Massachusetts, in June 1848 he found a possible soul-mate in Nancy Locke Heywood Richmond, but she was happily married. He was also intrigued by Sarah Helen Whitman, a forty-five-year-old widow from Providence, Rhode Island, whose published poetry he had noticed and whom he had seen though not met during a visit to Providence with Mrs Whitman's friend Frances

Osgood in 1845. His interest was heightened when some of the New York ladies passed on to him a Valentine written by Mrs Whitman:

> Oh! thou grim and ancient Raven,
> From the Night's plutonic shore,
> Oft in dreams, thy ghastly pinions
> Wave and flutter round my door —
> Oft thy shadow dims the moonlight
> Sleeping on my chamber door.
>
> Romeo talks of 'White doves trooping,
> Amid crows athwart the night,'
> But to see they dark wing swooping
> Down the silvery path of light,
> Amid swans and dovelets stooping,
> Were, to me, a nobler sight.

And so on in the same vein for six more stanzas. The verses were published in N. P. Willis's *Home Journal*, prompting Mrs Osgood, then dying of consumption, to comment in a letter to Mrs Whitman that Providence had better protect her if 'The Raven' swooped on her *dovecote,* for 'his croak is the most eloquent imaginable'. Edgar was flattered and replied with a poem of his own. Significantly, the title was 'To Helen', though it was not in the same class as the verses he had written for his first 'Helen', Jane Stanard:

> I saw thee — once only — years ago;
> I must not say *how* many — but *not* many.
> It was a July midnight; and from out
> A full-orbed moon, that, like thine own soul, soaring,
> Sought a precipitate pathway up through heaven,
> There fell a silvery-silken veil of light,
> With quietude, and sultriness, and slumber,
> Upon the upturn'd faces of a thousand
> Roses that grew in an enchanted garden,
> Where no wind dared to stir, unless on tiptoe —
> Fell on the upturn'd faces of these roses
> That gave out, in return for the love-light,
> Their odorous souls in an ecstatic death —
> Fell on the upturned faces of these roses
> That smiled and died in this parterre, enchanted
> By thee, and by the poetry of thy presence.

The blank verse goes on through 'mossy banks' and 'happy flowers' and 'repining trees' until:

> But now, at length, dear Dian sank from sight,
> Into a western couch of thunder-cloud;
> And thou, a ghost, amid the entombing trees
> Didst glide away. *Only thine eyes remained.*
> They *would not* go — they never yet have gone . . .

Romance was quite definitely in the air, and matters came to a head in June when Mrs Shew appeared to sink into some form of religious mania and began to regard Edgar as godless and therefore as unworthy of her friendship. Poe wrote her an impassioned letter. There is no better insight in any of his letters into his feelings towards women:

> Can it be true, Louise, that you have the idea fixed in your mind to desert your unhappy and unfortunate friend and patient? You did not say so, I know, but for months I have known you were deserting me, not willingly, but none the less surely — my destiny —
>
> 'Disaster, following fast and following faster, till his song
>   one burden bore —
> Till the dirges of his Hope that melancholy burden bore —
> Of "Never — nevermore".'
>
> So I have had premonitions of this for months. I repeat, my good spirit, my loyal heart! must this follow as a sequel to all the benefits and blessings you have so generously bestowed? Are you to vanish like all I love, or desire, from my darkened and 'lost soul'? I have read over your letter again and again, and cannot make it possible, with any degree of certainty, that you wrote it in your right mind. (*I know you did not without tears of anguish and regret.*) Is it possible your influence is lost to me? Such tender and true natures are ever loyal until death; but you are not dead, you are full of life and beauty! Louise, you came in . . . in your floating white robe — 'Good morning, Edgar.' There was a touch of conventional coldness in your hurried manner, and your attitude as you opened the kitchen door to find Muddie, is *my last remembrance of you.* There was love, hope, and *sorrow* in your smile, instead of love, hope, and *courage,* as ever before. O Louise, how many sorrows are before you! Your

ingenuous and sympathetic nature will be constantly wounded in its contact with the hollow, heartless world; and for me, alas! unless some true and tender, and pure womanly love saves me, I shall hardly last a year longer alive! A few short months will tell how far my strength (physical and moral) will carry me in life here. How can I believe in Providence when *you* look coldly upon me? Was it not you who renewed my hopes and faith in God? . . . and in humanity? Louise, I heard your voice as you passed out of my sight leaving me . . .; but I still listened to your voice. I heard you say with a sob, 'Dear Muddie.' I heard you greet *my Catarina* [apparently the spelling of the cat's name varied], but it was only as a memory . . . nothing escaped *my ear,* and I was convinced it was not your generous self . . . repeating words so foreign to your nature — to your tender heart! I heard her reply, 'Yes, Loui . . . yes' . . . Why turn your soul from its true work for the desolate to the thankless and miserly world? . . . I felt my heart stop, and I was sure I was then to die, before your eyes. Louise, it is well — it is fortunate — you looked up with a tear in your dear eyes, and raised the window, and talked of the guava you had brought for my sore throat. Your instincts are better than a *strong man's reason for me* — I trust they may be for *yourself.* Louise, I feel I shall not prevail — a shadow has already fallen upon your soul, and is reflected in your eyes. It is *too late* — your are floating away with a cruel tide . . . it is not a common trial — it is a fearful one to me. Such rare souls as yours so beautify this earth! so relieve it of all that is repulsive and sordid. So brighten its toils and cares, it is hard to lose sight of them even for a short time . . . but you must know and *be assured* of my regret and sorrow if aught I have ever written has hurt you. *My heart never wronged you.* I place you in *my esteem* — in all *solemnity* — beside the friend of my boyhood — the mother of my school-fellow, of whom I told you, and as I have repeated in the poem . . . as the truest, tenderest of this world's most womanly souls, and an angel to my forlorn and darkened nature. I will not say 'lost soul' again, for your sake. I will try to overcome my grief for the sake of your unselfish care of me in the past, and in life or death, I am ever yours gratefully and devotedly.

                                                            Edgar A. Poe

Here Poe lays open his ideals of love and beauty, his need for the tender care that only a woman can give, his fear that he could only survive if his soul were entwined with that of a woman who loved him. Perhaps it was the loss of Mrs Shew that caused Edgar to turn to drink on a visit to Richmond in the summer of 1848 when he was trying to gather subscriptions for the 'Stylus'. The then editor of the *Southern Literary Messenger,* John R. Thompson, reported that Poe got drunk every night (though he must have been quite sober some of the time, for he sold Thompson an essay on 'The Rationale of Verse'). But the second Helen was at hand to rescue him. Mrs Whitman had replied to Edgar's poem with another of her own, which she sent to Fordham before Edgar had left for Richmond. It did not reach him because the nearest post office was several miles away, and it was eventually forwarded to Richmond by Mrs Clemm. Edgar returned to Fordham and wrote to Mrs Whitman under an assumed name asking her to write to him because he was collecting autographs of 'the most distinguished American authors'. Of course, Mrs Whitman saw through the ruse and did not reply. Poe obtained a letter of introduction from a mutual friend and set off for Rhode Island towards the end of September. In spite of his cri de coeur to Mrs Shew, he was putting his trust in his new Helen. He had met Nancy Richmond in the meantime and had fallen in love with her, but she was not free. Only Helen Whitman could save him. He told her that a friend had described her to him:

> She had referred to thoughts, sentiments, traits, *moods*, which I knew to be my own, but which, until that moment, I had believed to be my own solely — unshared by any human being. A profound sympathy took immediate possession of my soul. I cannot better explain to you what I felt than by saying that your unknown heart seemed to pass into my bosom — there to dwell forever — while mine, I thought, was translated into your own. From that hour I loved you. Since that period I have never seen nor heard your name without a shiver, half of delight, half of anxiety ... The merest whisper that concerned you awoke in me a shuddering sixth sense, vaguely compounded of fear, ecstatic happiness, and a wild inexplicable sentiment that resembled nothing so nearly as a consciousness of guilt ...

He had thought that Mrs Whitman was still married, and 'it is only within the last few months that I have been undeceived in this respect'. There was nothing to stop him now. His feelings could be more than poetic. 'The Raven', it seemed, had been snared. During that autumn visit to Providence, he courted Helen and finally asked her to marry him.

Sarah Helen Whitman was passionate enough, and eccentric enough, to contemplate marriage with Poe, but her family were not so sure. She lived with her mother and sister, and they knew of Poe's bizarre reputation, of the Osgood scandal — indeed Mrs Osgood had described Edgar as 'a glorious devil' in a letter to Mrs Whitman. So while the prospect of marriage with such a man might seem excitingly dangerous to a romantic poetess, there were practical considerations, which her mother no doubt pointed out. Mrs Whitman sent Edgar back to Fordham while she considered and consulted about his proposal.

But Nancy Richmond — 'Annie', he called her — was still in his thoughts, and as he sat at home waiting for Mrs Whitman to make up her mind, he realized that his feelings for Mrs Richmond were something more than those of a poet for a kindred spirit. He wanted her purely as a woman. In October he was in Massachusetts for another lecture and although it was cancelled because of the presidential election, he stayed with the Richmonds and tried to ascertain the strength of Annie's feelings for him. She made it clear that, although she was fond of him, she could never be anything more than a friend: she had a husband and daughter whom she loved dearly. Disappointed, Edgar set off for Providence to renew his courtship of Mrs Whitman, who had written to him without giving any definite hope of marriage. What happened next can be told in his own words, taken from a letter to Mrs Richmond:

> I remember nothing distinctly . . . until I found myself in Providence. I went to bed and wept through a long, long, hideous night of Despair — When the day broke, I arose and endeavoured to quiet my mind by a rapid walk in the cold, keen air — but all *would* not do — the Demon tormented me still. Finally, I procured two ounces of laudanum, and without returning to my hotel, took the cars back to Boston. When I arrived I wrote you a letter, in which I opened my whole heart — to *you* . . . I told you how my struggles were more than I could bear . . . I then reminded you of that holy promise which was the last I exacted from you in parting — the promise that, under all circumstances, you would come to me on my bed of death. I implored you to come *then*, mentioning the place where I should be found in Boston. Having written this letter, I swallowed about half the laudanum, and hurried

to the Post Office, intending not to take the rest until I saw you — for, I did not doubt for one moment, that Annie would keep her sacred promise. But I had not calculated on the strength of the laudanum, for, before I reached the Post Office my reason was entirely gone, and the letter was never put in. Let me pass over — my darling *sister* — the awful horrors that succeeded. A friend was at hand, who aided, and (if it can be called saving) saved me, but it is only within the last three days that I have been able to remember what occurred in that dreary interval. It appears that, after the laudanum was rejected from the stomach, I became calm, and, to a casual observer, sane — so that I was suffered to go back to Providence.

This letter is of great importance because it throws light on claims that Poe was an habitual user of opium. Alexander Crane, the office boy at the *Broadway Journal* said he thought that drugs as well as drink were the cause of Poe's 'irregular' behaviour, and much has been made by critics and biographers of the repeated references to opium and its effects in the tales. Some argue that Edgar's apparent familiarity with opium indicates that he used it, while others suggest that his information came from books like De Quincey's *Confessions of an English Opium Eater*, published in 1822. The latter group believes that the Boston episode with the laudanum shows that Poe knew nothing about the use of opiates, otherwise he would not have miscalculated its effects. But the opposite could equally be true: if he did not seriously intend to kill himself but wished to make a dramatic gesture, he would perhaps have deliberately taken an amount of laudanum that his stomach would reject. Furthermore, we have only Poe's evidence that the event ever took place, and if he invented it he must have known that such an effect could be achieved with laudanum, which suggests that he was familiar with opiates. Again, though, that familiarity may not have been first-hand. The fact is, the Boston story proves absolutely nothing, and we have to rely on Poe's own testimony and that of people who knew him. His cousin, Elizabeth Herring, said that she had often seen him 'in sad conditions from the use of opium'; his sister Rosalie said that when she visited him in 1846 she heard him asking for morphine. One is tempted to ask how Elizabeth Herring knew the effects she was witnessing were those of opium — could they not also have been the results of heavy drinking, which Edgar admitted? And if Rosalie is to be believed, it is possible that the morphine her brother required was for medical reasons. Alexander Crane testified that Poe suffered from severe pains in his limbs, and the morphine might have been used to subdue them.

The question of the literary evidence for or against Poe's alleged opium addiction requires far too much explanation, example and analysis to have any place in a personal rather than a critical biography, and it is perhaps sufficient to say that because Poe described opium-related visions and compared certain emotional conditions to the after-effects of the drug, it does not mean that he was an addict. It is clear from the rest of his work that he was inclined to draw heavily on other writers for information, and among that information could well have been descriptions of opium-taking and its effects. Poe gave convincing details of Paris in 'The Murders in the Rue Morgue', 'The Mystery of Marie Roget' and 'The Purloined Letter'; he described Venice well in 'The Assignation' — but he had never been to either of those cities except in his imagination. I suspect the same is true when it comes to the opium dreams he records.

But let the final word on the subject come from Dr Thomas Dunn English, who disliked Poe and had every reason not to defend him. He said: 'Had Poe the opium habit when I knew him I should both as a physician and a man of observation, have discovered it during his frequent visits to my rooms, my visits at his house, and our meetings elsewhere — I saw no signs of it and believe the charge to be a baseless slander.'

The letter to Annie Richmond also shows much about Edgar's state of mind. He was clearly torn between the romantic attachment between himself and Mrs Whitman and his more physical need for Mrs Richmond, but even if the dilemma tipped him into temporary insanity and drove him to attempt suicide, the letter finds him balanced enough to describe his condition in a coherent and fairly unemotional way. Although Virginia's death had set him on a path to destruction, it was not downhill all the way. In any case, he had already written to Mrs Whitman apologizing for failing to call on her and saying that he was very ill (as a result of the laudanum, perhaps, though he did not mention it). Helen assumed he had been drinking and arranged a meeting, during which she showed him warning letters sent to her by friends in New York. Edgar wrote a denial of the charges contained in these letters, then called at Helen's home. He had, she said, 'passed the evening in a bar-room, and after a night of delirious frenzy, returned the next day to my mother's house in a state of great mental excitement and suffering, declaring that his welfare for time and eternity depended on me'. Mrs Whitman's mother became so afraid that a doctor was called, and Edgar was pronounced a victim of brain fever. He was taken to the home of a neighbour, William J. Pabodie, to recover.

Helen clearly felt sorry for Edgar, but her consent to an

engagement a few days later — with the agreement of her mother — may have resulted more from fear of what he might do if she refused his constant pleas for marriage. Mrs Whitman later admitted that, 'Our engagement was from the first a conditional one. My mother was inflexibly opposed to our union, and being in a pecuniary point of view entirely dependent upon her, I *could* not, if I would, have acted without her concurrence.' The conditions were that Poe would never drink and that he would sign legal documents that would prevent him from getting his hands on any money due to Mrs Whitman by inheritance if she were to die before him. These requirements had been discussed while Poe was away from Providence — he had gone home to Fordham as soon as he was fit enough after his attack of brain fever — and were put to him by letter. He returned to Rhode Island to lecture on 20 December, and two days later plans for the marriage were completed. Mrs Whitman takes up the story:

On the 23 of December Mr Poe wrote a note to the Rev. Dr Crocker requesting him to publish our intention of marriage on the ensuing Sunday — he also wrote a letter to Mrs Clemm informing her that we should be married on Monday and should arrive at Fordham on Tuesday in the second train of cars. We rode out together in the morning & passed the greater part of the day in making preparations for my sudden change of abode. In the afternoon, while we were together at one of the circulating libraries of the city, a communication was handed me cautioning me against this imprudent marriage & informing me of many things in Mr Poe's recent career with which I was previously unacquainted. I was at the same time informed that he had already violated the solemn promises that he had made to me & to my friends on the preceding evening. I knew that, even had I been disposed to overlook these things myself, they must within a few hours come to the knowledge of my friends & would lead to a recurrence of the scenes to which I had been already subjected, and felt utterly helpless of being able to exercise any permanent influence over his life. On our return home I announced to him what I had heard &, in his presence, countermanded the order, which he had previously given, for the delivery of the note to Dr Crocker. He earnestly endeavoured to persuade me that I had been misinformed, especially in relation to his having that very morning called for wine at the bar of the hotel where he boarded. The effect of this infringement of the promise was in no degree perceptible, but the authority on which I had received this & other statements concerning him, was not to be questioned. I listened to his explanations & his remonstrances without one word of reproach and with that marble stillness of despair so mercifully accorded to us when the heart has been wrought to its highest capacity of suffering. Nor was I, at that bitter moment, unsolaced by a sense of relief at being freed from the intolerable burden of responsibility which he had sought to impose upon me, by persuading me that his fate, for good or evil, depended upon me. I had now learned that my influence was unavailing. My mother on being informed of what had transpired had a brief interview with Mr Poe which resulted in his determination to return immediately to New York. In her presence & in that of his friend, Mr Pabodie, I bade him farewell, with feelings of profound commiseration for his fate — of intense sorrow thus to part from one whose sweet & gracious nature had endeared him to me beyond expression, and whose rare and peculiar intellect had given a new charm to my life. While he was endeavouring to win from me an assurance that our parting should not be a final one, my mother saved me from a response by insisting upon the immediate termination of the interview. Mr Poe then started up and left the house with an expression of bitter resentment at what he termed, the 'intolerable insults' of my family. I never saw him more.

That clear statement gives the lie to the story later circulated by Rufus Griswold that Edgar deliberately caused trouble so that the marriage should not take place. But that it would take place was in doubt from the start anyway. Edgar had told a friend he saw on his way to Providence that he was not necessarily going north to get married, and when he later wrote to Mrs Clemm saying that the ceremony would be performed on the Monday, he took no account of the fact that it would have been Christmas Day, hardly the time for a marriage. Finally, when he gave Pabodie his note to take to Dr Crocker, the worthy gentleman did not deliver it because he disapproved of the proposed union and either hoped that something would happen to stop it — or else knew that it was going to be prevented.

So Edgar did not marry his poetical love, Helen, and could not marry his other love, Annie. He seems to have been pretty philosophical about it all, and when the gossips got busy with stories of the broken engagement with Mrs Whitman, he wrote to her, via Mrs Richmond, assuring her that he would never speak ill of her, no matter what was said about him. At the same time he told Annie that 'from this day forth I shun the pestilential society of *literary women*. They are a heartless, unnatural, venomous, dishonorable *set*, with no guiding principle but inordinate self-esteem . . .' As for Mrs Richmond herself, there can be no doubt that Edgar loved her passionately, and he told her so in the letter that contained his account of his Boston suicide attempt. Angel, sister, soul-wife were the words of endearment he used, telling her that he would give anything to be with her and suggesting that he and Mrs Clemm might take a house in Westford, where she lived. She loved him, too, but as a loyal, devoted sister might, not in the way he wanted. He accepted this, though his own feelings did not change. He expressed them in a poem he sent her in the spring of 1849 — 'For Annie':

> Thank Heaven! the crisis —
>   The danger is past,
> And the lingering illness
>   Is over at last —
> And the fever called 'Living'
>   Is conquered at last.
>
> Sadly, I know
>   I am shorn of my strength,
> And no muscle I move
>   As I lie at full length —
> But no matter! — I feel
>   I am better at length.
>
> And oh! of all tortures
>   *That* torture the worst
> Has abated — the terrible
>   Torture of thirst,
> For the naphthaline river
>   Of Passion accurst: —
> I have drank of a water
>   That quenches all thirst: —
>   . . .
> And I lie so composedly,
>   Now, in my bed,
> (Knowing her love)
>   That you fancy me dead —
> And I rest so contentedly,

Now in my bed,
(With her love at my breast)
    That you fancy me dead —
That you shudder to look at me,
    Thinking me dead: —

But my heart it is brighter
    Than all of the many
Stars in the sky,
    For it sparkles with Annie —
It glows with the light —
    Of the love of my Annie —
With the thought of the light
    Of the eyes of my Annie.

Having come to terms with his emotional upheavals, Edgar had begun to write again. The masterly tale 'Hop-Frog', about a jester who takes revenge on his overbearing masters by incinerating them, was published by *The Flag of Our Union*, which also took 'For Annie'. To the *Southern Literary Messenger* Poe contributed a number of short essays under the heading of 'Marginalia', a technique he had developed in New York for other magazines, and he reviewed James Russell Lowell's *Fable for Critics* with its comment about Edgar being three-fifths genius and two-fifths sheer fudge. Poe quoted those lines in his review, then proceeded to attack Lowell for the omission of Southern writers in his 'Fable'. Nevertheless he ranked Lowell with Longfellow as, on the whole, the best of American poets.

The trek of the Forty-Niners to California in search of gold inspired Edgar to write another poem, 'Eldorado', and in July was published a verse on a more personal theme — Mrs Clemm. It was called simply 'To My Mother':

Because I feel that, in the Heavens above,
    The angels, whispering to one another,
Can find, among their burning terms of love,
    None so devotional as that of 'Mother,'
Therefore by that dear name I long have called you —
    You who are more than mother unto me,
And fill my heart of hearts, where Death installed you,
    In setting my Virginia's spirit free.
My mother — my own mother, who died early,
    Was but the mother of myself; but you
Are mother to the one I loved so dearly,

> And thus are dearer than the mother I knew
> By that infinity with which my wife
> Was dearer to my soul than its soul-life.

Then the idea of the Poe magazine was reborn. Edgar had some-how aroused the support of a certain Mr E. H. N. Patterson, from the unlikely quarter of Oquawka, Illinois, for his dream of a five-dollar magazine selling twenty thousand copies. He planned to publish simultaneously in New York and St Louis, Missouri, and the first issue was scheduled — in his mind at least — for 1 July 1850. With this deadline in mind, Edgar asked Patterson in May 1849 for a stake of fifty dollars to finance a subscription-raising trip. On the twenty-third of the month he arrived in Lowell to take his leave of Mrs Richmond before his journey, and back in Fordham a few weeks later he wrote his last goodbye:

> You asked me to write before I started for Richmond, and I was to have started last Monday — so, perhaps, you thought me gone, and without having written to say 'good bye' — but indeed, Annie, I *could not* have done so. The truth is, I have been on the point of starting every day . . . and so put off writing until the last moment — but I have been disappointed — and can no longer refrain from sending you, at least, a few lines to let you see *why* I have been so long silent. *When* I can go now is uncertain — but, perhaps, I may be off to-morrow, or next day: — all depends upon circumstances beyond my control. Most probably I will not go until I hear from Thompson, to whom I wrote five days ago — telling him to forward the letter from Oquawka, instead of retaining it until he sees me.

There had been some financial difficulty, it seems. He had tried to draw money against some articles he had sent to *Graham's*, but the draft had been refused because, according to Poe, the articles had been lost or delayed in the mail. No doubt the letter he had asked Thompson to send him contained the fifty dollars he needed to set out on his expedition. No doubt, too, he received a little something for a puff of Sarah Anna Lewis's poems he sent to Griswold for inclusion in the latter's *Female Poets of America* anthology — certainly Griswold got a bribe from Mrs Lewis's husband. On 28 June, Edgar and his mother-in-law left Fordham for Brooklyn, where Mrs Clemm was to stay at the home of Mrs Lewis during Poe's absence, and two days later, with high hopes of a new beginning,

Edgar boarded the steamer for the journey to the railway depot at Perth Amboy, New Jersey.

'God bless you, my own darling Mother,' he told Mrs Clemm as they parted. 'Do not fear for Eddy! See how good I will be while I am away from you, and I will come back to love and comfort you.'

It was the last time she saw him.

Chapter 15

The Final Tragedy

What happened to Edgar Allan Poe on the bewildering journey that ended in his death will probably never be satisfactorily explained. Perhaps he drank too much and his weakened constitution finally gave way under the strain. On the other hand, he may have been in a parlous mental state following Virginia's death, the Whitman debacle and his failure to win Annie Richmond: if that had been the case, his trip to Philadelphia, Richmond and Baltimore — all places associated with tragedy and unhappiness in his life — might have reawakened in him painful memories that his delicately balanced mind could not bear. Probably it was a combination of the two things. Throughout his adult life Edgar had been subject to periods of crippling depression, and I have no doubt that he was also the victim of some chronic illness, which I have suggested was diabetes. But diabetes was not the direct cause of his death.

Having left New York on 30 June, he arrived in Philadelphia on 2 July, but what he did then is a mystery. Mrs Clemm did not hear from him for ten days, and became worried. On 9 July she wrote to Mrs Richmond:

> Eddy has been gone ten days, and I have not heard one word from him. Do you wonder that I *am distracted*? I fear everything . . . Do you wonder that he has so little confidence in any one? Have we not suffered from the blackest treachery? Eddy was obliged to go through Philadelphia, and how much I fear he has got into some trouble there; he promised me *so* sincerely to write thence. I ought to have heard last Monday, and now it is Monday again and not one word . . . Oh, if any evil has befallen him, what can comfort me?

I wonder what she meant when she said she feared Poe had got into trouble in Philadelphia? She may have been thinking of drink, or perhaps the danger she had in mind was more specific. What is certain is that Edgar certainly did get into trouble in Philadelphia. On 9 July he burst in upon his old friend John Sartain, editor of the *Union Magazine*, whom he had known since his days on *Burton's*. Sartain gave a very interesting account of what happened in a little-known article published in the *Boston Evening Transcript* in 1893:

> I was at work, in my shirt sleeves, in my office on Sansom Street, when Poe burst in upon me excitedly, and exclaimed, 'I have come to you for refuge.' I saw at a glance that he was suffering from some mental overstrain, and assured him of shelter. I then begged him to explain.
>
> 'I was just on my way to New York on the train,' he said to me, 'when I heard whispering going on behind me. Owing to my marvellous power of hearing I was enabled to overhear what the conspirators were saying. Just imagine such a thing in this nineteenth century! They were plotting to murder me. I immediately left the train and hastened back here again. I must disguise myself in some way. I must shave off this mustache at once. Will you lend me a razor?'
>
> Afraid to trust him with it, I told him I hadn't any, but that I could remove his mustache with the scissors. Taking him to the rear of the office, I sheared away until he was absolutely barefaced. This satisfied him somewhat and I managed to calm him. That very evening, however, he prepared to leave the house. 'Where are you going?' I asked. 'To the Schuylkill [river],' he replied. 'Then I am going with you,' I declared. He did not object, and together we walked to Chestnut Street and took a bus.
>
> A steep flight of steps used to lead up from the Schuylkill then, and ascending these we sat on a bench overlooking the stream. The night was black, without a star, and I felt somewhat nervous alone with Poe in the condition he was in. Going up to the bus he said to me, 'After my death see that my mother (Mrs Clemm) gets the portrait of me from Osgood.'
>
> Now he began to talk the wildest nonsense, in the weird, dramatic style of his tales. He said he had been thrown into Moyamensing Prison for forging a check, and while there a white female form had appeared on the battlements and addressed him in whispers.
>
> 'If I had not heard what she said,' he declared, 'it would have been the end of me. But, owing to my marvellous hearing, I lost not a single word. Then another figure

appeared and invited me to walk with him around the battlements. He conducted me to a cauldron of liquid, and asked me if I wished a drink. I refused, for that was a trap. Do you know what would have happened if I had accepted? They would have lifted me over the cauldron, and placed me in the liquid up to my lips, like Tantalus, and gone away and left me there.'

By and by I suggested that we descend again and Poe assented. All the way down the steep steps I trembled lest he should remember his resolve of suicide, but I kept his mind from it and got him back safely. Three days after he went out again and returned in the same mood. 'I lay on the earth with my nose in the grass,' he said then, 'and the smell revived me. I began at once to realize the falsity of my hallucinations.'

Clearly Poe had been drinking, and the effect of the alcohol had turned his mind. It also affected him physically. On 7 July he had written to Mrs Clemm:

My *dear, dear* Mother, — I have been *so* ill — have had the cholera, or spasms quite as bad, and can now hardly hold the pen.

The very instant you get this, *come* to me. The joy of seeing you will almost compensate for our sorrows. We can but die together. It is no use to reason with *me* now; I must die. I have no desire to live since I have done 'Eureka'. I could accomplish nothing more. For your sake it would be sweet to live, but we must die together. You have been all in all to me, darling, ever beloved mother, and dearest, truest friend.

I was never *really* insane, except on occasions where my heart was touched.

I have been taken to prison once since I came here for getting drunk; but *then* I was not. It was about Virginia.

But what about the 'conspirators' on the train? The strange letter above was datelined New York, but Poe obviously knew that he was in Philadelphia, so it seems that he was trying to disguise his whereabouts. For some reason known only to himself, he feared he was being followed. Mrs Clemm did not receive the letter until some time later, for she had left the Lewis home — to which Edgar would have sent it — and returned to Fordham. In any case she could not have gone to Edgar's aid because his fear of the 'conspirators' had induced him to give the impression that he was in New York. In his confused state it did not occur to him that his subterfuge would throw not only the 'conspirators' off his track but also the 'dear Mother' he needed so desperately.

Edgar stayed in Philadelphia until 13 July, borrowing money from two friends, the writer George Lippard and the editor of the *Nineteenth Century* magazine, Chauncey Burr. By Saturday 14 July he was in Richmond, for he wrote despairingly once more to Mrs Clemm:

> Oh, my darling Mother, it is now more than three weeks [actually it was only two] since I saw you, and in all that time your poor Eddy has scarcely drawn a breath except of intense agony. Perhaps you are sick or gone from Fordham in despair, or dead. If you are but alive, and if I but *see you again,* all the rest is nothing. I love you better than ten thousand lives — so much so that it is cruel in you to let me leave you; nothing but sorrow *ever* comes of it.
>
> Oh, Mother, I am *so* ill while I write — but I resolved that come what would, I would not sleep again without easing your dear heart as far as I could.
>
> My valise was lost for ten days. At last I found it at the depot in Philadelphia, but (you will scarcely credit it) they had opened it and stolen *both lectures.* Oh, Mother, think of the blow to me this evening, when on examining the valise, these lectures were gone. All my object here is over unless I can recover them or re-write one of them.
>
> I am indebted for more than life itself to Burr. Never forget him, Mother, while you live. When all failed me, he stood my friend, got me money, and saw me off in the cars for Richmond.
>
> I got here with two dollars over — of which I inclose you one. Oh God, my Mother, shall we ever again meet? If possible, oh COME! My clothes are so *horrible,* and I am so *ill.* Oh, if you could come to me, *my mother.* Write instantly — oh *do* not fail. God forever bless you.
>
>   Eddy.

It seems he kept away from the bottle for the next few days, and he was comforted by receiving a letter from Mrs Clemm. By 19 July he was in better health. He told his mother-in-law: 'All was hallucination, arising from an attack which I had never before experienced — an attack of mania a potu. May Heaven grant that it prove a warning to me for the rest of my days. If so, I shall not regret even the horrible unspeakable torments I have endured.' He also wrote to his backer, Patterson, saying that an outbreak of cholera had held him up in Philadelphia, and to Lippard, asking him to search once more for the missing lectures.

Edgar was comfortably boarded at the Swan Tavern on Broad Street, near the centre of Richmond, and was meeting old friends and making new ones. In the latter category was Susan Archer Talley, a young poetess who had come to his critical attention and who was introduced to him by his sister, Rosalie. She clearly remembered the day he was brought to her home, Talavera, on West Grace Street:

> As I entered the parlor, Poe was seated near an open window, quietly conversing. His attitude was easy and graceful, with one arm lightly resting upon the back of his chair. His dark curling hair was thrown back from his broad forehead — a style in which he habitually wore it. At sight of him, the impression produced upon me was of a refined, high-bred, and chivalrous gentleman. I use this word 'chivalrous' as exactly descriptive of something in his whole *personnel,* distinct from either polish or high-breeding, and which, though instantly apparent, was yet an effect too subtle to be described. He rose on my entrance, and, other visitors being present, stood with one hand resting on the back of his chair, awaiting my greeting. So dignified was his manner, so reserved his expression, that I experienced an involuntary recoil, until I turned to him and saw his eyes suddenly brighten as I offered my hand; a barrier seemed to melt between us, and I felt that we were no longer strangers.

Edgar had fully recovered himself, although he had been warned by doctors in Richmond that another attack like the one he had suffered in Philadelphia would kill him. He joined the Sons of Temperance, and told the doctors that he would be all right if no one tempted him. Patterson had written to say that he would support a five-dollar magazine of the kind Poe wanted if Edgar could obtain a thousand subscribers to start with. To keep himself while he undertook this task, Edgar began lecturing again, starting with 'The Poetic Principle' at the Exchange Concert Rooms in Richmond on August 17. He made little money, but the lecture was well received, and he was able to tell Mrs Clemm: 'Everybody says that if I lecture again & put the tickets at 50 cts, I will clear $100. I *never* was received with so much enthusiasm. The papers have done nothing but praise me before the lecture and since . . .'

He was back among his own again, and the Southerners welcomed him as only they could. There was one welcome that was particularly gratifying — that of Sarah Elmira Shelton, by then a widow. They talked of their love all those years ago, and gradually it came out that Elmira's parents had objected, that Edgar's letters had been intercepted, and that she had been married off to Shelton. Now, though, there were no obstacles in the way, and she was a wealthy woman. He asked her to marry him and, though she delayed, he was certain that he would be accepted. As early as mid-August he was telling Mrs Clemm that friends were delighted by the engagement. And yet Edgar was not entirely committed. He wrote: 'I want to live *near Annie* . . . I *must* be somewhere where I can see Annie.' He even suggested that he and Elmira might go to live in Lowell. It was clear whom he really loved.

Elmira later denied that she ever was engaged to Poe. This is her version of the relationship:

> I was ready to go to church and a servant told me that a gentleman in the parlour wanted to see me. I went down and was amazed to see him — but I knew him instantly — He came up to me in the most enthusiastic manner and said: 'Oh! Elmira, is this you?' That very morning I told him I was going to church, that I never let anything interfere with that, that he must call again and when he did call again he renewed his addresses. I laughed at it; he looked very serious and said he was in earnest and had been thinking about it for a long time. Then I found out that he was serious and I became serious. I told him if he would not take a positive denial he must give me time to consider of it. And he said a love that hesitated was not a love for him. But he sat there a long time and was very pleasant and cheerful. He continued to visit me frequently but I never engaged myself to him. He begged me when he was going away to marry him. Promised he would be everything I could desire . . .

He had in fact written to Mrs Clemm suggesting that she sell up in Fordham and come to Richmond for the wedding. Mrs Clemm was in no position to do that, for she had no money. She had even written to Griswold trying to raise cash against the Lewis review Edgar had sent him. Poe himself was doing quite well. He had been offered a hundred dollars by the husband of a Philadelphia poetess to edit his wife's work, and his lectures were going well. On 18 September he wrote to Mrs Clemm:

> My own darling Muddy,
> On arriving here last night from Norfolk I received both your letters, including Mrs Lewis's. I cannot tell you the joy they gave me to learn at least that you are well & hopeful. May God for ever bless you, my *dear, dear* Muddy. — Elmira has just got home from the country. I spent last evening with her. I think she loves me more devotedly than any one I ever knew and I cannot help loving her in return. Nothing is as yet definitely settled — and it will not do to hurry matters. I lectured at Norfolk on Monday and cleared enough to settle my bill here at the Madison House [he had changed hotels] with $2 over. I had a highly fashionable audience, but Norfolk is a small place and there were two exhibitions the same night. Next Monday I lecture again here and expect to have a large audience. On Tuesday I start for Philadelphia to attend to Mrs Loud's poems — and *possibly* on Thursday I may start for New York. If I do I will go straight over to Mrs Lewis's and send for you. It will be better for me not to go to Fordham — don't you think so? Write immediately in reply and direct to Philadelphia . . . *If possible* I will get married before I start, but there is no telling . . . Muddy I am still unable to send you even one dollar — but keep up heart — I hope that our troubles are nearly over . . .

All was not well, however, for he asked Mrs Clemm to address her reply to 'E. S. T. Grey Esqre.' and to sign no name 'for fear I should not get the letter'. Clearly he was afraid of something in Philadelphia, afraid to have his identity and his whereabouts known. Perhaps he had outstanding debts and remembered those earlier occasions in Baltimore when he had been threatened with prison. Perhaps his all too recent experiences in Philadelphia were preying on his mind. Or perhaps he had been drinking again and his mind was affected by the feelings of apprehension associated with the hallucinations of delirium tremens. At his last lecture in Richmond it was noticed that he was excessively nervous and apparently fighting to retain self-control. His face was pale and his eyes betrayed inner agitation. The evening after the lecture he was at Talavera again, and Susan Talley reported that she had never seen him so cheerful and so full of hope for the future. The reunion with his old friends had been a great comfort to him, he told Miss Talley — yet he had written to Griswold asking him to become his literary executor if he should die suddenly. In spite of his optimism, there was some grim foreboding on his mind. Miss Talley recalled: 'We were standing on the portico, and after going a few steps he paused, turned, and again lifted his hat, in a last adieu. At that moment, a brilliant meteor appeared in the sky directly over his head, and vanished in the east. We commented laughingly on the incident; but I remembered it sadly afterward.'

Elmira Shelton, in spite of her later denial of any engagement with Edgar, had written to Mrs Clemm offering her friendship, even love, and making it clear that she was not attempting to supplant Virginia in Edgar's affections. After Edgar's farewell visit to her on 26 September, she wrote to Mrs Clemm again, saying that Poe had been quite ill, apparently suffering from a fever, and that she had doubted whether he would be fit enough to leave for Philadelphia the following morning as he planned. When she called at his hotel early on the Thursday, however, he had gone.

Edgar had spent the later part of Wednesday evening with friends at Sadler's Restaurant, on Main Street, having first called at the consulting rooms of Dr John Carter to say farewell and borrow the doctor's fine malacca cane. He did not drink at the restaurant and seemed in good spirits. In the early hours of the morning he boarded the boat for Baltimore — and vanished into his own nightmares.

The Baltimore boat arrived in that city on Friday 28 September, and Edgar apparently called at the home of his old friend Nathan Brooks, who was out. What happened next is a mystery. One story places Poe in Philadelphia, tired and ill and telling friends that he was on his way to New York. The only solid evidence, however, comes from Baltimore on 3 October, when Dr Snodgrass received a hurriedly scrawled note:

> Dear Sir, — There is a gentleman, rather the worse for wear, at Ryan's 4th Ward polls, who goes under the cognomen of Edgar A. Poe, and who appears in great distress, & says he is acquainted with you, and I assure you, he is in need of immediate assistance.
>   Yours, in haste,
>   Jos. W. Walker.

Walker, a compositor on the *Baltimore Sun,* had found Poe lying in the street outside an inn on East Lombard Street which served as a polling station in the congressional elections then going on. Perhaps, as a newspaperman, he recognized Poe, or perhaps he distinguished him from some poor drunk by the good malacca cane at his side. Whatever did make him stop, he soon learnt who Poe was and discovered his acquaintance with Snodgrass, who lived a few blocks away on High Street. When the doctor arrived, he found that Edgar was dressed not in the kind of clothes he usually wore, but in a poor quality suit that did not fit him. He summoned Poe's cousin, Henry Herring, and with his help took Edgar to the Washington College Hospital, where he was attended by Dr J. J. Moran, who later reported to Mrs Clemm:

> When brought to the Hospital he was unconscious of his condition – who brought him or with whom he had been associating. He remained in this condition from five o'clock in the afternoon – the hour of his admission – until three next morning. This was on the 3d October.
>
> To this state succeeded tremor of the limbs, and at first a busy but not violent or active delirium – constant talking – and vacant converse with spectral and imaginary objects on the walls. His face was pale and his whole person drenched in perspiration. We were unable to induce tranquillity before the second day after his admission.
>
> Having left orders with the nurses to that effect, I was summoned to his bedside so soon as consciousness super-vened, and questioned him in reference to his family, place of residence, relatives, etc. But his answers were incoherent and unsatisfactory. He told me, however, he had a wife in Richmond (which I have since learned was not the fact), that he did not know when he left that city or what had become of his trunk of clothing. Wishing to rally and sustain his now fast sinking hopes, I told him I hoped that in a few days he would be able to enjoy the society of his friends here and I would be most happy to contribute in every possible way to his ease and comfort. At this he broke out with much energy, and said the best thing his best friend could do would be to blow out his brains with a pistol – that when he beheld his degradation he was ready to sink into the earth, etc. Shortly after giving expression to these words Mr Poe seemed to doze, and I left him for a short time. When I returned I found him in a violent delirium, resisting the efforts of two nurses to keep him in bed . . .

What Moran was describing sounds very much like delirium tremens – the violent activity, the hallucinations, the thoughts of death, the loss of memory – which affects heavy drinkers most commonly in association with sudden illness. Poe's illness, if it was diabetes as I have suggested, was not sudden, but then neither was he what we understand by the term 'an alcoholic'. This being so, if he had never touched alcohol, he might have been expected to die in a diabetic coma, but since he did drink heavily from time to time, the toxic effect of the alcohol could have combined with the ravages of the diabetes to produce the violent and tragic result that Moran noted.

On the Saturday evening, Edgar began to call out for 'Reynolds! Reynolds' (Jeremiah Reynolds was the man who had inspired *The Narrative of Arthur Gordon Pym)*:

> ... And now we rushed into the embraces of the cataract, where a chasm threw itself open to receive us. But there arose in our pathway a shrouded Human figure, very far larger in its proportions than any dweller among men. And the hue of the skin of the figure was of the perfect whiteness of the snow.

At three o'clock on the morning of Sunday 7 October 1849, the chasm opened to receive Edgar Allan Poe. His last words before he died were: 'Lord help my poor soul.'

The funeral took place on 8 October (not the 9th, as is usually given) at the Presbyterian cemetery on the corner of Fayette and Green Streets, Baltimore, the service conducted by a Methodist minister. A passer-by, Colonel J. Alden Weston, gave an eye-witness account in the *Baltimore Sun* some time in March 1909:

> On a cold dismal October day, so different from the ordinary genial weather of that clime, I had just left my home when my attention was attracted to an approaching hearse, followed by hackney carriages, all of the plainest type. As I passed the little cortege some inscrutable impulse induced me to ask the driver of the hearse, 'Whose funeral is this?' And to my intense surprise received for answer, 'Mr Poe, the poet.' This being my first intimation of his death, which occurred at the hospital the previous day (Sunday) and was not generally known until after the funeral.
>
> Immediately on this reply I turned about to the grave-yard, a few blocks distant. On arrival there five or six gentlemen, including the officiating minister, descended from the carriages and followed the coffin to the grave, while I, as a simple onlooker, remained somewhat in the rear.

The burial ceremony, which did not occupy more than three minutes, was so cold-blooded and unchristianlike as to provoke on my part a sense of anger difficult to suppress. The only relative present was a cousin (a noted Baltimore lawyer), the remaining witnesses being from the hospital and the press.

After these had left I went to the grave and watched the earth being thrown upon the coffin until entirely covered and then passed on with a sad heart and the one consolation that I was the last person to see the coffin containing all that was mortal of Edgar Allan Poe.

According to Neilson Poe, the mourners were in fact himself, Henry Herring, Dr Snodgrass, and Z. Collins Lee, Edgar's classmate from the University of Virginia.

Colonel Weston added:

In justice to the people of Baltimore I must say that if the funeral had been postponed for a single day, until the death was generally known, a far more imposing escort to the tomb and one more worthy of the many admirers of the poet in the city would have taken place, and attended from Virginia and elsewhere.

The people of Baltimore were not the only ones who did not know of Edgar's death. Mrs Clemm, beside herself with worry after Elmira's letter in September, did not learn of the tragedy until news was published in the New York papers. She immediately wrote to Neilson Poe begging him to tell her it was not true. He replied: 'I would to God I could console you with the information that your dear Son, Edgar A. Poe, is still among the living. The newspapers, in announcing his death, have only told a truth, which we may weep over & deplore, but cannot change.'

But how had he died, and why? The assumption by many at the time, helped by Griswold, was that Edgar had drunk himself to death, and that view is still widely held today among people who know little of Poe except his 'horror stories' and a couple of poems. Later it was suggested that because he had been found outside a polling station he had fallen victim to a 'cooping gang', a group of thugs hired at election times to kidnap people, drug them and take them round the booths to register false votes for particular candidates. This sounds a likely explanation — indeed it was the one I accepted for many years — but a closer look raises some questions. Why, for instance, was Edgar found in a suit that was obviously not his own? The 'coopers' would hardly have gone to the trouble of changing his clothing. It is possible that he had simply been robbed, but in that case why was the handsome cane not taken from him? And if he had indeed gone on a binge, where did he get the other clothes?

Of course, these questions will never be answered now. But I venture to suggest a possible sequence of events that might go some way towards throwing light on Poe's last tragic journey.

We know, from Edgar's final letter to Mrs Clemm, that the balance of his mind was somewhat disturbed, and we know from the evidence of Elmira Royster that he was unwell when he left Richmond. What we do not know is what happened when he arrived in Baltimore on his way to Philadelphia (or, as has been suggested, having already visited Philadelphia and, meaning to carry on to New York, taken the wrong train). It is possible that, in a confused state of mind arising from his projected marriage to Elmira while he still really wanted Annie Richmond, and troubled by the fancies that caused him to ask Mrs Clemm to disguise her letters to him, he had been driven once more towards the alcohol which had anaesthetized him through other difficulties. As the drink took effect it increased rather than diminished his pain: he had just been in Richmond with old friends who remembered him from his happiest days; now he was in Baltimore, scene of his early struggles and also of his first meeting with his beloved Virginia. His mind would have been in a whirl and he would have sought more and more drink to quieten it. Perhaps he sold his clothes and bought cheap ones, buying more rum or brandy with the money he had left, while his remaining sense of decency prevented him from selling the cane he had borrowed from Dr Carter. In these circumstances, and given the havoc that drink caused in his mind and body, it would not have been long before he was reduced to the pitiable state in which Joseph Walker found him.

Do not be misled into thinking that the scenario I have just outlined might serve to confirm the rumours that Poe 'drank himself to death'. Alcohol may have played a part in his dying, it may have been the vehicle for his exit from the world, but it was not the root cause. There is a subtle difference between 'drinking oneself to death' and what happened to Edgar. I have suggested that he was a diabetic, and there is some medical doubt about what the effect of alcohol might be on chronic and untreated diabetes. The advice I have received is that a diabetic in Edgar's day might have been expected to die in a coma, quietly, but that the interference of alcohol could have produced a dramatically different result. At all events, only a small amount of alcohol would have been needed to finish the job that the diabetes began.

Apart from physical considerations, however, there is the state of Poe's mind to take into account. He himself admitted to Mrs Clemm, when he thought that Virginia might be taken away from him by Neilson Poe, that he went to pieces in a crisis — and his life had been one long crisis, its latest manifestation having been Virginia's death and Edgar's desperate attempts to find a substitute for her. One is reminded of 'Eleonora', where the dead loved one releases her man from his sacred vow; of 'Ligeia', where the wife's ghost murders her replacement and takes over her body; and of 'The Fall of the House of Usher', where Roderick's soul-mate returns from the very coffin to claim him. It may be that the imaginary 'conspirators' on the train were, in Edgar's mind, 'messengers' from his dead Virginia. The whole atmosphere of his last journey is that of an attempted escape, a desperate flight. In Philadelphia he almost surrendered, when he talked to John Sartain of throwing himself into the river, but his friend pulled him back from the abyss. In Baltimore, the only friend available was alcohol, and everyone knows how false that is as an ally. Urgently needing another woman to take over from Virginia, but fearful of the consequences of attaching himself to one, Edgar drank from the cauldron he had been offered in the hallucination he described to Sartain, and gradually sank into it. Perhaps there was no other possible end for the man who created Roderick Usher — the man who *was* Roderick Usher.

Epilogue

With his death, the sufferings of Edgar Allan Poe were, in a way, only just beginning. They were fostered by Rufus W. Griswold, of whom John Sartain said: 'He was a notorious blackmailer, and I myself had to pay him money to prevent abusive notices of Sartain's Magazine.' Griswold had nursed resentment of Poe's attacks on him for seven years when Edgar died and gave him the chance for revenge. Presumably Poe had made him his literary executor because he thought that, as a popular anthologist, Griswold was the best man for the job. He could not have been more wrong. On 9 October 1849, the day after Edgar's funeral, Griswold began his slanderous attack:

> Edgar Allan Poe is dead. He died in Baltimore the day before yesterday. This announcement will startle many, *but few will be grieved by it*. The poet was well known personally or by reputation in all this country; he had readers in England and in several of the states of Continental Europe; *but he had few or no friends*; and the regrets for his death will be suggested principally by the consideration that in him literary art lost one of its most brilliant, but erratic stars.

Griswold then reprinted biographical details from his *Poets and Poetry in America*, inaccurate details furnished by Edgar himself in order to enhance his reputation, and information which was for a long time accepted as true. Then came:

> The character of Mr Poe we cannot attempt to describe in this very hastily written article. We can but allude to some of the more striking phases.
> His conversation was at times almost supramortal in its eloquence. His voice was modulated with astonishing skill, and his large and variably expressive eyes looked reposed or shot fiery tumult into theirs who listened, while his own

face glowed or was changeless in pallor, as his imagination quickened his blood, or drew it back frozen to his heart. His imagery was from the worlds which no mortal can see but with the vision of genius. Suddenly starting from a proposition exactly and sharply defined in terms of utmost simplicity and clearness, he rejected the forms of customary logic, and in a crystalline process of accretion, built up his ocular demonstrations in forms of gloomiest and ghostliest grandeur, or in those of the most airy and delicious beauty, so minutely, and so distinctly, and yet so rapidly, that the attention which was yielded to him was chained till it stood among his wonderful creations — till he himself dissolved the spell, and brought his hearers back to common and base existence, by vulgar fancies or by exhibitions of the ignoble passions. ... He walked the streets, in madness or melancholy, with lips moving in indistinct curses, or with eyes upturned in passionate prayers (never for himself, for he felt, or professed to feel, that he was already damned), but for their happiness who at that moment were objects of his idolatry; or with his glance introverted to a heart gnawed with anguish, and with a face shrouded in gloom, he would brave the wildest storms; and all night, with drenched garments and arms wildly beating the wind and rain, he would speak as if to spirits . . .

And after suggesting that harsh experience had deprived Poe of all faith in man or woman, Griswold went on:

His had made up his mind upon the numberless complexities of the social world, and the whole system was with him an imposture. This conviction gave a direction to his shrewd and naturally unamiable character . . . his intellect . . . continually caused him overshots, to fail of the success of honesty . . . 'Passion, in him, comprehended many of the worst emotions which militate against human happiness. You could not contradict him, but you raised quick choler; you could not speak of wealth, but his cheek paled with gnawing envy . . . Irascible, envious — bad enough, but not the worst, for these salient angles were all varnished over with a cold repellent cynicism while his passions vented themselves in sneers . . . He had, to a morbid excess, that desire to rise which is vulgarly called ambition, but no wish for the esteem or the love of his species; only the hard wish to succeed ... that he might have the right to despise a world which galled his self-conceit.'

(The passage in quotation marks was taken verbatim from the description of Francis Vivian in Edward Bulwer's novel *The Caxtons.* Griswold later reprinted it without quotation marks, attempting to pass it off as his own description of Poe.)

Griswold's article, signed with the pseudonym 'Ludwig', appeared in the *New York Tribune*. Together with Griswold's later lies, forgeries and slanders, it gave the world a picture of Edgar Allan Poe which persists, in part, even today. And yet its falsehoods and distortions are so obvious. The idea, for instance, that Poe 'had few or no friends' and that 'few will be grieved' by his death. Poe, as we have seen, had a great many friends, and though they leapt to his defence in the face of Griswold's venom, the world preferred to believe the portrait that most unpleasant gentleman had painted — the stock picture of a maniacal Poe wandering the streets 'in madness or melancholy, with lips moving in indistinct curses'.

Writing off Edgar Allan Poe as a drunkard, a drug addict or a madman is, I suppose, an easy way out: his tales can be dismissed as fevered fantasies, diminished to the status of mere curiosities which serve as fodder for the insatiable and rather unpleasant human hunger for the novel, the bizarre and the macabre. The truth is harder to bear. Poe was not mad, neither was he befuddled by alcohol, nor hooked on opium. He *was* ill, weak and often foolish, and it is as descriptions of the all too sensitive mind collapsing under the stresses of illness, weakness and foolishness that his finest stories have their true significance. They show how feeble is our hold upon sanity, how unsure our footing as we search for direction along the perilous pathways of our souls.

John Allan said Poe's talents were of an order that could never prove a comfort to their possessor. I believe that Poe's talents offer no comfort to his readers, either. The achievement of the real, uncomfortable Edgar Allan Poe was to warn us in brutal and uncompromising terms of the evil within, to make us aware that inside each one of us there are demons which might one day rise up and overwhelm us. It is to be hoped that we have more luck with our devils than he had with his.

A Note on Sources

The Poe-Allan correspondence in the first half of this book is reproduced from transcripts of the original letters, through the kindness of the Valentine Museum in Richmond, Virginia. Other letters, accounts, etc. from John Allan's papers are reproduced from transcripts of documents among the Ellis-Allan Papers in the Poe Volume at the Library of Congress. The letters on pages 22 and 142 are reproduced by kind permission of the Enoch Pratt Free Library, Baltimore, Maryland, © Enoch Pratt Free Library. These and other documents, edited by Arthur H. Quinn and R. H. Hart, were published in volume form in 1941, under the title *Edgar Allan Poe Letters and Documents in the Enoch Pratt Library.* Details of Poe's army life and his period at West Point are taken from official records of the United States Army, except where otherwise stated. Other letters, the originals of which are difficult to trace or which are in private collections, have been reproduced from the biographies by Woodberry (1895), Ingram (1880), Gill (1878) and Harrison (1903), and the texts cross-checked with these and other sources. The recollections of Poe on pages 218, 246 and 254 were brought to light in *Poe Studies,* the newsletter published by Washington State University Press.

Select Bibliography

The best scholarly life of Poe is still Arthur Hobson Quinn's *Edgar Allan Poe: A Critical Biography*, published in 1941 and reprinted in 1969 by Cooper Square, New York, but this is more for the student than the general reader. William Bittner's *Poe: A Biography* (1962) is a highly readable summary of the life.

From the historical point of view, the following works are interesting:

J. H. Ingram: *Life, Letters and Opinions of E. A. Poe*, 1880

G. E. Woodberry: *E. A. Poe*, 1885 (reprinted in 1895 in the 'American Men of Letters' series); *Life of E. A. Poe, Personal and Literary, with his chief correspondence with Men of Letters*, 1909

J. R. Lowell: *A Fable for Critics*, 1848

S. H. Whitman: *E. A. Poe and his Critics*, 1860

S. S. Rice: *A Memorial Volume*, 1877

W. F. Gill: *The Life of Edgar Allan Poe*, 1877 (Boston), 1878 (London)

E. C. Stedman: *Essay on the Life and Works*, 1881

J. J. Moran: *A Defence of E. A. Poe*, 1885

J. Benton: *In the Poe Circle*, 1899

J. P. Fruit: *The Mind and Art of Poe's Poetry*, 1899

J. A. Harrison: *New Glimpses of Poe*, 1901; *Life and Letters of E. A. Poe*, 1903

J. A. Joyce: *E. A. Poe*, 1901

Susan Talley Weiss: *Home Life of Poe*, 1907

Arthur Ransome: *E. A. Poe, a Critical Study*, 1910

The 'golden age' of Poe biography was the 1920s, and the leading work from that period is Hervey Allen's *Israfel: The Life and Times of Edgar Allan Poe* (2 vols), published in New York in 1926. This is a very graphic account, but somewhat unreliable because it fails to discriminate between unsupported rumour and checkable fact. Almost completely unreliable is Mary Newton Stanard's *The*

Dreamer (1925), though it makes splendid reading for lovers of romantic fiction. Other interesting studies are:
C. A. Smith: *E. A. Poe*, 1921
J. W. Robertson: *E. A. Poe*, 1921, 1923
T. O. Mabbott: *Edgar Allan Poe*, 1924
Joseph Wood Krutch: *Edgar Allan Poe: A Study in Genius*, 1926
Mary E. Phillips: *Edgar Allan Poe the Man*, 1926

In the 1930s, the analytical and psychological approach to Poe became fashionable, with studies like:
A. P. Rossiter: *The Gold Insect*, 1932
Killis Campbell: *The Mind of Poe and Other Studies*, 1933
Una Pope Hennessy: *Edgar Allan Poe: A Critical Biography*, 1934

After Quinn's detailed and discriminating biography in 1941, the 'Poe rehabilitation movement' really got under way. Here is a representative list of modern biographical and critical works:
Marie Bonaparte: *The Life and Works of Edgar Allan Poe*, 1949
        (with an introduction written by Sigmund Freud)
N. Bryllion Fagin: *The Histrionic Mr Poe*, 1949
Philip Lindsay: *The Haunted Man*, 1953
Allan Tate: *The Forlorn Demon*, 1953
E. H. Davidson: *Poe*, 1957
Frances Wincar: *The Haunted Palace*, 1959
David M. Rein: *The Inner Pattern*, 1960
Vincent Buranelli: *Edgar Allan Poe*, 1961
Edward Wagenknecht: *The Man Behind the Legend*, 1963
Geoffrey Rans: *Edgar Allan Poe*, 1965
Haldeen Braddy: *Glorious Incense: The Fulfillment of Edgar Allan
        Poe*, 1968
Roger Asselineau: *Edgar Allan Poe*, 1970
John W. Robertson: *Edgar Allan Poe*, 1973

Among critical and incidental works on Poe, the following are the most interesting:
Perry Miller: *The Raven and the Whale*, 1956
Patrick F. Quinn: *The French Face of Edgar Poe*, 1957 (paperback
        edition 1971)
Sidney P. Moss: *Poe's Literary Battles*, 1963
Eric W. Carlson: *The Recognition of Edgar Allan Poe*, 1966
Robert C. Regan: *Poe: A Collection of Critical Essays*, 1967
Robert D. Jacobs: *Poe: Journalist and Critic*, 1969
Louis Broussard: *The Measure of Poe*, 1969
Floyd Stovall: *Edgar Poe the Poet*, 1969
Burton R. Pollin: *Discoveries in Poe*, 1970

William L. Howarth: *Twentieth Century Interpretations of Poe's Tales,* 1971
Daniel Hoffman: *Poe, Poe, Poe, Poe, Poe, Poe, Poe,* 1972

The latest academic research into Poe's life and work is chronicled in *Poe Studies,* a twice-yearly newsletter published by Washington State University Press, Pullman, Washington 99163.

As far as Poe's own writing is concerned, the following works were published in volume form during his lifetime:
Tamerlane and Other Poems. By a Bostonian, Boston, 1827
Al Aaraaf, Tamerlane and Minor Poems, Baltimore, 1829
Poems. Second Edition, New York, 1831
The Narrative of Arthur Gordon Pym, New York and London, 1838
Tales of the Grotesque and Arabesque (2 vols), Philadelphia, 1840
The Prose Romances of Edgar A. Poe (first volume only), Philadelphia, 1843
Tales, New York and London, 1845
The Raven and Other Poems, New York, 1845; London, 1846
Eureka: A Prose Poem, New York, 1848
(There was also, of course, the infamous *The Conchologist's First Book,* published in Philadelphia in 1839.)

Harvard University Press has undertaken a new edition of Poe's complete works, but since at the time of writing only the first volume is available, the best collection remains *The Complete Works of Edgar Allan Poe* (Virginia Edition), edited by James A. Harrison in 17 volumes, and published in New York in 1902. The most notorious collection is *The Works of the Late Edgar Allan Poe. With a Memoir by Rufus Wilmot Griswold* (4 vols), published in New York 1850-56. Other collections are:

The Complete Works of Edgar Allan Poe (editor, Ingram), 1874
The Works of Edgar Allan Poe (Stoddard), 1884
The Works of Edgar Allan Poe (Stedman and Woodberry), 1894, 1914
The Complete Works (Richardson), 1902
The Complete Works (Dole), 1908
The Complete Poems (Whitty), 1911, 1917
The Poems of Edgar Allan Poe (Campbell), 1917
Selected Poems (Mabbott), 1928
The Complete Tales and Poems (1 vol, introduction by Hervey Allen), 1938
The Complete Poems and Stories (Quinn and O'Neill), 1946
Complete Poems (Wilbur), 1959
The Poems of Edgar Allan Poe (Stovall), 1965

There have also been many volumes of selections from Poe's work. These are some of the most recent:

The Narrative of Arthur Gordon Pym, Hill and Wang, New York, 1960

Bizarre and Arabesque (tales, poems and 'Marginalia'), Panther, London, 1967

Tales, Poems, Essays, Collins, London, reprinted 1970

The Portable Poe (tales, poems, essays, criticism, letters), Viking, New York, reprinted 1973

Comic Tales of Edgar Allan Poe, Canongate, Edinburgh, 1973

Selected Writings (poems, tales, essays, reviews), Penguin, London and New York, reprinted 1974

The Poems of Edgar Allan Poe (facsimile of 1900 edition illustrated by W. Heath-Robinson), Bell, London, reprinted 1974

Tales of Mystery and Imagination, (Everyman's Library), London and New York, reprinted 1976

The Illustrated Edgar Allan Poe, Jupiter, London, 1976

Index

Allan, Frances Valentine, 31–9,
43–5, 50, 53, 56, 65, 72, 75,
85; death of, 86; 89, 91
Allan, John, 25–6, 28, 31–9,
42–5, 47, 50–4, 55–6, 64–7,
70–3, 80–9, 91, 95–100, 102–7,
109–14, 119, 120–3, 125–6,
133; death of and will, 134–5;
136, 162
Allan, Louisa Patterson, marriage to
John Allan, 107; 133, 134–5
American Museum, The, 170
Arnold, Elizabeth, 17–18
Arnold, Henry, 17

Baltimore Saturday Visiter, 125,
128, 134
Barnaby Rudge, 157, 192, 214
Bisco, John, 215, 220
Bransby, Rev. John, 39–42
Briggs, Charles F., 215, 219, 223
Broadway Journal, 215 et seq.
Brooks, Nathan C., 170, 171
Burrell, William, recalls E.A.P.'s
gambling, 69–70
Burton, William Evans, 172, 180–6

Chivers, Thomas Holly, 217
Clark, Lewis Gaylord, 170, 211, 216,
223, 224
Clark, Willis Gaylord, 160–1
Clarke, Joseph H., view of E.A.P.,
47
Clarke, Thomas C., partnership with
E.A.P., 200, 202

Clemm, Maria, 57, 92, 119, 122–3,
138, 139, 140–4, 153, 154–5,
164, 166, 168, 192, 210, 211,
231, 245, 247, 248, 249 et seq.
Collier, Edward, 34, 53, 65
Conchologist's First Book, The, 172
Crane, Alexander T., recollections of
E.A.P., 218, 237

Devereaux, Mary, description of
E.A.P., 126–7
Dickens, Charles, 157, 192; letter
to E.A.P., 194
Drayton, William, 79, 88

Eaton, John, 88, 98
Ellet, Elizabeth Frieze, 222–3
Ellis, Charles, 32, 35, 38, 44–5
Ellis, Tom, 48–9, 133–4
English, Thomas Dunn, 223; on
E.A.P. and opium, 238
Ewing, William, view of E.A.P., 34

Fable for Critics, 242
Fay, Theodore S., 158 et seq.

Galt, William, 32, 34, 42, 50, 56
Gentleman's Magazine, 172, 173,
180, 181, 183
George, Miles, recollection of
E.A.P., 61
Gibson, Thomas W., on E.A.P. at
W. Point, 108–9
Graham, George Rex, 189 et seq.,
192

Graham's Magazine, 189 et seq.
Graves, 'Bully', 87, 98, 104—5,
   109, 134
Greeley, Horace, 220, 228
Griswold, Rufus Wilmot, 61—2,
   195, 203, 204, 220, 240, 243,
   252, 255, 259 et seq.

Hoffman, E. T. A., 123—4
Home Journal, 224, 232
Hopkins, Charles D., 19—20
Horse-shoe Robinson, 136, 151

Jackson, Andrew, 35, 88, 128, 167
Jefferson, Thomas, 31, 59—60, 62

Kennedy, John P., 128, 130,
   136—8, 144—5, 151, 166, 190
Knickerbocker Magazine, 158, 211;
   comments on 'The Raven', 214

LaFayette, Comte de, visits
   Richmond, 49—50; 115
Latrobe, J. H. B., 128, 129, 130,
   131
Lewis, Sarah Anna, 231, 243
Longfellow, Henry Wadsworth, 215
   et seq.
Lowell, James Russell, 198—9, 200,
   201, 204, 214, 216, 242

Mackenzie, Jack, recollection of
   E.A.P., 49—50
Madison, James, 31
Moran, Dr J. J., describes E.A.P.'s
   death, 253 et seq.

Neal, John, 102
New York Mirror (later *Evening
   Mirror*), 158, 160, 211
New York Sun, 209
New Yorker, 159
Norman Leslie, 158—60

Osgood, Frances Sargent, 221 et
   seq., 231

Patterson, E. H. N., 243, 249
Paulding, James Kirke, 156

'Penn Magazine', E.A.P.'s plans for,
   187, 189
Philadelphia Gazette, 160
Pioneer, The, 198—9, 200, 201, 203
Poe, David Jr (E.A.P.'s father), 16,
   19—29, 85, 153
Poe, 'General' David, 16—17, 28,
   35
Poe, Edgar Allan, birth of, 20;
   adoption of, 28; in England,
   36 et seq.; at university, 59 et
   seq.; joins army, 75; discharged,
   89; goes to W. Point, 105;
   dismissed, 112; joins *Southern
   Literary Messenger*, 138; sacked,
   146; illness, 151—3; reinstated on
   Messenger, 153; marriage, 163;
   leaves *Messenger*, 167; replies to
   charges of drunkenness, 181—2;
   settles in N.Y., 207 et seq.;
   acquires *Broadway Journal*, 220;
   sues for libel, 223; proposes
   marriage to Helen Whitman, 236;
   'suicide attempt', 236; marriage
   called off, 240; last journey,
   245 et seq.; plans to marry
   Sarah Elmira Shelton, 250; dies,
   254; funeral of, 254
Poe, Edgar Allan, works of: 'The
   Lake', 37; 'The Murders in the
   Rue Morgue', 38; 'William
   Wilson', 39—41, 67, 199; 'Why
   the Little Frenchman Wears His
   Hand in a Sling', 43, 179; 'The
   Gold Bug', 49, 77—8; 'Arthur
   Gordon Pym', 49, 168—70; 'The
   Businessman', 51—2; 'The Literary
   Life of Thingum Bob', 51—2, 211;
   'To Helen', 54—5, 104, 116; 'A
   Tale of the Ragged Mountains',
   67—8; 'The Domain of Arnheim',
   68; 'Landor's Cottage', 69;
   'Tamerlane', 76; 'Song', 76;
   'Annabel Lee', 78—9, 117; 'The
   Imp of the Perverse', 85—6; 'Al
   Aaraaf', 93—5, 100; 'Fairyland',
   102; *Tamerlane and Other Poems*,
   104; *Al Aaraaf, Tamerlane and*

Minor Poems, 104; 'The City in the Sea', 116; 'The Raven', 117, 212 et seq.; 'Israfel', 117; 'Letter to Mr ——', 118–19; *Poems* (Second Edition), 115; 'The Duke de L'Omelette', 123; 'The Bargain Lost', 123; 'A Decided Loss', 123; 'A Tale of Jerusalem', 123; 'Metzengerstein', 123–5, 128, 129; *Tales of the Folio Club*, 127, 136; 'Epimanes', 127; 'Some Words with a Mummy', 127; 'Lionizing', 128; 'The Visionary', 128; 'Siope', 128; 'The Coliseum', 129; 'A Descent into the Maelstrom', 128, 129, 130; 'MS Found in a Bottle', 128, 129, 130, 132; 'The Assignation', 136; 'Berenice', 139–40; 'The Fall of the House of Usher', 141, 173–6; 'Eleonora', 141–2, 164–5; 'King Pest the First', 154; *Politian*, 154; 'Loss of Breath', 154; Drake-Halleck review, 161; 'Ligeia', 170–1; 'The Man That Was Used Up', 173; 'The Haunted Palace', 174–5; 'The Philosophy of Composition', 157, 176; *Tales of the Grotesque and Arabesque*, 179, 193; 'The Masque of the Red Death', 192; 'The Mystery of Marie Roget', 198; 'The Landscape Garden', 198; 'The Tell-Tale Heart', 199; 'The Black Cat', 202; 'Prose Romances', 203; 'The Conqueror Worm', 205; 'The Balloon Hoax', 209; 'The Premature Burial', 210–11; 'The Oblong Box', 211; 'Mesmeric Revelation', 210; 'The Facts in the Case of M. Valdemar', 217; *Tales*, 218; *The Raven and Other Poems*, 220; 'Ulalume', 228; *Eureka: A Prose Poem*, 229; 'The Bells', 230; 'To Helen' (second version), 232; 'The Purloined Letter', 238; 'For Annie', 241; 'To My Mother', 242; 'Hop-Frog', 242; 'Eldorado', 242

Poe, Elizabeth Arnold, 15, 17, 18–29, 31, 48
Poe, George, 22–3
Poe, George Jr, 154–5
Poe, James Mosher, 96
Poe, John, 16
Poe, Neilson, 120, 142, 153, 255
Poe, Rosalie, 15, 25–6, 47, 139, 237
Poe, Virginia Clemm, 92, 138–44, 153; marriage, 163; 164–6, 178, 192–4, 221 et seq.; death of, 224
Poe, William Henry, 15, 20–1, 28, 51–2, 56–7, 92, 119
Poets and Poetry of America, 89, 195, 204
Preston, John, 48
Prose Writers of America, 220

Ravenel, Dr Edmund, 77–8
Reid, Thomas Mayne, 197
Richmond, Nancy Locke Heywood ('Annie'), 231, 236, 238 et seq., 243, 245
Royster, Sarah Elmira (later Mrs Shelton), 57; marriage, 72; 76, 139, 142, 250

Sartain, John, recollection of E.A.P., 246; 259
Shew, Marie Louise, 224, 227, 230, 231, 233, 235
Snodgrass, Dr Joseph E., 170, 180–1, 189, 252, 253, 255
Southern Literary Messenger, The, 49, 138, 143, 146, 149, 153–4, 158, 160–2, 166, 235
Spy, E.A.P.'s column for, 209
Stanard, Jane Craig, 54–5, 104, 142
Stanard, Rob, 54
'Stylus', E.A.P.'s plans for, 200–2, 235
Sully, Thomas, comment on E.A.P. 48–9

Swallow Barn, 136

Talley, Susan Archer, recollection of
    E.A.P., 249, 251
Thomas, Frederick, 190–1, 195, 211
Tucker, Nathaniel Beverley, 156
Tucker, Thomas G., on E.A.P.'s
    drinking, 62, 74
Tyler, John, 190, 198
Tyler, Rob, 197–8

Valentine, Ann Moore (Nancy), 32,
    44–5, 73, 91, 100

War of 1812, 34–5
White, Thomas Willis, 138, 143; sacks
    E.A.P., 146–7; 149, 153–4,
    161–2, 167
Whitman, Sarah Helen, 231;
    Valentine for E.A.P., 232; 235
    et seq., 238, 239, 241
Willis, Nathaniel Parker, 211;
    recollection of E.A.P., 212
Wills, Elizabeth, 53, 65–6, 92, 107,
    134–5
Wilmer, Lambert A., 127, 139
Wirt, William, 83, 92–3, 95
Wyatt, Thomas, 172

7